PRAISE FOR

Present Parent: Connect.
Children in Five Minutes or Less

This book is masterful. So timely, so needed. I have enjoyed it profoundly.

—**Jason Hewlett**, DAD, speaker Hall of Fame 2016,
CSP Award from the National Speakers Association,
author, National Outstanding Eagle Scout Award
from the Boy Scouts of America

Mary Ann Johnson's book, *Becoming a Present Parent: Connecting with Your Children in Five Minutes or Less* has the potential to radically change families, and family situations, for the better. It's that powerful. *Becoming a Present Parent* delivers answers to questions you may not even know you're asking. But when you read certain chapters, you'll find yourself nodding, smiling, and then chuckling. Then, hopefully, taking action. Because, believe me, Mary Ann arms you with a whole bookful of ideas, strategies, techniques, concepts, and approaches. And all of them are *doable*. You may read *Becoming a Present Parent* all the way through one time. But then you'll come back to it time and again to refresh on certain topics at the very time you need them. My guess is your copy will become dog-eared and marked up and will become like a comfortable friend.

—**Norma Jean Lutz**, author, speaker, editor,
Novel Critique Consultant, ghostwriter

Connection is the key to healthy relationships. *Becoming a Present Parent* is chock full of ideas to build connection and bind hearts together. Mary Ann presents her vital information with a can-do attitude that w .... :ed and capable of growing stron;g .... Small changes in intention and practices will yield huge results in our hearts and most important, in the souls of our children. I hope this book makes it into the hands and hearts of thousands of parents!

—**Tracy Ward**, mother, scholar

This is a fantastic book—a real gift to parents.

—**Rochelle Cottle**, homemaker and homeschooling mom

This is such an important message. We need to hear it!

—**Sharilyn Bankole,** homemaker and homeschooling mom

I like to call Mary Ann the Connected Mother Coach because in our busy world, being home isn't always being present and she can help you reclaim that presence.

—**Elizabeth King Bradley**, mother and creator of the *Mama Mastermind*

Mary Ann is a master at helping you become a more present parent. Each chapter is filled with actionable insight and real-life steps in helping you stay "checked in" with your children, a difficult thing in this distracting world. I love how Mary Ann teaches us how to truly connect with our children.

—**Ann Webb,** teacher, lecturer, humanitarian and creator of *Life Vision*

Mary Ann is a masterful storyteller and has captured the art of being present in her latest book. She gives simple, easy, practical ways to create and maintain healthy familial relationships. I grew up in a "perfect" home and moved out feeling completely alone and unloved. I have often reflected on why that was the case and never wanted my children to feel that way when they left my home. I chose to show them love by giving them "quality time." After reading this book I discovered more ways I can increase the quality of that time and other ways my Presence would strengthen relationships. She shares simple ways we can help our children be seen, heard, loved, supported and to know they matter. When we give them the gift of Presence they will leave our homes with confidence and security. Reading this book is like sunlight kissing your cheeks as you wake up in the morning; you know it's going to be a good day. It will bring joy to your heart and to your relationships. Read this book and feel the warmth of good relationships in your life.

—**Tresta Neil,** homeschooling mom, speaker, and mentor

In an increasingly fast-paced world, Mary Ann has hit the nail on the head. She knows what struggling parents are lacking, what is making us feel overwhelmed and frustrated in our most precious roles as parents. It is Presence! This isn't just another how-to parenting book though. It's an honest, thought-provoking look on how to improve all of our relationships, especially those with our children. I'm already seeing the blessings, and the joy, that come from applying her counsel. Definitely worth a read for all parents!

—**Kamie Bushman**, mother of two

Becoming a
PRESENT
PARENT

CONNECTING
with your **CHILDREN**

in **5** Minutes or Less

Mary Ann Johnson

Plain Sight Publishing
Springville, Utah

ISBN 13: 978-1-4621-2021-5

33614080210221

Published by Plain Sight Publishing, an imprint of Cedar Fort, Inc.
2373 W. 700 S., Springville, UT 84663
Distributed by Cedar Fort, Inc., www.cedarfort.com

LIBRARY OF CONGRESS CONTROL NUMBER: 2017936764

Cover design by Kinsey Beckett
Cover design © 2017 by Cedar Fort, Inc.
Edited by Deborah Spencer

Printed in the United States of America

10 9 8 7 6 5 4 3 2 1

Printed on acid-free paper

Dedicated to God; my husband, Don; and my children, Jodie, Seth, Jenny, Marie, Andrew, Barry, and Kate. Together they've given me enough hard times so I could grow into a better and wiser person, and enough joy so I could endure the lessons.

And to the unnamed child who first helped me have *new eyes* to see. She was one of the lessons.

"Blessed are your eyes, for they see:
and your ears, for they hear."

—Matthew 13:16

CONTENTS

Contents

FOREWORD

My wife and I have welcomed four amazing children to this world. At the time the fourth arrived, we had four children under the age of five years, with no twins in the mix. We did our best to keep our sanity while the world seemed to gawk at us and look on.

"The Hewletts have arrived in the vicinity; we are not selling tickets to this traveling circus. Enjoy the free show!"

As parents, we attempted to create quality time with each child from the get-go. It didn't always happen, but when it did and it was Daddy's turn, the kids were excited. Because of this, I felt obligated to make it work and sadly didn't enjoy those moments as I should have. I often responded to emails and work needs during the entire date. Looking back, I just shake my head.

During one such daddy-son date, I remember looking in the rearview mirror seeing my son beaming with the widest grin. He was staring directly into the mirror watching me intently.

"What are you smiling about, Buddy?" I asked.

Innocently he replied, "I like it when you're nice Daddy, not mean Daddy."

My smile disappeared—his did not. I probed further, attempting to not be offended by a three-year-old—though I was. "When is Daddy mean?" I asked.

Without hesitation, he responded: "Just not right now."

My heart was shattered. I remember the exact place where this conversation took place. As we got out of the car, I reached down and picked up this perfect, sweet, beautiful little child. I embraced him and snuggled all the way into the restaurant. His grin seemed to grow, and the glow I saw on his face was unforgettable. As he played in the kid zone, I wondered how my son's perception of me could be so skewed. What had I done so wrong? I thought I was "The Fun Dad," but apparently not.

Upon returning home, I reluctantly related the conversation to my wife, hoping she might dispel my three-year-old's unfounded opinion. She affirmed he was correct and mentioned she had meant to bring up her disappointment in my tone of voice; my unrealistic expectations of infants to be quiet and perfect at home, at school, and at play; and the underlying rage she noticed spilling over at our children's natural way of doing things. I was mortified. I didn't sleep for two days. I just wrote in my journal and walked around outside.

Soon after this experience, I called a therapist. I wanted to know why I was such a great and fun guy on stages, yet, at home, I was a complete lunatic with angry militaristic expectations. Nothing about my work was congruent with my life, and I had to figure out why. I share this story for the first time in the foreword of this profoundly important book as a warning to parents everywhere, especially to dads. Don't be like me. I failed completely as a dad the first five years of my children's lives.

The process of righting my ship didn't happen overnight. I sought advice from my own parents, my wife, my siblings, and my friends. It became something of a full-time job. I sought help from my Higher Power, wrote in my journal like crazy, read every parenting self-help book available, and scoured the scriptures for examples of truly great parents. Slowly, I began to notice my mistakes and triggers, and I began to change.

Had I had the book *Becoming A Present Parent* when I went through this change process, it would have made my life so much better. The steps in this book are masterfully crafted and completely correct. The stories are real, heartbreaking, and yet redeeming. This book will change your life if you let it. The mission of Becoming a Present Parent is to help us push past the guilt and regret we all experience and commit to making small changes in every relationship until we become 100 percent present in life. It's as simple as that!

I am not out of the woods with my temperament, but things have improved drastically. Having spent the first eight years of my children's lives on the road around twenty days per month, I'm working toward being a stay-at-home dad/business owner who only travels five days per month. It is truly a balancing act of uncharted territory.

This is the life I want: not just quality time, not just quantity time, but all of my time with my family. I used to plan all of my time around my children going to bed, so I could get stuff done. When one of my children walked into my home office, I would keep typing and shoo them off without turning to look at them.

Now when I hear them coming, I stop what I'm doing, and I turn my chair completely around so they can run into my open arms for a hug. I answer questions. I help with problems. It only takes a couple of minutes to do this, and when I do, I have better focus when I return to my work. I have learned that when we get stuff done together, we have time to jump on the trampoline or to go bowling together. My life has been completely transformed as I have integrated my children into every part of my life.

I'm grateful I nipped my issues in the bud when I did, since I'm not sure I would still have the family I have had I continued on the same path. I encourage you to consider *Becoming A Present Parent* if your presence and focus are jeopardized by self-sabotage. This book is a how-to manual that can help you completely alter the course of your life. Learning to be fully present in the smallest of moments can create the greatest feelings of fulfillment this life has to offer us as parents.

I wish you the best and pray we'll all savor each moment.

—Jason Hewlett, certified speaking professional,
author of *Signature Moves: How to Stand Out in a
Sit Down World,* award-winning entertainer,
happy husband, full-time homeschooling Dad
(www.jasonhewlett.com)

ACKNOWLEDGMENTS

Tiffany Berg Coughran—Without her constant encouragement there would be no book. She read it and continued to affirm it was a message worth sharing.

Stefanie Miller—She read the book and kept me going with her wonderful comments about how it was impacting her family for good.

Sharilyn Bankole—She helped me remember the principle *less is more.*

Nathalie Bowman—She shared her talent for feeling energy and helped me know how the words in this book felt.

Kamie Bushman—She saw what everyone else missed.

My husband, Don—He was willing to watch television with a headset day after day so I could write and then read what I had written out loud. He took on extra home duties to give me space. Most of all, he believed I could write and what I wrote would be worth reading. Thanks, Don. I love you.

My son, Seth—He was brave enough to say, "Mom, take out the fluff!"

Norma Jean Lutz—A friend extraordinaire, who line edited the whole thing because she likes the book and me and is an extraordinary person.

My grandchildren—Michael, Kane, Maggie, Jack, Mary, Benjamin, Aubrey, Ashley, Elizabeth, Parker, Matilda, Tessa, and Elliott who gave me a second chance to practice and prove what I had learned through hard experience.

My children—Jodie, Seth, Jenny, Marie, Andrew, Barry, and Kate, who came to our family and endured the "hard experience" and love me anyway!

INTRODUCTION

As a young woman growing up in the '50s and '60s, I didn't contemplate any other occupation than motherhood. It was so much a part of what I expected to do that I didn't give it much thought. It was what everyone did. I looked forward to it. I expected to sail along doing what was required in the best way possible because I was made for it. It never occurred to me I wouldn't know what to do and how to manage.

Raising my family was "the best of times, it was the worst of times, it was the age of wisdom, it was the age of foolishness, it was the epoch of belief, it was the epoch of incredulity, it was the season of Light, it was the season of Darkness, it was the spring of hope, it was the winter of despair." These words from the Charles Dickens novel *A Tale of Two Cities* describe my parenting experience rather perfectly. In fact, in 1996 at the height of our family problems, that is what I wrote under our family photo.

Don and I didn't talk much about family and parenting before we embarked on this grand adventure. He was the second child in a family of two children. I was the oldest of nine. He assumed I knew what I was doing and I assumed I knew what I was doing. We never discussed how we would discipline, how we would manage chores, meals, vacations, schooling, the budget, and so on. Frankly, it didn't occur to us we might not agree on everything, that we might not have all the information we needed. After all, we were in love,

1

we shared the same faith, and parenting is what everyone did. It couldn't be all that complicated.

But it was complicated!

I have a belief that has carried me through all the hard times. I believe each person brings to their relationship and to their parenting a large bag of *stuff* they've accumulated along the road to becoming an adult—fears, prejudices, and stories about the why and what of their experience. I believe the stuff in our bag isn't because we are bad or were born into a troubled family. I believe we have our bag of stuff because the act of emptying it out helps us grow and become who we were meant to be. It's this bag of stuff we draw from as we determine *how* to parent.

Don and I had *big* stuff in our bags, which influenced how well we were able to communicate, connect, build esteem, manage stress, advocate for each other and our children, as well as how to manage daily life—alcoholism; sexual abuse; distant/controlling parents and grandparents; death; the usual growing up turmoil over friends, school, grades, and personal worth; not to mention what was in our bags that came from those who lived before us. You know, the stuff in our DNA.

Don and I had seven beautiful and amazing children, four girls and three boys. They currently range in age from twenty-seven to forty-five. I recall with great fondness camping, fishing, sewing, cooking, crafts, Christmas, Thanksgiving, dance recitals, band concerts, baseball games, wrestling competitions, and speech contests.

I remember the fun we had: breakfast on the tailgate of our old pickup truck at the park, a block from our home one early Saturday morning; quiet conversations with whichever child's turn it was to help me weed in the early dawn hours; canning while lots of kids snapped beans and peeled carrots; reading to our children; dinners together, a daily occurrence; bath time; night time cuddles; sitting together at church, filling a whole pew, while tickling backs and squeezing shoulders. These were memorable and satisfyingly ordinary days. These were the best of times.

I also have seared on my mind the struggles we shared as a family of nine—a husband who traveled for a living, drug abuse, premarital sex and a child born out of wedlock, thoughts of suicide, failure in school, smoking, alcoholism, lack of belief in one's value as a person, quitting school, abandoning church, a mother who raged and yelled, managing feelings of despair, and coming to terms with same-sex attraction. These were the worst of times.

When it's all shaken together and poured out, how did we fare? Well, far better than we expected or than you might expect. Don and I had done just enough right, and with a full measure of the grace of God thrown in that we all survived and, strangely enough, thrived. I stopped raging and yelling. Don came home off the road. We learned to communicate. Addictions were overcome. Stress was managed and we all live fully functional lives. We're connected and bonded in amazing ways. We look out for one another. The kids support each other and lean on each other. We're still a family!

Don's and my individual bags of stuff are lighter and get emptier each year. I think, as our children move along with their families, they'll empty their bags as well. We can see it happening now. Life isn't perfect and trouble-free for any of us, but we're all growing, contributing, and learning. The last four and a half decades have been the age of wisdom, the age of foolishness, the epoch of belief, the epoch of incredulity, a season of Light, a season of Darkness, a spring of hope, and a winter of despair. Family has been all of this for us.

Recently, I was impressed to read an old journal of mine. I hadn't read any of my journals since they were written. This one began in the spring of 1991. I was forty-one years old with a baby born the year before. We were in the throes of hard times with our children. Don and I felt like the worst parents on the planet.

As I read, I was overcome with all the things I'd forgotten. I'd forgotten how intense my desire for personal growth and change was and how diligently I worked on both. I'd forgotten how much I loved my children and how often I did more than was required to reach out and nurture them. I wept as I realized what a fine, although not perfect, mother I was, and what a great father Don was, despite being gone so much.

In my journal was an entry from one of my struggling children. She was involved in drugs and would eventually spend time in rehab. Despite her own significant issues, she had seen my discouragement and felt my fears. She wanted me to know I was doing a good job. Here's a small excerpt from her comments:

"You're doing everything you can to try and make our home and family what it should be. I wanted to let you in on a secret of mine. Our house is a temple. I love my home. I come here for protection and solace. This place is a haven, a place for love and spiritual replenishment. When times are the worst I long to be home where there's peace for my soul. No mother. Your efforts are far from in vain! I wanted you to know how much I love you and how much I love my home."

The story of our family is the story of an imperfect family. And ultimately, this is what this book is about. You won't and, frankly, can't do everything right. Your children will struggle as they grow. You'll struggle to do all that's required in your chosen vocation of parent. It's part of the process of being human, of being in a family. It's part of the process of emptying the bag.

I want to help you experience more joy right where you are, despite any troubles you may be experiencing or will yet experience, no matter what's in your bag. The steps in this book will help you do things now that will make all the difference for you and your children, regardless of their current ages. And with the grace of God, it will be enough.

Spring 1994   "It was the best of times, it was the worst of times..."

CHAPTER 1

HOW We Check Out

Do you feel you should spend more time with your family? Do you feel the time you do spend is lacking in real connection? Do you go to bed wishing you felt better about *how* you were with your kids during the day? Most of us can relate!

In order for time with our children to be most effective, it has to be Present time. One of the purposes of this book is to illustrate what Presence looks like in an average, busy family and demonstrate that it's doable regularly. I've been able to do this. You can do this, and it will make a difference in your family as a whole and in your relationships with your children.

I've been working with parents for many years and, as a mom myself, I can attest that being home with a child doesn't guarantee raising healthy, happy, well-adjusted children—children who feel a real and significant connection with their family. But then neither does quality time guarantee that unless we're clear on what quality time looks like.

A universal human need is to matter; especially to those we love. We all have the opportunity to help satisfy this need for others, especially in our families. Sending anyone, particularly a child, the

> **"Presence is more than just being there."**
>
> —Malcolm Forbes, American entrepreneur

message that they matter is dependent on being able to answer "yes" to their unspoken questions:

- Do you see me?

- Do you hear me?

- Do you love me?

Most of us have had the unnerving experience of being in a conversation and knowing the other person's mind is in another place. You're sure they don't hear you even as they nod their heads as if they do. We've likely all had this experience.

It's interesting how often moms and dads think they're sending positive, connected messages to their children, when in fact, their children are experiencing the kind of conversation I described above. How does this disconnect happen?

In today's world, it's become easier and easier to *check out*. We're a million miles away from our children, even when we're right there with them. We don't plan to be, we don't mean to be, but we are . . . a million miles away.

In *Highlights* magazine's annual State of the Kid Survey, a nationally representative sample of six- to twelve-year-olds were asked, "Are your parents ever distracted when you're trying to talk to them?" Sixty-two percent of children said yes (Highlights, 2014).

That's a lot of kids feeling as if they might not matter. We're distracted, overwhelmed, unrested, overworked, and so busy managing the things of life, it's difficult to hear and see our children.

Kids measure love primarily by our attentiveness to them. When you stop what you're doing to have a tea party, listen to what they have to share, look at a picture they made, or touch them with intention, it says you matter. I see you, I hear you, I love you.

Children need and want your Presence. They ask for it in many ways. They snuggle up beside you and say, "Whatcha doin' mom/dad?" They keep coming to you when they know you're busy; they ask silly questions. They throw a tantrum. Yes, they ask for your Presence in many ways.

SWEET MARIE

When my daughter Marie was three, she and I had an experience that opened my eyes to the importance of being Present—even for short amounts of time. It clarified for me, in a dynamic way, what being Present with a child looks and feels like.

I was in the middle of a sewing project. I'm not partial to sewing. Worse, this project had a deadline and it was fast approaching. Marie kept coming into the sewing room and bothering me. She asked questions, whined about this and that, asked for food, and on and on.

Finally, in exasperation, I decided if she came into the sewing room one more time, I was going to give her a swat. I had asked her repeatedly to stop interrupting me and she was just being naughty!

Fortunately for me, as she walked through the door for the umpteenth time, a thought came into my mind from outside of myself. I like to think God was teaching me this principle of Presence. The thought was, "Why not hug her instead?"

This new thought startled me! It was so far removed from what I'd intended, it brought me to a *stop*. I turned away from the sewing machine to face Marie. I looked at her, really looked at her, for the first time that day. I gathered her up and I gave her a long hug and said, "I love you." She went off happy as a clam and, interestingly enough, never came back. She wanted a moment of my Presence. She wanted to know she was on my list, in fact, at the top of my list.

WHAT IS PRESENCE?

The dictionary defines "present" as a gift or something willingly transferred by one person to another without thought of compensation (unselfishly) (Noah Webster 1828 Dictionary). In that transcendent moment, that's what happened for Marie and me. I gave her the gift of my full attention, my whole self, nothing held back. I wasn't thinking about the project or the deadline. I wasn't figuring out how to get her out of my hair. I wasn't looking for a solution to a problem—her. I was *present*. And she knew it, and me being Present was all she had needed from the first visit to the sewing room.

Jim Taylor, PhD, author of *The Power of Prime*, told his readers, "I thought you might find it interesting to learn of the findings of a survey of children four to eleven years old who were asked what they wanted from their parents. First, they wanted more attention from their parents and [for them] to be more available" (Taylor 2011).

This is exactly what Marie was asking; she wanted me to be available. She was saying as clearly as her three-year-old self was able to say, "Mom, see me. Hear me. Look at me and let me know you love me and that I matter."

What I know from working with hundreds of families is that most parents want their children to know they matter. Why then do we unknowingly send messages that make our kids feel they're in the way, that they're bothering us, or that they aren't as interesting as whatever else we're doing? It's because we're checking out!

Here are eight common ways loving, concerned, and dedicated parents check out. We all do it.

EIGHT WAYS WE CHECK OUT

1—THE BELIEF THAT IT TAKES A LOT OF TIME

I've practiced this idea of being Present with my children and grandchildren, and I've watched other parents practice it. I know it makes a *huge* difference in how parents and children relate to one another over the long term.

I've also researched it. I wanted to know what others had to say. There is a profusion of studies showing that when parents give their children *real* time, it has a big impact. Here's the problem. The majority of the research I've looked at advises parents to spend thirty minutes to an hour of alone time with each child, weekly. At times, the counsel is to have a date away from home with each child, weekly. Wouldn't that be terrific!

The question is, can you do it? I couldn't. I had seven children. Thirty minutes per child, per week would have been three and a half hours. I know it doesn't sound like much, but in a busy family, it was huge.

And think of it—a date per child, per week, away from home. Even a short date isn't short. What if all you did was go to the hamburger place down the street for ice cream? You drive there, order, eat the cone, and then drive home. This is still a big time commitment.

I've rarely talked to a parent who has been able to manage this type of time commitment over a long period. They begin with good intentions. Some manage it for a few months, but it doesn't last, as good as the advice may be. And so, because it doesn't seem doable, we check out. We let it alone. We give it up.

And think about this. Is it going to be enough to be Present once a week for a bigger block of time? I've practiced this. And I have to say *no*, it isn't. I believe small and simple things, done consistently over time, bring the greatest rewards.

I'm not saying we shouldn't take our kids on dates. We should. I'm not saying we shouldn't give our children time alone with us for serious conversations. We should. My fondest memories of my dad are the dates we went on. But that happened twice in my life. Looking back, I would have given a lot for more snuggles, more tickles, more mini-conversations, and more random touches. (More information on random touch and mini-conversations in chapter 3.)

What if you could connect in a Present way with each child, multiple times a day, for the full eighteen years they live in your home? Can you see this would be more beneficial than the occasional alone time?

I know many of you reading this book are thinking, "Well, that's just common sense. I connect with my kids every day." But do you? Do you really? Or do you, like many parents I work with, go to bed and lie there thinking, "Did I even hug John today—did I hug anyone? Did I talk about anything else but chores, homework, and not being rude?"

I want to take away the intimidation around being Present with your children. This myth of time causes good parents to check out. It doesn't require seven children to find it intimidating. Let's debunk this myth. In the following chapters, I'll illustrate many ways to be Present, with many taking as little as five minutes or less.

2—TECHNOLOGY

The digital age is exciting! But it's opened a Pandora's box for families. Let me give you three examples.

Example 1—For a time, I lived in a fourplex. There was a lovely high hedge separating our building from the sidewalk. One day, as I was returning home, I noticed the couple who lived below me sitting on their patio. They have very active children who were nowhere to be seen.

I made an assumption about them being out in the fresh air, on a warm and calm evening, with no children. I called out a cheery, "Hi. You guys must be having a date." They looked up at me, smiled, and replied, "Yes, we are."

As I rounded the hedge here's what I saw—They were each playing a game on their phones, independent of each other. This was the date. They

> "As parents, one of the most important things we teach our children is how to be in a relationship. No parent is going to be 100 percent responsive, but we can try to be more aware of when our children are looking for our attention. We can try to turn toward our kids in kind ways more often than away."
>
> —Eileen Kennedy-Moore, PhD.
> "Are You a Distracted Parent?
> How Not to (Smart) Phone
> It in as a Parent"

were together all right, and they didn't have any children distracting them. But I think it's safe to say they were not connecting in any meaningful way. Over the next few years, I noticed many of their quiet moments together were spent in this way.

Example 2—Across the hall from my apartment was a family with teens. One day, as I rounded the hedge, I saw one of the daughters and three of her friends on the stairs. Each had their phone in hand. They were texting friends and each other. I stood and watched them for a moment and they never spoke a word. It was all happening via a small handheld device.

What I observed was a quiet, intense focus on a phone and an unseen audience, even though part of the audience was within arm's reach. Those youth were missing out on a fundamental need of humanity: building relationships and understanding other people on a personal level. They had checked out from each other.

Example 3—My oldest daughter has four small children. Their home is a busy place. Jodie told me the computer and the world outside of her loud, busy, and demanding family could certainly be a siren's song to her. She confessed that many mornings she would get up and feel the need to check her email to see if anything important had come in. That would lead her to Facebook because the notices were in the email.

Soon she would be checking on other things, and before she knew it, the morning was gone, kids were not fed or dressed, and they were running late. The children's demands to be heard and seen had escalated. It got the morning off on a bad foot and made the family feel out of sorts. I know some of you are laughing because you've had the same experience!

Sherry Turkle, a clinical psychologist and professor at the Massachusetts Institute of Technology who studies how people use technology, says she has found children are worried their parents' love affairs with BlackBerries, iPhones, and computers are fracturing their families.

When she began writing her book *Alone Together*, her intention was to write about how teens and their technology were driving their parents crazy. She said in an interview with Nancy Shute, who writes for *US News and World Report*, "It turned out to be a much more compelling story of parents' texting in the car, parents' texting at dinner, and kids not knowing what to do. It was a surprising finding and very moving. The stories were about children wanting their parents' full attention."

Turkle spoke with many children and young people for her book. She discovered "[kids are] tired of being pushed on the swing with one hand while [Mom reads] her E-mail on the phone with the other" (Shute, "Parents, Not Kids, Are the Biggest Abusers of Technology").

She mentioned a mother who never looked up from her phone while picking her daughter up from school. In the interview, Turkle said,

> When children come home from school, that's the moment when they're desperate to make eye contact with you. In this case, a thirteen-year-old girl [emerges] from school [where] her mother's waiting in the car. And the mother never looks up from her phone. To make it worse, the [girl's] parents are divorced, [so] it may [have been] four days since she [last saw her daughter]. And she still won't look up. The car's moving, and she still doesn't look up. The girl describes such a sense of longing. What is [her] mother doing that's so much more important than looking at her? (Shute, "Parents, Not Kids, Are the Biggest Abusers of Technology")

Later, during an interview with the mother, Turkle discovered, "This is not an abusive, uncaring situation. This is a loving mother. But she's overwhelmed. Here's someone who's unthinkingly not giving her daughter something [she] so desperately needs. We can do better than this" (Shute, "Parents, Not Kids, Are the Biggest Abusers of Technology").

In *Highlights* magazine's 2014 survey, the kids said they know their parents are listening when their parents look at them (56 percent), respond (28 percent), and stop doing everything else (11 percent) ("National Survey Reveals 62% of Kids Think Parents Are Too Distracted to Listen").

And there it is. We love our children and want them to know they matter, but we're checking out with technology without even thinking about it. We're sending a different message than we intend.

As wonderful as technology can be—as helpful, relaxing, and fun—it's a double-edged sword that is cleaving our families into pieces.

3—WORK

A couple of days before Christmas, I found myself babysitting two of my grandchildren, Jack and Mary. Jack was almost three, and Mary was one. I hadn't been planning on having a house full of children the week before Christmas. I'm sure you know I had a ton of things to do before the twenty-fifth rolled around.

I was in the middle of writing an article with a publishing deadline. When Jack and Mary arrived at my home, I still had my *me not them* mind-set firmly in place. I set them down in front of Qubo (technology rearing its ugly head) and gave them a cubed cheese snack. "Ah, they're good to go, and I can finish my article."

But that isn't how it worked out. Jack needed a drink; he needed the toy closet opened; he wanted to know this and that. I could feel the worry about my writing deadline rising. I was stressed out!

Jack came into the office and climbed on my knee. "Can we look at rain sticks again?" he asked. The real question he was asking was, "Can you spend time with me?" I looked at Jack, took my own advice, and stopped working. What was the worst thing that could happen if I missed the 4:00 deadline? Nothing!

So I decided to spend some Present time with my grandchildren for the next hour. It was fun. I felt good as a grandmother. They felt good because they knew I loved them. Mary and Jack knew they mattered. It took a short amount of time and they were content for a while. I was able to finish my article.

The trap of work catches both parents who leave home to work and those who work at home. No parent is immune. Remember being in the same space with a child doesn't equate to Present time. It just doesn't!

A stay-at-home mom who wrote a blog for my website said in part, "It helps to physically remove myself from my distractions. If I'm [doing] something and I want to be present when my child wants to tell me all about their latest Lego creation, I need to physically remove myself from what I was [doing]; get up and go see what they are talking about. Or sit down with them on my lap and turn my whole self toward them. Otherwise, it's too easy to sneak a peek at what I was looking at before and get distracted again" (Humphries, "The Power of Focus ie. Being Present").

This mom has learned what I've learned. Work can get in the way of being Present. It doesn't matter whether you're bringing work home from the office or whether it's a pile of laundry calling to you. To be Present, even for small amounts of time, you have to leave it at the door, put it down, or walk away.

4—A HEAD FILLED WITH ANOTHER AGENDA

You all know what I'm referring to here. Those moments when you're looking at your child, you see their mouth moving, you hear the words, but you can't focus in. Your mind is filled with all the things you have to figure out, get done, or respond to. Here's a perfect example:

Recently . . . I got to learn . . . about the power of Being Present. . . . [Mary Ann] gave us a challenge that's been, well, challenging for me. It's a simple one, and I really needed it, but it's been harder . . . than I expected.

> "Kids can smell a rat when we pretend we're present."
>
> —Mimi Doe, author of *Busy But Balanced* and *10 Principles for Spiritual Parenting*

Here's what it is. You'll laugh; it sounds so easy. Commit to Be Present with one person each day for three minutes. Be totally focused on them, no multitasking or thinking about other things. No other agenda, no looking into the future, just looking in their eyes. Listening to them, and letting them know you value what they feel, say, and who they are by the way you are with them. Three minutes. Anyone can do that for three minutes, right?

Well, it turns out it's not so easy for me. I've gotten good at doing three or four things at once, which has served me well in some ways. But it often means I'm missing things that matter the most, opportunities to connect and teach and understand my kids better. Nursing a baby, while typing an email, while half listening to a child's request . . . have become a normal way of life for me. And it doesn't only zap my energy, it zaps my power to touch my children and be touched by them. Yes, I needed this exercise. I want to learn to harness the power of [being present]!" (Humphries, "The Power of Focus ie. Being Present")

I raised my seven children over a thirty-nine-year period. I understand what's involved in managing a home, making a living, working in the community, and helping children take lessons, be in sports, play instruments, do homework . . . I get it!

Here's something else I get. To be Present you have to learn to let it all go for a few minutes at a time so you can see, hear, and respond in loving and caring ways to your child. It isn't enough to just fill their needs.

You can't deceive children. They know when you're Present and when you're not!

5—FAMILY MANAGEMENT

Sharon Silver, a parenting educator, has said, "When a parent and a child connect, their hearts open. Both parent and child feel the love surging back and forth between them. When they're both filled up with the love that naturally flows between them, they feel renewed" (Silver 2015).

If this is the case, why wouldn't we engage in this type of connection regularly? Why wouldn't we take the time to make it happen?

I'm sure one of the reasons is because we're busy managing our home and family.

One busy father tackled the topic in a poignant *New York Times* essay called "Please Forgive My Spotless Home." David McGlynn writes about being "wracked with guilt" for ignoring and then yelling at his two sons in his effort to clean their house: "An entire weekend had slipped by, and we had barely looked each other in the eye until the moment I had spurned Galen's invitation to join him outside. . . . Our exchange on the staircase was the closest we had come to a conversation all weekend, and I had screamed at him" (McGlynn, "Please Forgive My Spotless Home").

Maintaining a clean home, teaching our children, being a role model, and making a living are struggles parents face. But the fleeting moments of childhood are passing by. So is the opportunity to create relationships with children who have the firm foundation of knowing they matter.

We frequently allow the time and effort it takes to manage our home and family come between us and the renewing moments of Presence we can and should have with our children daily. It's important to learn to *stop* managing, for moments at a time, in order to be Present.

6—THE NEED FOR SOLUTIONS

I'm embarrassed to begin this section with a true story about myself and my youngest daughter when she was thirteen years old. I'm embarrassed because I should have known better.

The school year was tough for Kate. She had difficult experiences with both teachers and students. She would come home and share what had gone on during the day, how she was feeling, who said what and why, and her response. And I, being the take-charge woman that I am, would come up with solutions. This went on for a few months.

One day she was relating a lunchroom experience, and I began giving her suggestions about what she could do. Finally, she looked me in the eye and said, "Mom, I don't need you to fix this for me. What I need is for you to listen." Wow, that brought me to my senses! How in the world could my daughter feel I was Present, hearing, and seeing her, if I was so busy in my mind figuring out what to say next, coming up with the solution?

While we're forming these solutions in our mind, we often miss the rest of the story, the part not shared with words.

When we're Present with a child, listening takes on a different quality. We're not listening to get enough information to make a judgment about what's being said and then pronounce a solution. When we're Present, we hear to connect with the speaker and to understand how they feel. It's active and engaged and seeks to hear the words and also to hear the heart. (More on active listening in chapter 3.)

If you want to be Present in conversations with your children, then you'll have to temper the temptation to offer solutions.

7—FEAR OF INVOLVEMENT OR MESS

Have you ever been listening to the ideas, thoughts, or feelings of your child and were inwardly cringing because you could see you would have to become involved or there might be a mess. Possibly their idea was totally impossible and unrealistic.

My daughters, Jodie, Marie, and Kate, have decided to listen with real interest and delight to their children no matter what. They say yes, to whatever it is, more often than they say no. I have to tell you it's working out for them and they have children who know they matter!

Jack, aged eight, will frequently talk up a storm about things that aren't possible. At one point, when he was seven, he was completely into Bigfoot. He talked incessantly with his grandpa, who was sincerely interested. They watched videos and looked at maps of where Bigfoot supposedly lived.

But soon the talk got serious for Jack. He was planning a trip to Virginia, which anyone knows is where you go if you want to trap a Bigfoot. He talked about it constantly. Grandpa and Jodie didn't know quite what to do. After all, no one was going to Virginia Bigfoot hunting.

Grandpa and Mom listened and agreed with Jack that it would be wonderful to take that trip. But they worried about Jack's feelings when he finally realized there wasn't going to be a trip. In the meantime, Jack experimented with traps, drew pictures, painted Big Feet, and created lots of little messes in his enthusiasm. Here's what happened after a couple of months.

One day Jack came to his grandpa and said, "We can't go to Virginia, can we?" "No," his grandpa responded. "Well, then I'll build a Bigfoot trap out in the yard," Jack replied. And he did.

It was a small plastic container tied to a rope. One end of the rope was thrown over a tree branch and then staked to the ground. He slept on the porch all night to see what would happen. It was a fabulous adventure and filled his small boy bucket. It did involve his mom a bit but let me tell you she got lots of points!

Mom and Grandpa did not tell Jack they weren't going to Virginia. They didn't squash any of his plans. They *saw* his interest and heard him. They waited patiently and when he needed help they gave what could be given. Jodie didn't worry about him making messes.

If we want to be Present with our children, or anyone else for that matter, we have to stop worrying that it might involve work or make a mess.

We certainly cannot indulge all of our children's fantasies and big plans, but we can listen and agree that if it could be done, it

> "By making eye contact, getting down to your child's level, offering a touch, or using a tone of your voice that conveys a desire to genuinely connect, you disarm yourself. You make it possible to reach your child more deeply and truly move forward together."
>
> —Hilary Flower, author of *Adventures in Gentle Discipline: A Parent-to-Parent Guide*

would be wonderful. We can let them dream. We can gather materials when asked. We can help clean up. We can also say yes a bit more often than we say no.

8—PLAY ADVERSE

I always felt I had a pretty ordinary family growing up. We didn't seem all that different than other families I knew. Looking back I can see one thing that made us different—kids and adults rarely played together.

I remember my sisters and I had a few late night chats with my mom. We sang in the car as we traveled, but we never played board games with Mom and Dad. I can't recall having tea parties or playing dolls with them. We didn't roughhouse or play any running games with our parents.

I spent a lot of time at my grandparent's house. I loved them and they loved me, but we didn't play together; no tickling or roughhousing. Occasionally I got to go to work with them. I know we never played any board games or things like that. It was the same with all of my aunts and uncles. Kids played with kids and adults sat around and chewed the fat, so to speak.

Play is what was missing from my relationship with my parents. Because of the lack of play, there were fewer moments of connection with them. There were fewer times when they were Present with me. That had an impact on our relationship as I grew up and became an adult. Although I had wonderful parents, and I know they loved me, the essential element of knowing I mattered to them was weaker than they probably knew.

As a young mother, I was play adverse myself. I enjoyed watching children play. I liked providing play resources for them. I even liked giving them ideas and getting them going, but I didn't want to play with them. I rarely roughhoused with my children. I played board games occasionally and infrequently did the block or doll thing. For my older children, the element of *you matter* was weaker than I would have liked it to have been.

You too may feel reticent about playing with your children. I talk to many parents who find it difficult to play with kids. They feel too busy to take the time. They often feel tired or they want to get their *stuff* done so they can have a moment to do what they like. Perhaps they grew up in a family like mine and playing with kids isn't appealing.

I've found it helpful to recognize that what play looks like can be different for each family. If you're play adverse, then find something you can do with your child that is play and is enjoyable for both of you. Remember, it doesn't have to last long, often as little as five minutes. (We'll discuss solutions for how to play in chapter 3.)

IN SUMMARY

Quality or quantity? It doesn't matter unless we learn that quality is being Present. It isn't what we do with a child, where we take a child, or the level of excitement and fun. It's the gift of our full attention, our whole self, nothing held back, and it can take as little as five minutes or less.

No matter how much we love our children, if we fail to be Present consistently over time, they will fail to feel they matter. And as any adult child knows, love isn't always enough! We all want to know we matter!

CHAPTER 2

THE COST of Checking Out

W hen we check out, there are consequences. We will, as a family, pay a price. Sometimes the cost of checking out isn't apparent until our children are grown.

A while back, my then thirty-eight-year-old daughter said, "When I was a kid I didn't get any one-on-one time and it has impacted my life." You need to know Jenny loves me madly. But what she missed was my Presence.

We can all choose to be Present. The choice isn't dependent upon where we work, our finances, our health, our energy level, or anything else. Whether we're Present with our children is a choice.

When we face an important life-altering choice, it's helpful to be able to see the consequences of the choice. In this chapter, we'll consider the consequences to our children and family when we choose to check out. These consequences include

- Loss of esteem

- Poor parent responses and poor parent messages

- Less enjoyment

- Missing what matters most

- Regret

LOSS OF ESTEEM

I was forty years old when my youngest child was born. She was seven years younger than her next oldest sibling. When Kate was twelve, the sibling closest in age turned nineteen, and I was fifty-two. Something happened to me. I was done. I kept cooking and cleaning and helping with homework, going to concerts and sporting events—all the *things* we equate with good parenting. But I stopped being emotionally Present with Kate.

Until that time, I had made real progress in understanding what being Present looks like, and I found I liked it. It was fun being with those last two children. Kate and I would help Barry deliver his paper route, talking and laughing and finding giant icicles.

We had wonderful bedtime routines, which were a lot of fun and made us laugh. I read and sang to them. I was a better listener. I hugged more.

That year, Barry graduated from high school and went away to work for the summer and, as I said, something happened to me. It was a hard time for Kate. Not only was her brother gone, but so was her mom. I was there physically to manage home and family, but I was not as emotionally Present as I had been.

Now, I have seven physically beautiful children, but Kate is elegantly beautiful. She's my tallest girl and looks like a model. She's bright and charming and has a beautiful smile. Here's the interesting thing. When she was twenty years old, I realized this beautiful, amazingly talented woman had little esteem.

I couldn't get over the situation and pondered it for a long time. I began to pray because praying is what I do when I need answers to difficult questions. One day, as I was driving across town, a thought came into my head. You know, one of those thoughts you're sure didn't originate with you. Here was the thought: "Kate has a hole in her soul, and it won't be filled until you're Present."

Wow! This experience was years before I began organizing and teaching my thoughts on what it means to be Present. But I had started thinking about this issue, and I could go back to her earlier childhood and I knew how it had been.

So I began figuring out how Presence would look with an adult child. It's been five years since that day. I'm not sure the hole has been totally filled, but I do know I've worked on it, doing small and simple things consistently, over the intervening time. I think it's making a difference. Our being Present does matter to our children's belief in their personal value.

In a study of adolescents from 1997, we read, "Youths who experience higher levels of parental involvement and a closer relationship with their parents are less likely to exhibit behavioral problems and to engage in risk behaviors. In addition, they tend to achieve better grades and higher levels of education and to experience better emotional health" (Resnick et al. 1997).

And in another study: "Youths whose parents exhibit love, responsiveness, and involvement tend to have higher levels of self-esteem and internal self-control" (Gray and Steinberg 1999).

How our children *feel* because of the messages we send matters far more than anything we can *do* for them. I did all the right things for my youngest daughter, but it was how she felt in her teen years that ultimately mattered the most when it came to her sense of worth. Far more than attending concerts, helping with homework, cooking great meals, and all the rest was her need to know that she mattered. She needed me to be Present, and when I wasn't, her sense of worth took a *big* hit.

> "Children desperately need to know—and to hear in ways they understand and remember—that they're loved and valued by mom and dad."
>
> —Gary Smalley, family counselor and founder of Smalley Relationship Center

When it comes to esteem, being Present matters to both children and youth.

POOR PARENT RESPONSES AND POOR PARENT MESSAGES

Here's an excerpt from an article a mother wrote for my blog:

In the past, I've believed the myth that giving of myself to my children will drain me of the little energy I have. . . . I have so many worries to focus on, who has time to be present?! . . . It leads to a vicious cycle of me pulling away, them reaching out more desperately for me, and my responding with even more protective withdrawal. Or sometimes I give in grudgingly and half-heartedly. Both of these responses on my part leave my children feeling unloved and empty. (Schetzel, "Being Present: My Cure for a Busy Life")

This mom has learned the importance of being Present. She knows how she responds makes a difference in how her children feel about themselves based on the message she is sending. She also knows if she checks out, it affects her response.

When we're checked out in some way, our responses to our children are compromised. Their needs, comments, and behaviors can seem intrusive. They can feel like naughtiness. They can appear overwhelming or excessive. It isn't that they're any of these things. It's that our mind is fully occupied elsewhere and our distraction affects how we respond.

One of my clients is a self-employed mom who works at home. She felt stressed because her seven-year-old son seemed whiny and needy and he constantly interrupted her work. Their relationship was strained. She had begun to worry because it was having an effect on how he felt about himself.

As we talked, it became evident to her that she was checking out often and that was causing her to respond in ways that made them both feel bad, and those responses colored how he perceived her feelings for him.

Let's look at a few scenarios you'll probably relate to.

1. It's been a long day and you're standing at the kitchen counter playing a game on your cell phone before you begin dinner. This is a game you find relaxing and you're fully engaged.

Your child comes into the kitchen and asks you to help him with something. You reply, "Okay. In a minute," while continuing the game. Your child repeats the request. This time, you feel a bit of irritation. While continuing the game you reply in a sharper tone, "I said I would. Just a minute! Be patient."

As children will, your child repeats the request and this time in a demanding voice. You finally look at your child and reply, "Don't talk to me like that. It's disrespectful. I said I would help you in a minute!"

2. You have created a to-do list for the day. It's long and everything on it feels urgent. Your brain keeps revisiting all you have to do. Your child comes into the laundry room and starts to tell you about her day. You half-hear and occasionally nod your head while still working on your current project and thinking about the next thing on the list. Finally, she stops talking and wanders off.

3. You have put your six-year-old to bed. As you get ready to walk out of the room, he says, "Dad, can I have a drink of water?" After the drink, he asks for his favorite stuffed animal and you search the closet for it. He wants to know if you'll read a story.

It was a busy day at work. You still have some stuff to finish for the next day. You know your child wants time with you and you feel you should give it. But work is calling. You reply, "Listen, it's time for bed. Stop stalling and go to sleep." Then you turn out the light.

All of these parents had checked out in one way or another and it colored their responses, which sent a "you don't matter" message to their child whether that's what they meant to say or not.

When we've checked out with technology, work, or are totally involved in what comes next on our list, it's easy to be irritated and frustrated with our children, which leads to poor responses on our part.

Children don't hear "I'm busy. I'll help you later." They don't sense you're overwhelmed or tired. They aren't old enough or experienced enough to give you the benefit of the doubt. They hear, "You have no value." "You don't matter." "This is more important than you."

Poor responses lead to poor messages we don't mean and don't intend to send.

LESS ENJOYMENT

When we check out, we enjoy family life less! The ways we check out often leave us feeling irritated, frustrated, or overwhelmed by our family members. But when we're Present, we feel and respond differently. We're able to enjoy being with them.

Mealtime is a good example. If we're anxious to get to our favorite TV program, check our email and Facebook, or are consumed with all we still have to do, we want our family to hurry and eat so we can move on to the next thing.

However, when we're Present, we smile at our children, hold conversations and laugh, despite spilled milk and tipped chairs. We allow the time it takes to eat together and enjoy one another's company. A feeling of happiness, contentment, or gratitude is generated.

Sometimes we think if we can check out for a minute, we can recharge, get a grip, and have a rest. But that isn't what usually happens. While we're checked out we miss important, energy-giving moments *with* our children. Deep inside we know it. When we check out, we cheat ourselves of what we could have experienced with our family.

Happiness reduces the burdens that come with living. Happiness increases our ability to manage the hard things in life. So doesn't it make sense to work at accumulating as many moments of happiness as you can each day?

If you can do it in five-minute increments *with* your child, why wouldn't you? This is what can happen when you learn to be Present. If you make the effort to change your *way of being* with your family and learn to be Present more often—to stay checked in—you'll enjoy your family more. You'll miss less of the things that matter most.

MISSING WHAT MATTERS MOST

Five years ago I wrote something I want to share with you:

The windows are fog covered from soup steam and the air smells of baking bread. It's cold outside on this wintery Montana day. I hear the children clattering through the gate and up the back steps, coming home from school. "Don't bang the screen door."

The kitchens filled with bodies, wet coats, boots, and mittens are strewn on the floor. "You guys pick up those coats and hang them up. Put your mittens away."

What in the world made me think of this most ordinary moment in my past with such an ache? It was the shower. The shower's where I think, random thoughts about what I need to do, what the day was like, the book I'm reading. Tonight I had this thought, this memory, and it pierced my heart fiercely.

How could such an ordinary memory cause such emotion? Why would I even remember this past day?

It's because it wasn't ordinary, it was miraculous. This is how the moments of our days with our children are; they're miraculous.

We rarely perceive it as so because we're busy taking care of the business at hand. We just don't see the beauty.

Forty-five years ago I was twenty-one, a new mother starting out. If I live to be one hundred, and I think I will, I will have lived another forty years. Since that day so long ago, how many ordinary, magical days have I missed seeing? Was today miraculous? In forty years will I remember my days with such happiness and nostalgia as the memory I had today? Have I learned what matters most in life? (Johnson, "What matters most in life")

As I look back over the years, I know I missed much of the beauty of life with my children because I was so busy managing it all. I wasn't always Present in the beautiful, everyday moments.

I want to help you grasp a few more precious moments with your children so you stop missing them. The day will come when you'll wish you could listen to the happy prattle of your child or youth as they tell you about their day. That's how it will be!

We move through life taking care of business. We worry too much. We hug too little, smile not enough, and push away the joy that we could have. We get confused about what matters most. We check out and miss the Present moments we could have with our children.

It's funny (and sad) how it's the things that you can't get back, like being Present with your kids, are the easiest things to put off. We put them off in favor of stuff that will always be there, such as dishes, phone calls, work and errands, texts and games.

That exact moment might not ever come back, no matter

> "KIDS. They know a BRIBE when they see one. They want a PARENT, not a PAYOFF. They don't care if you're Jack-King-Rodeo or Mister-You-Own-New-York. All they understand is time spent WITH YOU or WITHOUT YOU. It's that SIMPLE."
>
> —Carew Papritz, author of *The Legacy Letters: His Wife, His Children, His Final Gift*

how much you might try to recreate it when it fits in the schedule. Taking five minutes or less to stop, turn, and take in your child completely means capturing something irreplaceable.

Remember my thirty seconds with Marie? That happened more than thirty years ago, and sometimes it's such a sweet memory that it can bring me to tears, and I almost missed it. If I hadn't taken thirty seconds to be Present, I would have missed it!

This is worth remembering when you're tempted to put your children off for work, text messages, games on your cell phone, laundry, cooking, and all the other things that make up your life. It's worth remembering when being Present isn't convenient. If you take this to heart, you'll have less regret when it's all said and done.

REGRET

My sister, Cindy, has a saying: "Regret will come knocking. Open the door and acknowledge it, but don't invite it in for tea." I love that because we all have regrets. I have regrets of my own. Nevertheless, I believe that as we learn new ways of being, we can lessen the regrets that will come knocking, especially those from parenting.

Lauren Revell, from Huggies Little Swimmers, commissioned some research as part of the campaign to encourage more parents to take their children swimming. They asked two thousand parents what regrets they had from their parenting.

Researchers found that more than three-quarters of parents have at least one thing they regret doing, or not doing. And two-thirds admit they would do things differently if they could relive that period again (Waterlow 2012).

The top three responses were

- Working too much

- Worrying about the little things

- Not playing with my children more

Isn't it interesting that these are some of the things I've mentioned as ways we check out, and when we check out, whether intentionally or unintentionally, we will regret it?

Dr. Angharad Rudkin, a clinical psychologist who works with families, surveyed his clients asking them for their top five regrets. Number one was spending too little time with their children.

He said, "You're not just spending time with them—you're laying foundations that help them feel important and valued. Even a short amount of time every day, when you're completely with your children, can work wonders to make them feel other people are interested in them" (Rudkin 2013).

One of my big takeaways from parenting is that checking out will bring regrets of the heart whether we believe so now or not. As parents, we love our children, and we want what's best for them. In the hustle and bustle of busy days, it's easy to lose sight of what *best* looks like. As they grow and life begins to calm down, we look back, and it becomes apparent to us.

One of the costs of checking out is that we lose precious time with those most valuable to us, and we can't reclaim it. We carry the regret with us, and it's a heavy weight.

I have a friend, Tiffany Berg Coughran, who has five children. Two were gone from home, two of them married in a six-month period and a third left home for school. In a short amount of time, she was faced with the empty nest time of life.

Here's what she told me in a conversation. "I truly believe that my lack of regret and my confidence, gratitude, and clarity about my children's growing up was that I decided when they were little to do everything in my power to be *present* with them. For me that meant getting creative with my income, juggling and innovating so I could work from home. I included them in my charity work and my businesses. Including them and working around their needs allowed me those incredible, ordinary, irreplaceable moments. Ahhh. I *loved* it all!"

Tiffany understood what it means to be Present, and she worked at it all her children's growing up years—not perfectly, but consistently, in all the everyday moments.

When we choose to be too busy to be Present with our children for even a few minutes each day, when we decide to check out, there's a price we will pay. It will come in the form of regret. Regret for the beautiful moments we missed. Regret for the times when our responses were poor. Regret for the messages we sent and didn't mean. Regret for the happiness and joy we let slip away in our distracted and checked out moments.

> **"As your kids grow they may forget what you said, but won't forget how you made them feel."**
>
> —Kevin Heath,
> Australian soccer player

IN SUMMARY

Remember that when we check out there are consequences for our children, ourselves, and our family:

- Loss of esteem

- Poor parent responses and poor parent messages

- Less enjoyment

- Missing what matters most

- Regret

We have our children for only a short while. In fact, we have only about nine hundred weeks before they leave us to build their lives. Wouldn't you rather look back on those nine hundred weeks with fondness rather than regret? You can if you learn to check back in.

In the next ten chapters, I'll teach you ways to be Present through simple applications.

Chapter 3 will help you develop skills that will facilitate greater Presence.

Chapter 4 illustrates specific actions to take that are simple, readily available, and require only small amounts of time, some less than five minutes.

In chapters 5 through 13, I'll offer information that can help you adjust your thinking when you're with your children to achieve a Present mind-set.

CHAPTER 3

MASTER Important Skills

Being Present consistently will become easier if you master a few important skills. These skills can help you tune in to your children. They assist you to hear what they're saying. They help you learn more about your kids so you can appreciate who they are even when you may not be happy with a behavior. They allow you to connect more often in your daily activities.

Being Present isn't as much about time as it is about our understanding of how to find moments to be present when we're busy.

We're going to consider six skills:

- Active listening

- Mini-conversations

- Random touch

- Sparks

- Play

- Being silly and having Fun

Don't assume being with your children is the same as connecting with them. Connecting involves being Present, and you can be Present more often as you learn to use these skills. They'll help you remain checked in. You will be able to use some of them daily, and others multiple times a day. It can be a relief to have a quiver full of possibilities for connecting with your children.

1—ACTIVE LISTENING

When we're Present, we listen to connect with the speaker and to understand how they feel about what they're saying. It's active and engaged and seeks to hear the words and, more important, to hear the heart.

Because this type of listening doesn't come naturally, I've had to develop steps to make it happen more often. They may be helpful to you also.

A. STOP what you're doing. Turn away from any technology, book, or project. If you truly can't stop, tell your child you can see this is important to them and you want to hear what they have to say. Set a specific time when you'll be free and keep it. Saying "we'll talk about it later" is not specific and sends the message you're not available to them, that whatever else you're doing is more interesting or more important. If at all possible, *stop* and listen now!

B. Make eye contact with your child. I remember reading that an infant can tell the difference between a face that is in order and one with the features jumbled.

From my experience, I know babies are interested in their parent's faces. They look at their parent's faces constantly and reach out to touch them. Infants want us to look back at them. As we grow older, desire for eye contact with the people in our lives that matter to us remains.

Eye contact is looking directly into your child's eyes and not looking away at other things or looking down. When we look at our children as we listen to them, it sends a powerful message that we care, we hear them, and they matter.

C. Respond to what your child is feeling, not only what they're saying. When you're Present, you'll respond to feelings more quickly and more accurately. This helps your child feel heard. You can say things like, "Boy—how maddening!" or "You didn't like that, did you?" or "How did you feel?" This helps your child know that you view their feelings as valid and important.

D. Listen with patience and interest. Whatever you're feeling, your child will know! They're like energy magnets. If your energy is inwardly impatient, they'll know. If you're dying to get back to your stuff, they'll feel it. If you're bored out of your mind, it's coming across loud and clear. It may all be on a subconscious level, but they know. Hold thoughts in your mind that will help you maintain interest and patience.

For example, you can think, "I sure love this kid. They're so interesting, funny, kind, thoughtful," whatever. Hold thoughts that allow you to embrace fully the moment you're sharing with your child.

Avoid interrupting. Ask only those questions that help clarify. Your job at this moment is not to teach, reprimand, or *fix*. It's to listen.

Being present with your child is an end in itself. It isn't about resolution, teaching, making progress, none of that. It's about connection, pure and simple. You can always teach later. Right now, be Present!

During a day, there are dozens of opportunities to stop and listen. We can't actively listen in all of them. But if we can increase those times we do, it will have a big impact on our relationships.

Remember, being Present is a gift we give another person without thought of return. It means giving full attention, our whole self, nothing held back.

2—MINI-CONVERSATIONS

This is one of my all-time favorite ways to connect with kids. Conversing with children can be so much fun, and it's relaxing and energizing.

The purpose of a mini-conversation is to hear what your kids have to say and to make a connection that's enjoyable. Sometimes you share cool stuff, sometimes they share cool stuff, and through it all, you stay Present and listen. Mini-conversations always feel enjoyable to both parties! They never feel like a lecture.

Here are three mini-conversations. One lasted less than three minutes, and one spanned five weeks.

Conversation 1—Jack, my grandson, who was two at the time, had a dear friend who turned ninety. He gave Jack a bunch of helium-filled balloons from his party. Jack and I took one balloon to the front yard and let it go. As it floated upward, we had a mini-conversation. It went like this:

> **"By familiar conversation, children's curiosity may be roused much more effectually, and by it they may be taught a great deal more in a little time than can possibly be done in the austere magisterial way of calling them to a lecture."**
>
> —George Turnbull, author of *Observations Upon Liberal Education, In All Its Branches: In Three Parts*

Jack: "Look at the balloon go up!"

Me: "Pretty isn't it? Do all balloons float up like these?"

Jack: "No."

Me: "Do you know why this balloon floats up into the air?"

Jack: "No."

Me: "Well, they have gas inside called helium. It makes the balloon go up."

Jack: "Cool!"

That's it; that's all there was to the conversation. We stood and watched the balloon until it was out of sight. We held hands. It was a pleasurable moment. We felt connected as we did something we enjoyed together.

Conversation 2—Austin was six, and he was the son of a friend. We had a *great* relationship. His mom always commented on what interesting conversations we had. Part of the reason this was the case was because I consciously worked at keeping the conversation going. I wanted to talk with Austin, to know what he thought and felt, because I wanted to know him better. He was a fun little boy.

Week One—"Where do you live?" "Do you have kids?" "How many kids do you have?" "How do you know my mom?" "Are you coming back?"

Austin's questions came rapid fire because we had just met.

"Hi, I'm Mary Ann. What's your name?"

"Austin."

"Well, it's good to meet you, Austin." Then he was shooed away by adults who felt he was bothering me.

Week Two—"Hi there. Now, what was your name again?"

"Austin."

"Oh yes, Austin. I remember now." But I hadn't remembered.

Week Three—"So tell me your name again, one more time."

"Austin."

"I'm going to remember your name, Austin." I wondered how in the world I was going to remember his name, this new friend of mine. Let's see, Austin, the capital of Texas. Great! Now I'll never forget.

Week Four—"Hi, Austin."

"Hey, how did you remember my name?"

"Well, I used a name remembering trick. Do you know what Texas is?"

"No."

"Well, it's a big piece of land in the United States, and it has a big town in it called Austin. So when I see you, I think of Texas and it helps me remember your name is Austin."

"Cool."

"Austin, do you know my name?"

"No."

"Well, it's Mary Ann. Let's see, how you could use the name trick to remember my name? Can you think of a poem about a Mary?"

"Oh yeah, 'Mary Had a Little Lamb.'"

"Good job. Now you'll never forget my name. Cool trick huh!"

Week Five —Austin was sitting on a stool in the kitchen. His face lit up when I walked in.

"Hi, Austin how are you?" He gave me a satisfied smile and said deliberately, with emphasis on the word Mary, "Hi, Mary, I'm fine." I could tell he was happy with himself.

"Good job, Austin, I can see you used the name remembering trick."

"Well now I know your name, and so I don't need the trick."

"Right, Austin, we only have to use it when we first meet someone, until we know their name well. Then we don't need the trick anymore."

"Cool."

Austin told me how he was learning other people's names. We had quite a few conversations about names. This led to conversations about his friends and school.

Conversation 3—One day, while I was working at my computer, Benny, my two-year-old grandson, came and climbed into my lap. He watched what I was doing for a short time and asked, "What this?" while pointing to the cord connecting my computer to the wall outlet.

I responded that the cord brought electricity to the computer and a computer needs electricity to work. He repeated, "Electricity."

He pointed to the printer cord and said, "What that?" "It's a cord to the printer, Benny. It lets the computer tell the printer to go to work." I pointed out the cursor and hit the printer icon. We watched the page print.

He pointed to the cord connecting the mouse to the computer. "What that?" "It's called a mouse, Benny. See, when I move it, this little cursor moves on the screen and lets me pick what I want." He repeated, "Cursor." He was fascinated by this stuff.

Finally, he pointed to the thumb drive I was using for my project. "What that?" I told him it was a thumb drive and it had pictures on it. He said, "Thumb drive." I moved the mouse and pointed out the cursor on the screen, and he watched while I opened a file of pictures. We took a moment or two and scrolled through the pictures while he named off the people.

Then Benny climbed off my lap and went off happy with himself. The whole conversation took less than five minutes.

The three conversations I've shared were simple. There was no preparation or planning ahead. They happened because I wanted to connect with the children involved. This leads us to the first tip to having great mini-conversations with kids.

TIPS FOR HAVING SUCCESSFUL
MINI-CONVERSATIONS

A. Desire the conversation. I'm a great conversationalist with kids of all ages because I want to talk to them. I want to know them. I want to know what they think. I want to know how they feel. Do you want to know more about your children? Do you want to hear what they have to say? This is the number one key to having successful mini-conversations.

B. Listen more than you talk. You may have to ask a question or make a statement to get a mini-conversation going but then listen as much as you can. Pose the question or make the statement and wait to see what happens. If there's no response, the conversation is over. You wait a while and try again with a different question or comment.

As your child or family begins to respond, keep asking questions with an occasional comment. If you spend most of the time being quiet or asking questions, you'll avoid giving a mini-lecture.

C. Listen without judgment or giving your opinion. A conversation goes much further with a child when we withhold our judgments and opinions. There's great value in focusing on a child's feelings or reactions in any given situation rather than sharing what we think or feel. When we can listen without judgment, it helps children process their emotions.

I have to laugh when I think of a conversation a friend and blogger shared. She was riding in the car with her teenaged daughter, and it went like this:

"Mom."

"What?"

"I don't think I should have a baby now."

"Is this a consideration?"

"I thought about it, but now I've realized something."

"What's that?"

"I only really want to buy lots of cute little baby shoes."

"Oh, that's very different from having a real baby."

"Yeah, that's what I think too."

When this mom listened calmly, without judgment or sharing her opinion, she found out what was really going on. It was all about cute baby shoes and not sex. She learned something about her daughter. The conversation lasted long enough to know what her daughter was thinking (Moore, "What I learn while driving . . . ").

Here's another example of listening without judgment or opinion.

"Mom, I don't like David."

"Hmm, why not?"

"He's dumb."

"What happened to make you feel that way?"

"He pushed me off the swing."

"Oh really? How did you feel?"

"Not good! I really wanted to swing, and it hurt my leg."

"You didn't get to swing."

"No, and it wasn't nice! I would never do that to someone!"

Notice that in the above conversation the child was not called out for using the word dumb, which may have derailed the conversation.

Listening without judgment also applies if your child makes an incorrect statement. Here's a conversation I had with a four-year-old.

Child: "All caterpillars are green, and I hate caterpillars."

Me: "Is that so? Why?"

Child: "I don't like that creepy feeling."

Me: "Ewww. I don't like that creepy feeling either."

Child: "We're the same." Big smile.

The conversation may not have had the happy connection at the end if I had informed the child that all caterpillars are not green.

Mini-conversations will go much better if you stay away from judgment and giving your opinion.

D. Listen with interest. Use active listening. Listening with deep interest shows that you care about what your child is saying in contrast to simply listening because it's what parents do. If you question whether your kids can tell the difference, *don't*. They can, and it matters.

E. Ask open-ended questions. How did that work out? How do you feel about that? What do you think you can do? Why don't you like that? Would you go there again? Are you considering that?

F. Believe that kids like talking with adults. Occasionally, adults feel that kids wouldn't enjoy conversing with them, but that's not true. Most kids enjoy speaking with adults because, for some, it gives them a sense of maturity. For others, it feels connecting and kids like that.

For all children and youth, it helps them feel that what they have to say is important. Conversing about world events, sports, hobbies, interests, what happened at school, the past, and so on will open the door for your child to feel comfortable enough to come to you if they need advice or help later on.

G. Take advantage of *wait times*. There are wait times often in a family: at the doctor's or other appointments, waiting for the school bus to come, while Dad runs into the store leaving the family in the car, when a pan of cookies is baking, when the light's red, and so on. These wait times are perfect for having mini-conversations.

Try having a mini-conversation when your family's in the potty-training mode. Tiny children say such cute things. When you put your two-year-old on the potty, say any old thing that comes to your mind. "I think worms are slimy." "I think birds sing pretty." "Blue is my favorite color." It doesn't matter. You want to get them talking because you're working on the relationship. And frankly, wouldn't that be more fun than saying, "Go" or "Pee" every minute and a half?

H. Have mini-conversations at the most important touchpoints: mealtime, car time, and bedtime. Have dinner mini-conversations no matter who spills milk, slurps their soup, or tips over their chair. You can get it going by saying, "Guess what I saw today," or "Do you know what my boss did?" or "Hey, did anyone have anything fun happen today?" Try the Conversation Game explained in chapter 4, in Touchpoint 1—Mealtime.

Coming back from your fifth trip to the kitchen to get something for someone—smile and say, "Did you know that . . . " If your purpose for the meal is to work on your family relationships, you'll be able to let go of the frustrations of repeated trips to the kitchen and focus on Presence.

While helping your kids get ready for bed, take advantage of tooth-brushing time. While your little kids are brushing their teeth, sit on the toilet and strike up a mini-conversation. Again, ask questions or throw out a statement. "I love red socks!" "I hate the squishy feel of peas in my mouth." "Do you like baseball?" Kids will respond, mouth full of toothpaste or not!

Have mini-conversations no matter how many times you have to play referee on the way home from the store or whether your favorite show starts right when you put Janet to bed. Mealtime, car time, and bedtime happen daily, and these are perfect mini-conversation moments.

3—RANDOM TOUCH

I love random touch! This is an effective tool for connecting in astounding ways with your children. Random touch helps reduce the need for discipline, opens pathways to mini-conversations, melts stony hearts, and bonds children to parents.

When I was a younger mom, I had a challenge hugging my children. I could hug and snuggle babies, but as they moved past their toddler years, I found it more difficult. Recently on a walk, my forty-four-year-old daughter commented that touching wasn't part of our family culture. I felt a bit badly about that.

> **"We need four hugs a day for survival. We need eight hugs a day for maintenance. We need 12 hugs a day for growth."**
>
> —Virginia Satir, American author and social worker

There were reasons why I had this difficulty and in time those reasons were worked out, but my older children grew up without as much physical contact as they would have liked. However, all we can do is move forward when we learn a better way.

Hugs and snuggles are vital for deep and abiding child-parent relationships and as things in my life righted themselves, I was able to begin connecting in more physical ways with my two youngest children. Their experience was completely different than their older siblings'. We hugged often. I rubbed their backs. I was comfortable sitting next to them and having them cuddle with me.

When my youngest daughter, who is currently twenty-six, is with me, she holds my hand when we're walking together. On her last visit, after we had all gone to bed, she came in our room and snuggled between her dad and I so that we could talk for a while. She has no problem hugging me.

I want to emphasize that touching your children matters when they're small; it matters, even more, when they're youth and it will continue to matter when they're adults.

WHAT A RANDOM TOUCH LOOKS LIKE

Here are a few examples of what a random touch looks like in real life:

- If you see your child sitting on the couch, at the table, on their bed or anywhere, stop, sit close to them, stay for twenty to thirty seconds, squeeze a knee or give a quick hug, and go on your way. No need to say a word.

- When you go into your child's room to wake them up, give them a hug. Don't stand in the hall and yell "Get up." Go in; give a gentle shake to the shoulder and a hug. Say, "Hey buddy. It's time to get up." It's going to take a few more seconds than yelling from the hall, but remember to stay out of management mode and build your relationship instead.

- As you walk through a room or down the hall and see one of your children, look them in the eye and smile. Touch them on their back, arm, or shoulder as they pass by. Don't say anything; just give a squeeze or a pat. You can do this a dozen times a day and use up only a few minutes.

- When you're moving from one room to another (as you go through your day) and you see one of your children, make a small detour. Grab your child and tickle them for a few moments, just long enough to get a little tussle going. Then gently punch a shoulder or tousle a head and move on.

- Hold your child's hand when you're walking together or keep your hand on their back or shoulder for a few moments at a time.

- Rub your child's back while sitting in church, in the doctor's waiting room, and so on.

Random touches are just that, random. They don't require any reason for the touch or hug. They happen whenever you're in close proximity to your child. They're effective with children, youth, and adult children.

I want you to understand how powerful this one skill can be in changing the dynamics of your family. It's easy to do, takes only moments and practically shouts "You matter" to your child. **If you do only one thing in this book, use random touch. It will make a difference!**

If you have a child or youth who doesn't like to be touched, then respect their boundaries. You may have to use some of the other techniques and skills that have been addressed first. Remember that I was a bit touch adverse but I still wanted to connect in meaningful ways and so do your children. Experiment to find out what is acceptable to your child. A teen may not want to be hugged, but may allow you to rub their back.

A SUCCESS STORY

I worked with a mother who was having significant relationship issues with her seventeen-year-old daughter, who was getting ready to graduate. The mom was often irritated by her daughter.

As we talked about how she could reconnect their broken relationship, she decided to experiment with giving her daughter as many random touches as she could remember to each day. I've seen random touch produce amazing healing in relationships, so I felt confident in offering it to this mother as an experiment.

In one week it improved her and her daughter's relationship significantly. They were beginning to talk more. Mom felt less annoyed by her daughter. She was more aware of her daughter. She had begun responding in calmer and more loving ways. They had even made plans to go to lunch together.

Mom said later that using random touch had changed *how* she was with all of her children. And in turn, it has changed how they have responded to her.

Physical touch matters to our children. Children need and want to be touched, hugged, and kissed.

4—SPARKS

What's a Spark, you may ask? Well, a Spark is anything that a child says or does that lets you know they're interested in something right now. We can find opportunities to be Present as we watch for and recognize our children's Sparks.

One of my friends, Hana, has two boys. At the time this experience took place they were six and four. Her boys had begun burping and belching on purpose. They were giggling about farts and other bodily functions. Many mothers in that situation would be reminding them to say excuse me and chastising them for being rude. After all, it's your job to teach them manners, right?

Because of her knowledge of being Present and Sparks, Hana did something quite different. Here's the email she sent me:

> I picked up five books at the library last night. One of the books is about the human body and burps (lol! yes, two boys in my family) and I was following a spark! Their obsession with bodily functions is hilarious, and they're wondering why these things happen! What fun! (funny! is more like it!) Anyway, I will keep you posted! Thanks so much for your wisdom . . . really and truly. Luvs, Hana (Freeman, quoted in Johnson, "Listening and responding to children")

Hana told me later:

- She went back to the library and checked out all of the interesting books she could find on urine, blood, gas, snot—all of it.

- For a whole month, her boys were deeply interested and pored over the books with her and with each other.

- They talked with her and her husband. They wanted to know how their bodies worked.

- They had *interesting* dinner conversations.

- They drew bodies and tracked bodily functions in them. How does a burp go from the top of you to the bottom of you?

When our kids are burping, most of us spend a lot of time saying, "Stop that, it's rude," because we are in a box so to speak. We can only see the need to teach manners and help our kids to not be rude. But once we begin to see differently we say, "Oh my gosh, this is a terrific opportunity." It's what you're looking for, an opportunity to have joy with your children and to connect with them in fun and interesting ways.

> "Take an interest in each other's fascinations. Your son's obsession with Star Wars novels may seem like a waste of time (Why isn't he reading the classics?) but your interest in hearing about the plots, even if they all sound the same at first, will go a long way toward making him feel comfortable talking with you about what's important to him when something's bothering him. Aha!"
>
> —Parenting.com

Another friend, Leah, had dug some dirt in her yard to plant flowers. Before she could plant, the family took a short trip. When they got home, her boys discovered the dirt. They began to play in this spot daily and called it the water game.

They made mud, built cities, created a mine, dug for artifacts, and had a blast all summer. Eventually, there was a four-foot hole in their front yard. You and I might have had a fit and put a stop to all the messy foolishness, but Leah has learned a lot about Presence and Sparks. She went with the flow.

At dinner, they would talk about the water game and all they had done and learned during the day. Mom, dad, and neighbors would come out and ask what was happening, and the boys and their friends were happy to share.

This family had amazing Present moments together in a situation that could have created serious contention. Instead, the parents saw a Spark and used it to have mini-conversations and a lot of fun with their boys. They valued the relationship over a perfect front yard.

Here's what Leah had to say: "I'm so grateful for the shift in my thought process . . . or I would have missed out on an incredibly magical . . . summer (and fall). Now I have a hole so deep they can stand in it to their chests . . . The crater in my yard will last a few months whereas the memories . . . will last forever."

This same mom had another advantageous Spark moment with her oldest son. He was eight at the time. Miles was in love with rocks and left them all over the house. They were in the dryer, on the floor, in his pockets, everywhere. It was very annoying and frustrating and had become a point of contention between mother and son.

One day Leah realized this was a Spark and an opportunity to get Present with Miles. So she asked him, "Miles will you tell me all about your rocks?" He did for the next hour. Leah, like you, had a million other things to do, but she cleared her mind and actively listened (Spencer, quoted in "Example of learning style in children— The Spencer Sparks").

Later, she helped Miles design a very simple system for displaying his precious rocks. The result was that Miles, Leah, and the whole family had a great many activities and conversations in the following year, all based on Miles's love of rocks. It was fun and afforded his parents many opportunities to be Present (Spencer, Leah, quoted in

"How to assist your child's love for learning by responding to their sparks").

I could go on and on giving you examples of parents who have had more opportunities to be Present because they saw a child's Spark, honored it, and spent time learning about it.

Are you wondering if your kids have been giving off any Sparks lately? Believe it or not, the thing that's making a mess, which bugs you or is causing you frustration or annoyance, is probably a Spark.

HOW TO SEE SPARKS

A. Be Present. Do you want to know the number one way to see and hear your child's Sparks? *Be present.* When we're Present in all the mundane moments of a family's day, we will see and hear what we've missed up until now.

It's hard to see a Spark if your head's filled with another agenda or if you're totally engrossed in your technology. It's hard to see if you're trying to avoid becoming involved or prevent a mess. You can't see if you're so busy working that the Spark appears to be an irritation or problem.

B. Ask good questions. You can jump-start your ability to see your children's Sparks by asking yourself questions:

- What activity do you have to make them stop doing to get them to eat or go to sleep?

- What activity are they doing when they seem most engaged and alive?

- When they get to choose what to do on a free afternoon, what activity do they choose?

- What did they love to do when they were three years old? Five years old?

- What are they currently doing that bugs you?

- What do they do that's making a mess?

- What do they collect?

C. Have mini-conversations.

- Share your Sparks and they may share theirs

- Say "You're very good at this"

- Say "You seem interested in this"

- Say "This appears to make you happy/excited"

- Ask "Have you ever thought of . . ."

- Say "I had a great day today"

- At dinner ask "What was the best part of your day?" and have each one share

Pay attention to what keeps coming up over and over again in their answers and their conversations.

5—PLAY

There are real advantages when children play with adults. Sharing laughter, roughhousing and fun can

- Foster empathy

- Build compassion, trust, and intimacy

- Help kids want to cooperate

- Keep you feeling young and energetic

- Keep the relationship fresh and exciting

- Bring joy, vitality, and resilience to the relationship

- Relieve the stress of parenting

- Promote a sense of well-being

- Improve brain function

- Ward off depression

- Provide moments when we can be Present

If you search for pictures on the Internet of children playing with adults here's what you find: adults and kids playing with Legos, dolls, having tea parties, doing puzzles, puppet shows, blocks, trains, and a multitude of activities on the floor. This is what we think of when we think about playing with children, and these types of activities don't appeal to lots of adults. So if it isn't about kid's toys and floor time, what else could it look like?

> "We don't stop playing because we grow old; we grow old because we stop playing."
>
> —George Bernard Shaw, Irish playwright

I'm confident as you think on it and as you read the following ideas, you'll begin to see how you can play with your children even if you're a bit play adverse. Make a mental shift about what play needs to look like and then start playing with your kids regularly.

I know a dad with a three-year-old daughter. She has spent a lot of her life up in the air. She's been thrown onto the couch or bed often. And she *loves* it. They laugh so much. This is how Dad plays with his daughter, and they have a tight bond. No matter how busy he is, and he's an active doctoral student, he can find time to rough-house with his daughter. This is how they play.

I know another family who converses. Yup, this is how they play. They have stimulating conversations at meals. They speak of education, politics, or the latest movie. They converse about silly topics. What would you do if you had a million dollars? If you were on a deserted island, what would be the top five items to have with you? At their table, there's a lot of debating going on, as well as laughter and energy. This is how they play.

A third family is into board games. Mom and Dad spend a few evenings a week playing board games after the kids are in bed. When the kids are awake, they play board games with them. Their kids are little, so the games are Candy Land and Chutes and Ladders. It doesn't seem to matter to these parents; they like board games. Their children like them too. This activity brings energy to the family and lots of laughter. This is how they play.

I love being outdoors and I've found a fun way to play with my grandchildren. It pleases me and pleases them. We walk. As we walk, we search for treasures (pine cones, gum wrappers, pretty stones) that we carry home. We talk and talk and talk. Kids have the most interesting things to say if you get good at having mini-conversations with them. I enjoy it, and so do my grandchildren. This is how we play.

Another way I'm comfortable playing is with craft projects. I like them. I enjoy coming up with a plan and helping the kids do whatever it is. I like watching them use scissors, glue, paper, and glitter. I'm calm with the messes. I enjoy this creative process with my grandchildren.

A few women I know cook for play. They enjoy cooking with their kids, and they do it a lot. Their children help with meals and with baking projects for holidays and gifts. When they're baking, it isn't serious business. The whole family joins in; there's talking and laughter and fun. It's playing for them, and the adults maintain an energy that allows it to feel like play for everyone.

I knew a family who played music together. Each of the kids played an instrument. They and their mom jammed together regularly. The family played at farmers markets, senior citizen centers, and schools. They had a lot fun. They even made a CD. Their mom began this when the children were young. When I knew them, the most inexperienced player was six years old. This is one of the ways this mother played with her children.

We can even turn work into play. When you want the family room cleaned, call everyone in and while they're groaning because there's work to do turn on energetic music. Dance while you clean. It takes a bit of silliness to pull this off, but if you're an adult with a silly bent, this will work for you.

I've known active families who love to use their muscles. These families hike, bike, ski, and frankly run crazy in the backyard. They play touch football or soccer. They use their bodies regularly in strenuous ways. This is how they play.

In our family, we use cross country skis. We bought some and went skiing on a groomed course. We also used the city park and our quiet, small town streets.

I skied with my youngest son, an afternoon kindergartner, to school and brought his skis home on my back. When I asked him what his favorite memories of growing up were, skiing to school was on the list. It was a bonding time for us. I was totally Present for the fifteen minutes it took to ski to school. It was fun! It was playing.

The focus of play is on the experience, not in accomplishing any goal. There doesn't need to be any point to the activity beyond having fun and enjoying each other's company.

Find what type of play will work for you and then play with your family regularly. The word "regularly" is the key. Simple things, done consistently over time, make all the difference.

6—BE SILLY AND HAVE FUN

Life can feel hard. Both parents may work. A home might have a single parent. Money may be tight. Illness may come. Jobs may be lost. A parent may return to school. There's work and stress. Life is hard sometimes.

Joy and happiness come naturally to children, and if we want to be Present with them, we need to shrug off our problems and stress occasionally and be a bit silly and have fun despite the challenges of life. Remember Being Present is a choice we make. Having fun is also a choice.

Being silly and having fun is good for both children and youth. Your little kids will join right in without any encouragement. Your older ones may roll their eyes at you or say, "Oh Dad, stop it." However, deep inside they'll like it, and it creates a point of connection.

Don and I were having trouble with our oldest son. He thought we were lame. He wasn't interested in cooperating or in keeping family rules. It was a tough time.

One day I was doing the dishes and singing "I Love Rock 'n' Roll" at the top of my lungs and dancing at the sink. My son happened to come in, and you can't believe how wide his eyes got. He said, "Mom I didn't know you liked *that* song." I replied by singing even louder while smiling at him. He smiled back, rolled his eyes, and walked out of the room.

That silly moment didn't fix his problems. In fact, he went on to have even more difficult issues. But I felt a connection being forged. As an adult, he's brought the event up in conversation a few times. He always smiles while sharing that memory. It did create a bond that helped hold him to us during those troubled years.

I know that dancing and singing each night to my two younger children did the same. It was fun, and it lightened the troubles of the fading day for them and me.

I have the best witch laugh ever! I'm not kidding. I have to gear up to do it, and I always feel so silly when I do. But my grandkids and my kids ask me for it.

In fact, this morning my three-year-old grandson was asking me to do the "witchy laugh" but not to make it too scary. It's a silly thing that binds us all together. So go ahead and be silly. Make faces, sing silly songs, and dance around your house.

IN SUMMARY

Being Present is simple but that doesn't always equate with easy. It isn't always easy to listen, put your technology to the side, clear out your head, and focus or give a child T-I-M-E.

Try this experiment: Begin by being Present with one of your children daily for a week; just one child, three minutes, once a day for a week. The next week pick a different child. Do this until you've had a week with each child—one child, daily for three minutes, for one week. That's all you have to do. Practice!

After a while you'll do it without thinking and you'll be Present with them all, every day. Being Present will become *how* you are, not what you *do*!

Experiment with the things you've read so far and those you'll learn about in later chapters. Give it a try and you'll begin to see and hear better, and you'll find many opportunities to be Present with your children, who will begin to open up. You'll find yourself frustrated less and amazed more with the fascinating people that live in your home.

CHAPTER 4

UTILIZE Touchpoints

At the end of a live event, a father with teary eyes told me he had always wanted to connect with his children consistently but hadn't known how. He was short on time!

This father was gone each day working eight or more hours. When he came home it was difficult to connect with each child in a meaningful way. There was so much competing for his time in the few hours they had before bed. There was the deluge of homework, mealtime, and the chaos of getting kids to sleep. Not to mention his need for down time to unwind from a busy day.

What brought tears to this father's eyes was the comfort of knowing he could connect in meaningful ways with the time he had. He felt the information was life-changing.

It's helpful to know and understand that moments of connection can happen during the daily activities we engage in already. It needn't be out of the ordinary or planned ahead. The purpose of this chapter is to illustrate simple and practical ways you can connect with your children daily, in relatively short bursts of time, by recognizing and utilizing Touchpoints.

WHAT IS A TOUCHPOINT?

A Touchpoint is a point of contact between two people or entities. The word is usually used to describe contact between a buyer and a seller or a buyer and a product. We're going to use it this way: the point at which one person feels seen and heard by another person; when they know they matter. Most touchpoints happen daily and many require five minutes or less.

In the Highlights magazine 2014 State of the Kid survey, here's what kids said they consider touchpoints to be with their parents: "When it comes to finding focused time to talk to parents, kids say the best time is during a meal (33 percent), closely followed by bedtime (29 percent) and in the car (18 percent)" ("National Survey Reveals 62% of Kids Think Parents Are Too Distracted to Listen").

So let's begin with these three: mealtime, bedtime, and car time. Then we'll go on to discuss others we can easily add into our families as well.

TOUCHPOINTS THAT OCCUR DAILY

TOUCHPOINT 1—Mealtime

When I asked my children, "What are your fondest and most meaningful memories of growing up in our home?" some of my kids said, "Eating together." When it came to this one thing, I was doggedly consistent. I had a large family, was active in community organizations and at church, and I homeschooled later on. I was busy! But when it came to mealtime, I was determined to make it happen.

It wasn't perfect, but we talked. We laughed. We spilled milk together; we fell off our chairs together. We were a family together. Mealtime is one of my fondest memories also.

Dinner can be a time to reconnect and leave behind individual pursuits. It's a time to relax, recharge, laugh, and tell stories. You can catch up on the day's ups and downs while developing a sense of who you are as a family.

It's interesting that in American culture we treat mealtime so casually, as if its main purpose is to get the food in and move on to more important things. We eat in our cars as we run errands. We eat standing at the kitchen counter, solo, not just busy parents but kids, alone. We hurry family dinners so we can get to the next thing.

> "I had a friend whose family had dinner together every day. The mother would tuck you in at night and make breakfast in the morning. It just seemed so amazing to me."
> —Moon Unit Zappa, American actress, comedian, sculptor and writer

As Cody C. Delistraty mentioned in his article "The Importance of Eating Together" (published in *The Atlantic*),

> In many countries, mealtime is treated as sacred. In France, for instance, while it's acceptable to eat by oneself, one should never rush a meal. A frenzied salad muncher on the métro invites dirty glares, and employees are given at least an hour for lunch.
>
> In many Mexican cities, townspeople will eat together with friends and family in central areas like parks or town squares. In Cambodia, villagers spread out colorful mats and bring food to share with loved ones like a potluck." (Delistraty, "The Importance of Eating Together")

If we stop looking at eating together as one more thing on our long list of to-dos and instead begin to consider it *sacred* family time, we'll be better able to pull it off more consistently.

It might not work out all the time, but what would work? Can you manage it four times a week? Two? Wherever you're willing to set your intention, make it happen consistently!

Remember consistency, in simple things, over time, is what ultimately brings significant results. But just so you know, most studies have found medium and high levels (three or more days per week) of frequent meals yield the most positive benefits for children.

REASONS TO EAT TOGETHER

Here's a list of reasons why you might want to implement this particular touchpoint more regularly.

A. It will help you get what you want. Eating together goes a long way in helping you create the family culture you see in your mind or have written in a Family Mission Statement. (In chapter 7 you'll learn more about knowing what you want in your family.)

B. It will unify your family. The dinner table can be a place of unification. It can give your family a sense of belonging to something that matters. During the years, when some of our children were making poor choices, the time at the dinner table held us together. If we couldn't agree on the best way to live, we could at least gather once a day and eat together. It kept us face-to-face and heart-to-heart.

We didn't try to teach or reprimand during these meals. We stayed out of management and worked on the relationships. This effort didn't stop our children from making choices we didn't agree with, but it kept our children bonded to us until they were ready to make changes. It kept us unified as a family.

C. You can de-stress. A family meal provides a chance to de-stress, to breathe, and to give you space. If you determine that spilled milk and children falling off chairs are not interruptions and catastrophes but significant family life moments, then the dinner hour will bring you joy.

Even when mealtimes feel hectic or disorganized, they have long-term benefits for children because if parents remain calm, kids aren't stressed by dinnertime chaos. Remember they think and see like kids and not like adults.

D. You can build close relationships. Family mealtimes are opportunities to develop more intimate family relationships. Although families live together, we each go about our business of living independently of one another. We aren't all doing the same things each day.

When we eat together, we have a few moments to reconnect, talk, laugh, and enjoy one another. Meals are a prime time for communication and understanding where we each are in our daily walk through life.

E. You'll have an improved sense of well-being. Anne Fishel, PhD, said, "Over the past fifteen years researchers have confirmed what parents have known for a long time: sharing a family meal is good for the spirit, the brain and the health of all family members" (Fishel 2016).

F. You can practice Being Present. Eating together gives you an opportunity to implement Present strategies. You could discuss a book the family's reading together. You could memorize a scripture or quote you like. You could tell jokes and laugh. You could share what happened in the community or thoughts you had during the day.

When having a conversation, include everyone. Keep it positive. Avoid nagging, complaining, or controlling the discussion. Listen more than you talk.

> "One of the simplest and most effective ways for parents to be engaged in their teens' lives is by having frequent family dinners."
>
> —Joseph Califano, Jr., of Columbia University

If up until now, dinner hasn't been a productive time to connect and build relationships with your kids, try playing the Conversation Game. This game can get the flow going. Go around the table and have each person share a high point of the day and a low point.

Eventually, when done consistently over time, it will begin to feel safe, and your family members will open up more. This game is fun and you can practice seeing and hearing your children. You'll also notice Sparks.

Dinner's the perfect time to turn away from your technology. Turn off cell phones while at the table. Mute your landline. Even the ringing can be a major distraction. Turn off the TV! Having the TV on negates many of the benefits of a family meal and prevents you and your family from being Present with each other. The comfort of the food will make practicing this less painful.

Eating together is an opportunity to empty your mind of your endless to-do list and focus on your children. What are they saying? How do they look? What's their body language? What did you miss in the rush of getting out the door in the morning and as you moved through the day? Mealtime is a perfect time to practice being Present.

G. You can give your kids T-I-M-E. If you need one more reason to eat together as a family, ponder this: in a nationally representative Internet-based survey of 1,037 teens (ages twelve to seventeen), 71 percent said that they consider talking/catching up and spending time with family members as the best part of family dinners. These comments come from kids, just like your kids. They want and need time with you. They want your Presence, and one of the easiest ways to give it to the whole family at once is at the dinner table (National Center on Addiction and Substance Abuse at Columbia University, "The Importance of Family Dinners")!

TOUCHPOINT 2—Bedtime

Far too often, bedtime feels stressful for both children and parents. A child isn't always ready to disengage from life and go to sleep. So they fight having to leave whatever it is they're doing and go to bed. Parents are weary from all they've had to manage during the day, and they want to get bedtime done and over so they can rest and have some peace.

Despite your weariness, if you switch your mind-set, bedtime can become one of your most cherished times with your children and a productive time for Presence.

It's like dinnertime. What's the purpose? Dinner isn't just about eating and bedtime isn't just about sleeping. They're both touchpoints where we can connect and work on the most important relationships we have. Time invested here will pay huge dividends.

TWO EXAMPLES OF THE POWER OF BEDTIME

Example A—Let me share a poignant story with you. I know a mom whose fourteen-year-old daughter was cutting herself. The daughter was in significant pain, but the parents were clueless as to what the trouble was. Therapy had been ineffective, since the girl was unwilling to talk with anyone.

This mom took to heart the counsel to be Present at bedtime. Each evening she would go to her daughter's room after she was in bed. Mom sat quietly on the bed and touched her daughter, rubbing an arm or putting a hand on her back for a few minutes. And she would wait. For the first few nights nothing happened.

However, it didn't take too long until her daughter began to open up and talk. The three-minute nightly ritual turned into thirty.

This mom had things on her to-do list. She probably hadn't planned on giving an extra thirty minutes to one of her children each evening. But she felt immense relief at having found a way to break through to her daughter.

Their situation is not healed. I suspect they have a long way to go. But taking time at the close of the day is paying dividends for this family.

Example B—Bedtime isn't always this dramatic, but it can always be this impactful. Let me share another example, much lighter in tone. When my son Barry was nine, he began asking me many questions. It became a bit overwhelming, and I needed a way to satisfy his need for answers and still keep my sanity. So I bought him a pocket notebook.

I told him to write down questions that came to his mind and at bedtime, I would answer them. Often, after fifteen minutes of answers, he would still have questions on his list. So I told him to keep those questions safe in his book until the next night and to add any new questions. We continued this for almost a year.

Despite the hectic nature of my life at that time, this evening ritual was one of the most energizing experiments I ever entered into with any of my kids. I know it was impactful for Barry. It said what I could never have verbally communicated—"I see you. I hear you. You're on my list, in fact at the top of my list."

MAKING BEDTIME WORK FOR PRESENCE

It's not necessary to spend thirty minutes with each child or even fifteen; you can't and you won't. But make it a habit of giving each child at least three good minutes. No feeling rushed. Let the mental agenda go. Whatever TV show is coming on will not matter to you ten years from now, but the relationship you have with your child will. Lie or sit down by them. Touch them. Have a mini-conversation.

If you need to, set your child's bedtime a wee bit earlier to give you time for visiting and snuggling in the dark. When you make space for these safe, companionable moments, your child will be able to share feelings they're currently grappling with. Listen and hear. There's always tomorrow for problem-solving. Right now, in this three-minute space, you're busy working on the relationship. You'll be amazed at how much deeper it will begin to feel.

If you have youth—even angry, belligerent, closed youth—give this a try. Safe, quiet moments in the dark can be soothing. Often bedtime is the only time youth will open up, so take advantage of it. And if they don't open up, it's okay. Be with them, give a random touch, and be Present without a word being spoken.

If you have multiple children and this feels a bit daunting to you, have different nights for different children. Get both parents involved—divide and conquer! Snuggle with two kids on Monday and the other two on Tuesday. Then begin again. You might only be able to do one child each day of the week if you have lots of kids.

Avoid letting your mind get stuck on having this nightly routine with each child, every night. If you can do it, great! But if it's not possible, all is not lost! Remember simple things, done consistently over time, make *big* things happen. Consistency long-term is the key.

If you give a few minutes to your child once a week, that's fifty-two times a year you make the effort to work on the relationship. If your child is ten, you have eight years left with him. At once a week, you will have given him 416 quiet, safe, and Present moments. Even if you're not perfect (and you won't be) and miss a few of those nights, can you see how successful you could be, despite your imperfection?

Give bedtime some thought; focus on what you can do. What are you willing to commit to? Whatever it is, do it! Remember anything done consistently over time brings *big* results.

TOUCHPOINT 3—Car Time

The twenty-first century is an incredible time to be alive. However, one of the results of life in this era is we spend lots of time in our cars. Adults tend to keep themselves company with the radio or CDs.

We often use these tools to check out, to block out the distractions coming from the back seat. But time in the car time can be truly well spent when we use it as a place to be Present.

Isn't it interesting so many children listed car time as one of the top three times when they can get their parent's attention? Possibly it's because we're all trapped inside a moving piece of metal, and there are fewer ways to check out. Occasionally there are fine moments of connection. We can, by choice, have those moments happen more often.

"Turn off the cell phone and the radio when you're in the car and use that time to connect with your child. Try hanging a tag in your car that reads "Here, now" or "Just this moment." Or simply ask yourself over and over, 'what am I aware of right now?' This question can help mothers tap into what's happening in their bodies, like clenching jaws or holding breath, as well as what's happening around them, like the sky looks incredibly blue today."

—Mara Kormylo, mother of two, licensed clinical social worker and adjunct professor of Family Systems at Naropa University in Boulder, CO

CONVERSATION IS KEY

No matter whether you have one child or seven in your car, car time is a great time to throw out questions that help you hear what your kids have to say.

- What was good today?

- What are you looking forward to?

- Was anything disappointing?

- Was anything sad?

- What's something new you've heard about?

- Did anyone hear a good joke?

- What was the best thing for lunch?

- Look at the goofy sign!

- Don't you love that guy's coat?

- You can make car time more successful if you remember to

- Keep questions from becoming lectures

- Accept all comments as valuable

- Listen more than you talk

- Stop trying to problem solve; just hear and see. You can problem solve later

- Avoid pointing out one person's faults or errors

- Remember building relationships and practicing Presence is the goal

Car time can be the perfect time to bring up tough family subjects. The car's sort of a neutral ground. You can discuss family schedules, family rules, the upcoming family vacation and what needs doing, family values, and so forth.

You're not trying to solve anything. You're working at hearing your children. What are they saying? How are they feeling? Are your children on the same page with you or are there misunderstandings you pick up on that can be resolved later? What Sparks do you notice?

Relationships are built in everyday moments; the seemingly mundane and often overlooked. Car time is an excellent opportunity for practicing Presence, sharing, connecting, and growing relationships.

TOUCHPOINT 4—Chores and Family Work

Thinking about the word "work" can make a parent groan inside, because work is often a point of contention in a family. But work can be a place where we create a touchpoint rather than a point of contention if building relationships is our ultimate goal.

CHORES

Often we get so involved in the management portion of family life that it's difficult to address the relationship portion. We'll cover this topic in depth in chapter 9. For now, know that when we're Present, things work out better.

Everyone wants support when facing a tough job. No one wants to be isolated in a mess. We sometimes forget our kids feel the same way we do.

Moms have had the experience of walking into a disaster of a kitchen after a long day. Your family's watching TV and here you are, in this messy kitchen. Where do you start?

How does it feel when your husband abandons his show, comes in, and begins helping you pick up? And how does it feel when he also asks you how your day went? It's amazing!

This happens to dads in garages and backyards. How does it feel when your seventeen-year-old volunteers to help get the backyard in order? How about when your thirteen-year-old offers to spend time helping you organize the garage? It feels better, doesn't it?

When a child is faced with what seems like a daunting task, check on them. Put your hand on their back or rub a shoulder and say, "Let me give you a hand." Help them for two to three minutes while having a mini-conversation. Then head off to the next child or to your own work. It makes all the difference in how chores feel and in how well they get done. It solidifies relationships. It allows you to be Present with your child for a few minutes. Chores can be a touchpoint!

> "Last year, I planned to paint a room in our house by myself but realized this was an opportunity to teach and connect with all the kids. We transformed painting from a chore into a wonderful memory."
>
> —Clem Boyd, author of *Build Relationship With Your Child*," published by Focus on the Family

FAMILY WORK

Family work is another time when you can create a touchpoint rather than a point of contention.

When working as a family, we need to keep in mind the objective isn't just to get another item off the to-do list—we're creating relationships and bonding our family.

I love gardening alone. I love the quiet and feeling the dirt in my fingers. But I understand it's an opportunity for me to teach and connect with my grandchildren. Gardening can be transformed into an enduring memory for us all when I remember the garden isn't what's important, the relationship is.

Add fun to any work you do as a family—sing, dance as you clean, play great music, tell jokes, laugh, and have mini-conversations and lots of random touches.

Things aren't going to work out all of the time. You'll have family work that turns into chaos or contention. We're all imperfect, we get tired, and we have grouchy moments. It's inevitable. But what if you could make family work more pleasant even one-quarter of the time?

If you can be Present as you work together even one-quarter of the time, your family members will feel supported and relationships will be built up. You'll experience *great* results in the happiness level of your family.

TOUCHPOINT 5—Transitions

Families have moments of transition during their day. A working mom or dad leaves the home and possibly leaves a child at day care. Kids go to school and come back again. Mom and Dad go on a date. Youth go out in the evening. We all have transitions, and we have them multiple times a day. These are perfect moments to be Present. They're touchpoints. Here are three examples:

Example A—As a youth, when I left home, I would go out the door and yell, "Bye Mom." From some far-flung place in the house, I would hear her call back, "Bye Mary. Be safe." This scenario was repeated often.

There isn't anything wrong with this. But what if my mom had replied, "Wait a minute," and had come quickly to the door? What if she had looked me in the eye, smiled, laid a hand on my shoulder, and said, "Bye Mary. Be safe"? Can you feel the difference? Can you sense the Presence I would have felt at sixteen? Do you think it would have made a difference for me?

Coming to see me off would have cost my mother something. It would have cost her T-I-M-E. Time is a precious commodity. This is why it's so powerful when we give our precious time to our children and are Present. There's an innate knowledge that you have received a gift and it's valuable.

Example B—School is out. The front door bangs open and in charge three children. They call, "Mom, I'm home." Out of another door flies a mother. She begins chasing the children. They run around the living room squealing. As she catches them, she gives each one a big kiss and hug. These kids are six, nine, and twelve.

Finally, they all fall onto the couch and talk over each other as they relate the day's experiences to their mom. She looks at them and smiles, making an occasional comment. Soon they scatter off to different parts of the house.

This scenario is repeated most days at the home of my friend Kim. She's a work-at-home mom who runs a successful business. Daily, at the same time, she stops what she's doing. She prepares for the onslaught of coats, boots, book bags, and kids. Then she participates in their catch-and-kiss ritual and gives them her full attention. It takes around twenty minutes of her day, and it happens before her work day is finished.

For these twenty minutes, Kim is Present. It's a gift she gives to her kids. It helps them transition back into their family. It rekindles that *family* feeling for all of them. (Kim Flynn, UT. CEO at Entrepreneur Simplified.)

Example C—Let's say you're dropping your child off at day care. As you drive you sing a favorite song. You look at your child in the rearview mirror, and they look back at you. You smile. You ask them, "What's the best thing that's going to happen today?" and they tell you. You get to the day care. You open the car door, unbuckle your child, and rub noses. You say, "I love you." They respond, "I love you," and you take them in.

Maybe they begin to cry. You soothe them, hand them to the aide, and head out the door. But you can feel okay because you've had a few minutes of Present time together.

TRANSITIONS WITH YOUTH

When I was raising my children, I had many opportunities to use transition times to be Present with my youth. As our kids age, it gets more challenging to be Present because we're busy and they're busy. They can seem distant. They may act as if they don't want to be with us.

When they return home in the evening or late at night is a perfect transition time to connect and help them ease back into the family. Be prepared to pay the price required to connect with youth—a small amount of your T-I-M-E.

Leave the TV, the ironing, the email, and Facebook. Meet them when you hear the door open. Look at them and smile. Touch a shoulder. Say, "I'm so glad you're home. How did it go?" You may get nothing more than a quick "okay." That's all right because they'll feel your Presence. Now and then you'll get more. They will, in turn, be Present with you and share feelings. These can be precious, sweet, and, at times, crucial moments.

This can also work in reverse when you're returning after a long day. My friend Tiffany has a teenage son. One day when she returned home from shopping, he met her in the driveway and offered to carry in the groceries, an uncommon occurrence.

Although she was tired and anxious to get things put away and dinner started, she got Present. She watched her son as he carried in the groceries and paid attention to his body language. When the groceries were on the counter she asked, "What happened today?" Her son opened up and shared an experience that was bothering him.

My friend said, "I almost missed this opportunity because I was transitioning back home and I was tired and had an agenda. I'm so glad I stopped and got Present."

Are you getting a sense of how you can use transitions to be Present? You won't be able to do this all the time. You'll run late for work. A work-at-home parent may have a deadline. You may miss a youth coming back. But as much as possible, we should use transition times to be Present with our children. When we do, we build relationships, we bond our family, and, frankly, we are happier.

TOUCHPOINTS TO ADD TO YOUR FAMILY

TOUCHPOINT 6—Family Night/Meeting

Many parents work at getting what they want by having a weekly meeting or activity. My church has encouraged this for many years.

When Don and I had a young family, we had a family night on and off. I hate to admit we didn't take it as seriously as we should have. In retrospect, it would have been helpful to gather our family together consistently to have fun, to share family stories, to eat treats, to share values and so forth.

It's easy to check out from your family. Life is busy. It was busy back in the day before computers and cell phones, and it's gotten busier. I would think about our family night, but put it off for the laundry's sake, the garden's sake, a friend's sake, time-to-myself sake, and "I haven't prepared anything's" sake. But when you consistently gather your family together, you send a powerful message that your family matters more than anything else.

Let's look at two significant reasons to make the effort to gather your family together weekly.

A. Practice Presence—This family gathering time is a perfect place to practice being Present, to shut out the world, to actually see and hear your children, and to show them they matter to you.

You have the opportunity to shut off all of the technology for a short time and focus on your children. You put work on hold—the outside-of-the-home work and also the inside-of-the-home work. When you do this, you clear the agenda out of your head. You make your family, being with and enjoying them, the agenda.

I remember hearing a story once, told by a son. His dad was a successful man and in high demand. The circus was coming to town, and he had promised his boys he would take them. During dinner on the night of the proposed trip, the father received a call. The boys were relieved to hear their father respond, "I'm sorry, I can't come. I have an appointment." This father said, by his actions, loud and clear to his sons, "I see you, I hear you, you matter to me!"

B. Create your family culture—While a family mission statement can provide the big-picture vision for your family, regular family night/meetings are how you take your vision and turn it into action. It's the doing part of the equation.

A healthy family culture doesn't just happen. (We'll cover family culture in more detail in chapter 7.) Weekly family night/meetings are an effective way to reinforce your family's culture and values. They offer opportunities to teach principles you want to instill in your children, as well as discuss how to apply them in real-life situations.

Teaching and connecting with your kids is why you take the time to decide what you want. A weekly evening together is a rare opportunity in a chaotic and busy world to implement what you've decided.

When I presented this information in a webinar series I gave, one mom named Stefanie Miller responded, "I guess that means we have to be on our game and not tired and annoyed with our kids when we go into these family night/meetings. Wow. Not sure how to bridge the gap." (We will talk more about nurturing yourself in chapter 12.)

She's right. Gathering your family together can be a bit exhausting and chaotic at the end of a long day. So what can we do? If we remember enjoying our family *is* the agenda, we'll manage better.

If your family night/meeting is going south, shift gears. Throw out your notes. Stop trying to accomplish anything. Sing a song, play a game, roughhouse on the floor, or go for a walk. You can even troop into the kitchen for lemonade. Then try again next week.

A FEW MORE ICING-ON-THE-CAKE REASONS

C. Family solidarity—Gathering together weekly will help establish a firm foundation of solidarity for your family. Dedicating time each week to play together, teach, and plan helps families withstand the storms of life. It gives your children a clear sense that they have a support group they can count on.

D. Resolve problems—When we're all together, it provides a family the opportunity to talk and resolve problems.

E. Teach skills—These weekly family night/meetings are a chance to teach and pick up valuable skills that will serve your children well and help them develop into contributing members of society. They'll pick up skills like problem solving, planning, conflict resolution, and communication, for example. Letting kids teach a short lesson or lead a discussion helps them practice teaching and public speaking skills.

You can also dedicate this family gathering to teaching specific life skills: how to budget, how to take care of a car, how to civically engage, how to write a letter, how to sew on a button, how to use proper manners (teaching what they are), and so forth.

F. Get in sync—At this gathering, you can reduce the stressors that occur in most families. You can sync calendars and get your family on the same page concerning what's going on in the household.

MONITOR YOUR EXPECTATIONS

When Don and I had our family evenings, we would become discouraged because they didn't always turn out as we planned. There were always the yawning teens, the arguing ten- and twelve-year-olds, the chaotic and noisy little kids, as well as an occasionally crying infant. Yikes!

Keep expectations from getting in the way of enjoying your family. Avoid the trap of giving up because, well, what's the use, what can they possibly be getting out of this? Keep the perfect from becoming the enemy of the good. The point is not what you teach, or how well it looks, but being together while you're Present.

Even if your family night/meetings seem chaotic, there's still value in holding them. You'd be surprised how much your kids are picking up during the chaos. I've passed from having kids at home to having adult children with families of their own. I know they appreciated those evenings together because many of our children now have these same types of evenings with their kids.

I've sat in on their family night/meetings and have seen the gamut from utterly chaotic and "I am never going to do this again," to "Wow. Can you believe how well that went? We have to keep doing this." And they do keep doing it regardless of the individual outcomes, because the cumulative effect, over time, will bless their family. And family night/meetings can bless yours too!

ORGANIZING A FAMILY NIGHT/MEETING

- Lead and stay Present

- Shoot for once a week

- Make it a priority—keep it sacred family time

- Have an agenda your family members can count on (opening, teaching, ask what is working, who needs help, sync calendars, have fun, treats, and so on)

- Have reasonable expectations

- Keep it simple

- Ask for weekly feedback

  -What was successful in our family this week?

  -What went wrong in our family this week?

  -What will we work on this coming week?

- Avoid discussing individual problems or grievances (you'll have time later and in private)

- Be flexible, vary the length depending on ages, and get everyone involved

Family night/meetings help you send the message to your children that they matter and help you accomplish the goals in your Family Mission Statement. (You'll learn how to write a Family Mission Statement in chapter 7.)

Thoughtfully consider and determine what you can and are willing to do and what will most effectively benefit you and your family. Then be consistent!

TOUCHPOINT 7—Family Reading Time

From Scholastic's Kids and Family Reading Report, we learn only 17 percent of parents of kids aged nine through eleven read aloud to their children. Yet 83 percent of kids aged six through seventeen say being read to is something they either loved or liked a lot (Scholastic Inc. and YouGov 2014).

One of my warmest memories is of my mother reading poetry to us. She didn't read to us often, but when she did it was magical for me!

As I think back on those reading moments with my mom, I know what made them so special. I knew my mom loved us. That's why she was reading to us. I just knew in my little girl heart this was true.

MAKING FAMILY READING WORK

The number one reason to read to your children until they leave your home and go out on their own is to establish an intimate experience filled with feelings of warmth and belonging.

There are many ways to find time to read as a family. Each family will find what works best for them. You may have to try a few things out, but go ahead and experiment. Snuggle together in the family room before the little ones go to bed. Have a Sunday morning or afternoon reading time. Have Dad read at the kitchen table before dinner. Read right after breakfast, before everyone heads out for the day.

Reading as a family can last past the time children begin to read on their own, as long as you're choosing books a notch above the readers in the group. You want to challenge your older one's thinking, open a door to discussion, and create the possibility of broaching difficult topics if needed.

The question arises as to how you keep the littles engaged if you're reading to engage the older youth. I found my Presence, warm snuggles, pillows, and popcorn did the trick.

For small children, cuddling with Mom and Dad and feeling a kinship with older siblings goes a long way to keeping them engaged. Another tip is to allow them to do quiet activities that require no help from anyone else—coloring, stringing beads, Legos, and so on. Even if they seem deeply engrossed in these activities, they hear more than you know.

Some families read every day. Others read a few times a week. There are those that have a once a week routine. It isn't as important how often you read as that you do read, consistently, and that while you're reading, you're Present with your family.

WHY YOU SHOULD READ AS A FAMILY

There are many reasons to make the effort to read together. Here are a few:

A. Physical closeness—Reading aloud gives you and your children an opportunity to achieve physical closeness. Small children enjoy sitting on your lap or draping themselves across your body.

You may snuggle less with older children, but this is not a given. If you're open to having older children sit next to you or lay a head on your shoulder, the chances are it will happen often. That has been my experience.

B. A sense of security—Gathering together as a family and reading create a sense of security and safety—a feeling of all is right with the world. When children feel secure and safe, they function better out in the world. Love is important to a child, but feeling safe is as important and often, even more important.

C. A sense of belonging—There's a sense of belonging that comes from everyone being in the same room, snuggling and listening to the same story, having a shared experience. This can be especially helpful as our children begin to mature. They're trying to figure themselves out as well as figure out where they fit in the world. This process of personal growth can bring a sense of isolation. Reading as a family is one of the ways parents can create a sense of belonging.

> "When you talk about a book together, it's not a lecture, it's more like a coach looking at a film with his players, going over the plays to find out what went right and what went wrong."
>
> —Jim Trelease, author of *Read-Aloud Handbook*, as told to GreatSchools.net

D. A chance to tackle difficult subjects—Reading as a family allows you to introduce difficult subjects to your children and have safe discussions. I've read books to my children dealing with honesty, integrity, kindness, bullying, God, social issues, beliefs, and feelings. It made it possible to bring up ideas and thoughts I wanted my children to consider and ponder on. It was a safe and comfortable way to experience great life lessons.

E. A shared language and a sense of intimacy—When families read together, they often create a unique language. It can provide inside jokes. I read an article that described the experience of a family who loved the Mercy Watson books. In their family, they frequently heard the call at breakfast for "Mercy Watson toast, please!" (Johnson, "Why You Should Read Aloud to Older Kids").

I queried the families I've worked with the question, "What quotes and phrases do you use in your family?" Here's a sampling:

- From *Little Britches*: "Is your (choice) taking care of building your character house?" —Colleen Cubberley

- From *The Phantom Tollbooth*: "Are you jumping to conclusions?" for my son who freaks out before he knows what's going on. —Christine Owens

- From the title of the easy reader *No Fighting, No Biting* by Else Holmelund Minarik: "No Fighting, No Biting." —Theresa Raymond

- Something Ma and Pa say to their kids in the Little House on the Prairie series by Laura Ingalls Wilder: "Don't contradict." —Darla Stevenson

It is fun, as well as bonding, when families share a phrase from a good book that means something to all of them. It creates a sense of intimacy.

F. It can strengthen struggling children and youth—When one of my daughters was fifteen, she was making unwise choices. She knew it, but she was struggling to make changes.

At the time, the youngest two children read with me. We read in the middle of my bed before lights out. Although my daughter wasn't usually home, I noticed when she was, she would come to my bedroom door, lean against it and listen, no matter what the book was.

This did not resolve her issues and she had a tough road, but I'm certain it helped her stay connected to our family in a way that was vital to her eventual success.

I worked with a single mom who was struggling with her children ages eight, eleven, and fourteen. They were argumentative and disobedient. One of her sons was withdrawn, and other people commented on how hyper her kids were. There was a fair amount of chaos in the home.

This mother wanted to learn to be more consistent in her life. I suggested she experiment with reading as a family regularly. She was doubtful it would be successful but decided to give it a try.

As she began reading aloud to her children, it didn't appear it was going to work out well. The kids were restive and quarrelsome. But I encouraged her to keep it up no matter how it looked or felt because the goal was to practice consistency. Her job was to provide a comfy spot and to read, no matter how her kids behaved. So she did.

She committed to reading to her children twice a week. They would all gather in her room, in the middle of her bed and they would read. It wasn't always easy, but as time went by it became more and more enjoyable. The surprising part is there began to be a sense of cooperation and peace while they read together and this feeling moved into other areas of their lives.

They felt it at mealtimes, in conversation, and when working together. People began commenting that her children seemed more patient and calm. Her withdrawn child seemed happier and had begun to sing around the house. The family's problems didn't vanish away and life wasn't a bed of roses, but change was happening. Her family culture was changing for the better.

If you're struggling with any of your children, for any reason, the closeness generated by reading together can go a long way to keeping you connected while issues are worked out. Reading together is comforting.

TOUCHPOINT 8—Daily Devotionals

Family devotionals are valuable for families of any religious faith and for families who don't ascribe to any religious faith. I realize the word devotional connotes a religious belief, so if the word doesn't fit your family, call it something else. Each morning at one of my daughters' homes you can hear the call, "It's time for Good Morning." The family knows what that means and they come running.

One of the synonyms for devotion is *reverence*. A definition of reverence is "to treat with respect." Whether you're a religious family or not, it's of great value to teach your children to respect the family. Your devotional can help you accomplish this. Devotionals are shorter than a family night/meeting. They usually last less than fifteen minutes and can be as short as five. A family devotional is your opportunity to call your family together daily before they all scatter for school, work, and so on.

Here are possible components for family devotionals:

- Praying

- Reading a classic book

- Sharing the best thing that happened the day before

- Sharing each person's schedule for the day

- Reading out of your spiritual canon

- Memorizing a verse of scripture

- Reading the family mission/vision statement

- Sharing a thought

- Memorizing a quote

- Watching a short online video (four minutes or less) emphasizing how you want to behave as a family or as people

> **"Other things may change, but we start and end with family."**
>
> —Author unknown

- Watching a short video story from your spiritual canon

- Singing a hymn or children's song

- Discussing what you're reading or what you're watching or what you're memorizing

It's not as important what you do as that you do it consistently and have a predictable structure. The younger your children, the more important the structure. Children like to know what's coming next. They feel safe when they can depend on things happening regularly, in a predictable way.

When planning the elements of your devotional, take into consideration the ages of your children. If they're all under five, your devotional will, by necessity, be simple and short.

If you have youth, it may contain more complex elements and be a bit longer. Then again, if you have youth with busy schedules, it may be as short as those who have children under five. You determine what's going to work best for your family, and then be consistent.

Family devotionals are effective in the morning but can happen any time during the day. What works best will depend on your children's ages and your family's schedule. But whatever time you choose, you want the whole family together on a fairly regular basis.

If the family schedule changes and one person would miss the devotional consistently, then you need to find a new time slot for it. You want everyone to be there as often as possible; experiment to see what works best.

One important caveat—have your devotional when you have it planned even if someone is going to be gone. As your children get older, they may miss a devotional occasionally.

IN SUMMARY

Eating together, bedtime rituals, time in the car, chores and family work, and transitions give you plenty of opportunities to connect daily. You needn't plan and carve out extra time. You can take advantage of these moments to be Present and build solid relationships with your children.

Family night/meetings, reading together, and daily devotionals are touchpoints you can implement into your family without a big time commitment or a lot of preplanning.

Remember, you get to choose to have touchpoints in the daily affairs of life or points of contention. It's always a choice.

As you work on being Present in your relationships with your kids, it will cease to be about what you do for them. It will become how you are when you're with them. That's when your relationships will take off and soar.

CHAPTER 5

CHANGE Your Story
for Greater Presence

I
s this Mrs. Johnson?"

"Yes."

"Do you have a daughter, Jenny, who lives in Eureka, CA?"

Those few words sent me on a four-month odyssey with my daughter who was facing a six-year journey. Jenny had been hit head-on by a drunk driver. He had been going the wrong way on the freeway on a foggy December night in 2006. She hadn't seen him coming until seconds before impact. He'd been going eighty miles an hour.

Those few terrible seconds changed Jenny's life forever. She was ready to graduate with her BA—it was weeks away from the end of the semester—but the accident left her unable to walk or find words for simple things such as orange or shoe. She couldn't track conversations or make sense out of what people were saying. Her center for receiving social cues was damaged.

In 2012, Jenny's six-year journey to get her life back ended when she graduated with her master's degree in speech therapy. She set out for a new life, in a new city, at a new job, helping other people put their lives back together.

It was beautiful to sit in the auditorium and watch her walk across the stage. It was incredible to see all the people who came and who loved our daughter. They wanted us to know what a fantastic job we'd done in raising her. It caused me serious introspection.

We did a good job of raising our children. Not a perfect or pain-free job, but a good job. We know this from the fruit we've harvested: seven loyal and kind adults with integrity.

But when I think of Jenny's experience, I know her recovery was less about what we had done and more about some crucial steps she had taken long before the accident.

WE CONTROL OUR STORIES

Jenny had her rough years. She had used drugs as a youth, but when she'd regained control, she'd set out on a course to make her life what she wanted it to be. Jenny began by choosing to manage her thoughts. She took control of the stories she told herself.

Quotes decorated her walls and reflected how she wanted to view herself and life. When something bad, confusing, embarrassing, or hurtful happened to her, Jenny would recite one of her quotes in response. Then she would move forward.

These quotes became the building blocks of her life. They helped her form the core of who she had decided to be and how she had decided to see the world. Despite her horrific accident, she was able to walk the path of six years of recovery with grace and humor.

> "The wonderful thing about story, 'real' or otherwise, is that because we create it, we can change it—in any given moment."
>
> —Stephanie S. Tolan
> Children's book author

Here are a few samples of quotes she chose to look at and believe before and after her accident:

"If you correct your mind, the rest of your life will fall into place." Lao Tzu

"Life is not about finding yourself; life is about creating yourself." George Bernard Shaw

"When I started counting my blessings, my whole world turned around." Willie Nelson

"Turn your face to the sun and the shadows fall behind you." Maori Proverb

A quote from the movie *American Beauty* sheds a beautiful light on life and Jenny posted it on her wall and embraced it:

I'd always heard your entire life flashes in front of your eyes the second before you die. First of all, that one second isn't a second at all—it stretches on forever like an ocean of time. I guess I could be pretty pissed-off about what happened to me, but it's hard to stay mad in a world where there's so much beauty. Sometimes I feel like I'm seeing it all at once, and it's too much; my heart fills up like a balloon that's about to burst. I remember to relax and stop trying to hold onto it, and the beauty flows through me like rain, and I can't feel anything but gratitude for every single moment of my little life. You have no idea what I'm talking about I'm sure, but don't worry, you will—someday. (*American Beauty* 1999)

CAN CONTROLLING YOUR STORY MAKE A DIFFERENCE?

Many of you may have a difficult time accepting you can control how you feel by taking charge of the story you tell yourself. I was in a similar place years ago. I was a reasonable person, and I lived a good life but, darn it, stuff was always happening. I couldn't control all the circumstances in my life and when bad things happen, what can you do? Naturally, it makes you feel low.

I mean, if the kids are acting crazy, it's going to make you feel crazy. If milk keeps getting spilled, if the house is getting trashed, and if grades are down, you feel down yourself. When money's tight or your spouse isn't helping you out, you feel overwhelmed. If you feel unsupported or if you have a health issue, all of this is going to mess with how you feel, right?

I knew the answer was a big fat *yes!* This was my belief until one day when I had an experience and a light bulb went on in my head. It changed my life forever.

I was mentoring with a woman I loved and trusted. I was mentoring because, well, I wasn't as happy with my life as I felt I should be. Each week we talked about things that were seemingly out of my control, which were making me miserable.

One day I was complaining how my husband managed money. I was fed up with having the same discussion over and over again. Finally, my mentor said, "Mary Ann, you're not a victim. You can choose to leave." I was shocked. No, I couldn't. After all, he was my husband, and I loved him. My religion would make leaving difficult and I had seven kids and . . . .

Suddenly I realized I could. I could leave. I wasn't a victim. I had the ability to choose how I was going to respond to this situation. I was in control of the story and the outcome.

I'm happy to say many years have passed, and I'm still married to the same man. I love him and occasionally we still have a money conversation or two but it has changed because my story changed.

You see, at the time, this was my story. "My husband doesn't care how I feel. If he did, he would spend money differently. He does what he wants to do. My life is painful because of my husband." *Wow!* Feels dreadful, doesn't it?

Now, years later, here's my story. "I have a great relationship with money. I always have what I need. Don's making progress on his relationship with money. I'm supporting him, sharing what I've learned, and enjoying my healthy relationship with both Don and money." Doesn't that feel better?

You might be thinking, *That's the dumbest thing I've ever heard! You still have to live with the results of his choices. How can you be happy? Nothing has changed. You're hiding your head in the sand and being a Pollyanna.*

If I weren't living my life, I would agree with you. But I have firsthand experience that has proven when we change our story, everything changes.

> **"Man is not fully conditioned and determined but rather determines himself whether he gives in to conditions or stands up to them. In other words, man is ultimately self-determining. Man does not simply exist but always decides what his existence will be, what he will become in the next moment... every human being has the freedom to change at any instant."**
>
> —Viktor Frankl, Man's Search for Meaning

One of my favorite quotes is from Viktor E. Frankl, a Holocaust survivor. He said, "When we're no longer able to change a situation—we're challenged to change ourselves." He reminded us in his book *Man's Search for Meaning* the one thing that can never be taken from a person is their ability to choose how to respond (Frankl).

I would add that their responsibility to mentally write a story leading to the best response is also completely within their control.

Frankl explored why a portion of those in concentration camps were able to maintain their humanity while others lost theirs. Both groups were experiencing the same things, but what made the difference in their response was the story they told themselves about what was happening to them (Frankl).

In the case of my husband, myself, and our money conversation, when I changed my story it changed me. I no longer felt threatened, put upon, hurt, scared, or angry. It stopped impacting me as negatively.

Let's take one last look at Jenny's situation. In a time of darkness, confusion, and both physical and mental pain, she chose to look at life through a lens of light. She decided to embrace happiness no matter how hard the day. She controlled her thoughts, and she controlled her words. She controlled her story!

I don't want you to think the years after her accident were easy—they were long and painful—but she had decided to believe life was beautiful and there were lessons of value in each experience for her as a result.

When she began her master's program, I was concerned. She was still dealing with issues from the brain injury she had sustained in the accident and she will for the rest of her life. While talking to her on the phone, I asked her how school was going.

She replied, "Mom, it's hard to follow the lecture and I have a hard time remembering stuff. But I've learned I can make notes on my hand, and it helps me remember. Sometimes when I get home, the list is up to my elbow." She laughed.

As her mom, I wanted to believe her life was going along well, that she was able to traverse all of the new pitfalls, but I knew from other conversations she had shed many silent tears for the changes in her life.

She had lost her beautiful ankles and the ability to easily converse and know what was appropriate to say and what to withhold. More important, she had lost herself, so to speak. Her personality changed, and she had to learn to live as a different person in many ways. She was no longer as carefree and untroubled. She had a new, more serious nature. It was a big adjustment for her. It was a more significant change for her friends. It complicated her life.

Despite all of the difficulty and loss, Jenny would not discuss, in negative terms, the man who hit her. She wouldn't listen to others who wanted to talk negatively about him. Jenny said she wished him well, she hoped for joy in his life and she wasn't going to waste one minute on anger.

Jenny wouldn't verbalize the bad but chose instead to think and talk positively. She behaved this way before the accident and maintained this *way of being* after the crash. Jenny told her story in a way that did not include her as a victim.

THOUGHTS CREATE OUR STORIES

Perspective is an amazing thing. It is, simply put, the story we tell ourselves: what we think is happening in our lives right now, what we believe happened in the past, and even what we think will happen in the future.

It all begins with a thought. Once we have a thought, if we hold it in our minds, it becomes a story because our brain does its job and goes to the files and finds evidence that our thought is correct; usually evidence based on past experiences. This process takes fractions of seconds.

> "If I think something long enough—with images and conversation to support it, it will translate into movement, and I will get the results I was thinking of."
>
> —Kirk Duncan, CEO of 3 Key Elements

Once we have our story, feelings are generated. These feelings move us to an action or response. Our response produces a result, either good or bad. This little scenario repeats itself hundreds of times each day.

Once I had a teacher show a visual that helped me see how our thoughts shape our stories and, in turn, get us a result, either good or bad. It looks like this:

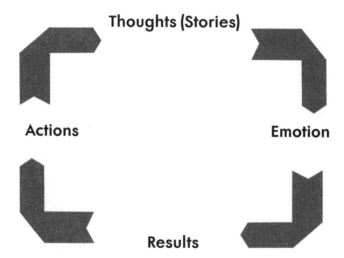

Thoughts (Stories)

Actions

Emotion

Results

You change your story by controlling your thoughts. You manage your emotions by controlling your story. When you do this, you take more positive actions and you get better results. Jenny has proven this to be true! I've proven it to be true in my own life as well.

HOW YOUR STORIES
AFFECT YOUR RESPONSE

You've all heard this old saying or something like it, "What you say is what you get." It's true.

If you say "My kids are driving me nuts," they'll drive you nuts. If you say "I can't stand my kids today," or "My kids are so sloppy, messy, noisy, naughty, and so on," that's what you'll get. It's what you perceive is happening, regardless of what's actually going on. This will influence your response and your ability to be Present.

James Clear wrote for the *Huffington Post*, "Your brain is . . . programmed to respond to negative emotions . . . by shutting off the outside world and limiting the options you see around you."

He gave the example of seeing a tiger standing in front of you. When you see the tiger, your thoughts tell you tigers are dangerous. You might even bring up a visual memory of something you've seen on TV or read in a book. You immediately feel fear (Clear 2013).

Clear writes,

Researchers have long known negative emotions program your brain to do a specific action. When that tiger crosses your path, for example, you run. The rest of the world doesn't matter. You're focused entirely on the tiger, the fear it creates, and how you can get away from it.

In other words, negative emotions narrow your mind and focus your thoughts. At that same moment, you might have the option to climb a tree, pick up a leaf, or grab a stick—but your brain ignores all of those options because they seem irrelevant when a tiger is standing in front of you." (Clear, "The Science of Positive Thinking")

This same thing happens whether you're facing a daunting to-do list, having a fight with your spouse, feeling sorry for not exercising, or feeling overwhelmed because your kids have been playing in the mud. Your brain shuts everything else off and focuses on the negative emotions of fear, anger, frustration, or stress— just like it did with the tiger. You can't see other options or choices. It's your survival instinct at work, and it's great if you're facing a tiger in the jungle.

It's not helpful, however, when you're parenting a houseful of active children, who are experimenting with life. If you allow your mind to focus on the negative, you'll be limiting your ability to choose wise and helpful responses, to be Present. You'll see your children and how they're behaving in a negative way even if that isn't the real story at all.

POSITIVE STORIES INCREASE YOUR INTERNAL RESOURCES

The negative stories you tell yourself over and over again impact how you feel about your children and your ability to be Present with them. Negative thoughts hinder you from achieving things you want. Positive thoughts do the opposite.

Barbara Fredrickson is a positive psychology researcher at the University of North Carolina. She's been able to demonstrate positive thoughts can create real value in your life.

Here's a summation from James Clear's *Huffington Post* article:

Fredrickson tested the impact of positive emotions on the brain by setting up a little experiment. During this experiment, she divided her research subjects into five groups and showed each group different film clips.

The first two groups saw clips that created positive emotions. Group One saw images that created feelings of joy. Group two saw images that created feelings of contentment.

Group three was the control group. They saw images that were neutral and produced no significant emotion.

The last two groups saw clips that created negative emotions. Group four saw images that created feelings of fear. Group five saw images that created feelings of anger.

Afterward, each participant was asked to imagine themselves in a situation where similar feelings would arise and to write down what they would do. Each participant was handed a piece of paper with twenty blank lines beginning with the phrase, "I would like to . . . "

Participants who saw images of fear and anger wrote down the fewest responses. Meanwhile, the participants who saw images of joy and contentment wrote down a significantly higher number of actions that they would take, even when compared to the neutral group.

In other words, when you're experiencing positive emotions like joy, contentment, and love, you'll see more possibilities in your life. These findings were among the first suggesting positive emotions broaden your sense of possibility and open your mind up to more options. (Clear, "The Science of Positive Thinking")

To read more about Fredrickson's study, visit www.ncbi.nlm.nih. gov and search for "Open Hearts Build Lives: Positive Emotions, Induced Through Loving-Kindness Meditation, Build Consequential Personal Resources."

In chapter 2 I mentioned the self-employed mother who was telling herself a negative story about her son's actions. She felt he was whiney and needy. He was a bother when she was trying to work. Her responses to her son were causing a strained relationship between them. She was having difficulty figuring out how to fix the situation.

Here's what happened when she began telling herself a more positive story. When I asked her to tell me more about her son, she replied that he was bright, loving, and responsible. So she decided to remind herself of these qualities each time she began to experience annoyance or frustration.

When I talked with her next, I asked her how it was going. She replied she and her son were no longer at odds. She enjoyed his company. She could see that he was just interested in what she was doing, and they had had opportunities to connect on and off during the day. She was able to respond positively to him more often. She was able to be Present more frequently.

When her story was negative, she had fewer ideas on how she could deal with the situation in positive ways and, in fact, dealt with her son in negative ways. She often checked out.

When she checked out, it set up a negative cycle between them. Her son tried harder to be heard and seen, her annoyance was heightened, and she responded in more negative ways. Her son would try even harder to be heard and seen, and the cycle would repeat.

When she changed her story and generated more positive feelings, she found more creative ways to respond. The new responses changed the dynamic or cycle with her son. This mom got better results because her feelings were positive. Her feelings were positive because she changed her story about her son. She found ways to be Present despite her work or his needs.

Again from the research of Fredrickson, "Positive emotions broaden an individual's momentary thought-action repertoire: joy sparks the urge to play, interest sparks the urge to explore, contentment sparks the urge to savor and integrate, and love sparks a recurring cycle of each of these urges within safe, close relationships. The broadened mind-sets arising from these positive emotions are contrasted to the narrowed mind-sets sparked by many negative emotions" (Fredrickson et al, "Open Hearts Build Lives").

All parents could use lots of helpful inner resources. These internal resources improve your odds of responding well when you're dealing with a tired child, a discontent child, a misbehaving child, or a child who has a need. And when you keep your thoughts and the resulting stories positive, you increase your inner resources to be Present. This is a great cycle to set up!

OUR WORDS TELL THE TRUE STORY!

Our negative thoughts and the resulting stories trip us up in our efforts to be Present Parents. Our words can do the same.

We say things without thinking. They're only words after all. We don't mean what we say but . . . the truth is *we actually do*. What we say is an indicator of the story we're holding in our minds.

No parent wants to admit their thoughts might honestly be negative about their child because we love our kids. If we love our children, we couldn't truly mean the things we say. We're responding to frustration or anger, like anyone else, but we don't mean it.

I submit that we do mean it. I submit that we must begin taking full responsibility for the words we say, because those words are telling you your real story; the one you're repeating to yourself over and over again; the one driving your responses that either expand or limit your inner resources.

Saying, "My kids are so messy" or "My son doesn't respect me" generates low energy. This low energy attracts the very thing that is distressing us. If our words are, "I love being with my kids," "My daughter is sure helpful today," or "I'm having a peaceful day," we generate high energy that attracts what we want to have happen.

I have a friend who believes everyone is out to get her. She constantly says the people she hires are going to take advantage of her. And guess what, they do!

I've been around her long enough and often enough to have been able to observe what happens. Even if someone she hires does a great job and is fair, she finds a way to feel as if they've taken advantage of her. The story she repeats out loud is a self-fulfilling prophecy.

I know a man who has difficulty walking. When he's going anywhere, you can hear him say, "I always find the perfect parking spot." It amazes me how often he actually does find the perfect spot. Frequently, as he drives up, someone in the perfect space pulls out. It's incredible!

I know another woman who is constantly saying, "I can't believe how blessed I am." And she is. Marvelous things happen to her all the time, both large and small. Even when something in her life might look bad to another person, she'll say, "I live the most blessed life," because she sees the good in even the bad.

Think of all the phrases we say and hear over and over again about kids:

- You're driving me crazy.

- You're so messy.

- You're so noisy.

- I can't get a minute's peace.

- Why can't you listen to me? You never listen!

- You're so irresponsible.

- I don't know what I'm going to do with you!

- You make me so mad.

- You're so sloppy, disobedient, messy, argumentative, quarrelsome, and so on.

- You're wearing me out.

- I can't listen one more minute.

If we want better outcomes, we need to watch our words. Say what you want, not what you don't want. Words are your thoughts/stories put into concrete form. Words generate emotions. You'll feel the way you speak. How you feel moves you to an action that gives you a result, either good or bad. Your words move you closer to or away from the ability to be Present.

TIPS FOR HAVING BETTER STORIES

TIP 1—Take responsibility and stop blaming

When we choose to tell ourselves stories that blame others, we decide to become victims. Victims parent poorly. I hear parents blame their kids all the time for how they're feeling.

- You make me so mad.

- You have ruined my day.

- I can't think straight because you're so noisy.

- I wouldn't be yelling if you would listen.

Blame is always an indicator there's a problem with our way of being or how we perceive what's happening, or in other words, the story we're telling ourselves.

Let me illustrate—Don is a gadget man. One fall he bought a new stove top grill at the county fair and was excited to use it. The next morning was Sunday, and we needed to get to a very important reception right after church. I said to Don, "Honey, there isn't time to grill chicken today and make it to the reception. You'll have to do it tomorrow."

After church, Don was nowhere to be seen. I knew he had left early to go home and grill chicken! Sure enough, when I got home the grill was on and he was cooking.

When we got to the reception, they were cleaning up. The bride and groom had left. We ate at a table alone while others cleaned up around us. I was *so* angry!

Here was my *heat of the moment* story—"There are only two reasons Don would have done this. Either he didn't hear a word I said because he doesn't listen to me, or he didn't care what I said." I was practiced at controlling my thoughts by now, and I knew this particular story was blaming and would color our relationship for weeks. Not appealing at all.

So I looked for a new story. "I know Don. He loves me. He isn't insensitive. There must be a reason he went ahead and grilled chicken."

Later in the evening I calmly said, "Don, remember when I said there wasn't time to grill chicken today. I can see two reasons why you went ahead and did it. Either you didn't hear what I said this morning, or you didn't care what I wanted. But I know you, and you love me. You're not insensitive. So there must be a reason I haven't thought of."

> **"When you blame others for what you're going through, you deny responsibility—you give others power over that part of your life."**
>
> —Author Unknown

He looked at me with a stricken face and replied, "Gosh Mary, I thought I could do it in time. I thought the whole thing would take thirty minutes. I didn't know it would take so long."

I had to laugh because I could tell from his poor face he had really believed it would only take thirty minutes and was shocked to find out it wasn't true. He never intended to ignore me or hurt me or make us late. He didn't plan anything of the kind. He was moving forward based on an unrealistic expectation.

I was able to revise my story because I took responsibility. I stopped blaming. I could see my story was the issue, not Don's actions.

Knowing this, I was able to control my thoughts and tell a story that felt better. With those positive thoughts in my mind, I was able to devise a plan of action that eventually resulted in a positive outcome. I was able to get Present with Don and that made it possible for him to clear up the issue for me.

Taking responsibility for how we perceive what's happening can and does make a difference in our outcomes, as April Hiatt has discovered. She told me the following:

I opened the dryer door to discover wet clothes. Jonathan (my fourteen-year-old) didn't press the start button when he transferred loads. I was three words into my grumble when I heard myself say out loud "Oh, I'm so glad I checked the dryer." The next words were of understanding, with a deep feeling of love [for my son]. "I've done this same thing before [myself]." This whole cycle took under three seconds, and it happened without me really thinking about it. Wow, I'm amazed.

TIP 2—Decide to think the best of others

Ron McMillan, in an online magazine, shared an experience a father had with his sixteen-year-old daughter. She was supposed to be home by a certain time and she was late. Very late!

He did what we're prone to do. He began writing a mental story. He imagined all sorts of scenarios for why she was late. She lacked respect for family rules. She was thoughtless. She was irresponsible. The later she was, the bigger the story grew and the angrier he became.

As she opened the door, he exploded with, "You're late! You know the rules, and you broke your promise. You're grounded, young lady." Of course, his daughter ran to her room crying.

To let you in on the facts, the girl's date had taken her to a drinking party after the movie. When she asked him to take her home, he refused. She had tried to call home, but the line was busy. So she called a friend who got off work at midnight and came and got her. In the meantime, she sat on the curb in the dark because the party was out of control and not safe.

The father's story was at the heart of the problem, not his daughter's lateness. If he'd stayed away from negative, judgmental thoughts he could have staved off feelings of anger, frustration, and offense, which would have helped him act differently as his daughter came in the door.

He could have felt relief at her return rather than anger. He would have been able to ask questions when she got home instead of the next morning. He could have been Present with his daughter whether she was innocent or guilty. He could have built the relationship rather than damaging it.

As McMillan explains,

> The key to overcoming the natural man's tendency to assume the worst about others' motives is not to polish our apology skills nor learn to control our anger and frustration. Rather, the key to overcoming this destructive chain of events is to question our story.

> Examining the negative story we tell ourselves . . . causes us to consider alternate explanations for their apparently hurtful behavior. To accomplish this, ask yourself one question: "Why would a reasonable, rational and decent person do this?" Or, if this is too unwieldy, ask, "Why would a decent person act this way?" (McMillan, "Master Your Stories and You Master Your Life")

The lateness of the daughter did not make her dad mad. The story Dad told himself is what made him mad. If he had changed his story/thoughts, he would have changed his emotions, which in turn would have changed his response and the result.

Again from McMillan,

> If, after recognizing his escalating anger, Dad had asked himself, "Why would my responsible, decent daughter be late for her

curfew?" he might come up with various answers. The first might be, "Because she's being rebellious!"

But after mastering his story, he'd come to consider the possibilities of car trouble, bad traffic, or that she was innocently having fun and lost track of time. The valuable revelation is all of these reasons are possibilities, and Dad can't know which reason is true until he has a conversation with his daughter. (McMillan, "Master Your Stories and You Master Your Life")

When we decide to think the best of others, we can manage our thoughts and the resulting stories more effectively.

TIP 3—Choose words wisely

Dr. Wayne Dyer has said, "What's in you is what comes out" ("Why the Inside Matters").

It's true! Pay attention to the words you say in frustration, sorrow, and anger; you'll get a good idea of what you're holding onto in your subconscious mind.

Earlier in this chapter I gave numerous examples of the power of our words and how they reveal what we truly feel. The words that we allow to come out of our mouths are what ultimately drive feelings and actions and bring you the results you live with daily.

Watch the words you use when thinking or speaking:

- Childlike vs. naughty

- Young vs. clumsy

- Needs more direction vs. oppositional

- Tired vs. grumpy

- Preoccupied vs. lazy

- Angry vs. rebellious

- Being a kid vs. messy

- Wants my presence vs. needy

- Has a need vs. pushing my buttons

> **"Happiness is found along the way of this journey, not at the end of the road."**
>
> —Howard W. Hunter, former president of The Church of Jesus Christ of Latter-day Saints

You're in control of your thoughts and words. You're in control of your stories. When you accept this idea and take responsibility, you'll be in control of your life. You'll be able to be Present more often when things aren't going your way.

TIP 4—Check your core beliefs

We can get an idea of the beliefs we've formed growing up by paying attention to the stories we tell ourselves over and over again and by listening to the words coming out of our mouths. These beliefs may not be supportive or helpful in having good relationships with others or in our ability to be Present and parent well.

Once we've found a core belief that is not helpful, we can get rid of it by rewriting the story. Here are two powerful examples.

Example 1—One day I was busily helping a friend organize and clean her home. Her children were just as actively messing and un-organizing. My friend said, "Doesn't that get to you? You get it cleaned, and they mess it up. It seems like a losing battle."

It seems like a losing battle! I'll bet you've heard your parents say this. I'll bet you've said it to your kids.

I looked up and smiled. I replied, "It used to upset me. It did seem like a losing battle. But one day I changed my story. I decided I wasn't at war. It wasn't me against them. It wasn't a zero-sum game where if I win they lose and if they win, I lose. I realized the reason I was cleaning and organizing, baking bread, changing diapers, cooking food, gardening, and sewing were all for the same reason. I was ministering to the needs of my family."

The meaning of "to minister" is to give aid or service and I would add to do it with joy. It felt good when I stopped going to war daily and went to minister instead. It freed me up. I no longer had to worry if I got it all done before they could mess it up again. In fact, I no longer had to worry if I got it done at all. All I had to do was look for ways to minister. Being Present was one of those ways!

The mom I was talking with had an inner belief that parenting could be a no-win job. It affected her ability to deal with the messiness, chaos, and noise that naturally come with raising children. I had thought the same, but changing the belief by altering my story made it much easier to manage the day to day stresses of keeping up with a family.

Example 2—After many years of marriage, I realized I felt a lot of resentment. But when I learned and accepted I was in control of my thoughts and the resulting stories, I stopped pointing the finger of blame for my resentments. I began searching for what story fueled my feelings. When I found it, I could see why I was so unhappy.

Here it is: "I'm alone. I have to do it all myself, no one will help me. I'm invisible." This story came from my childhood.

Once I had the story, this deeply held core belief, I could see the impossibility of feeling supported in my relationship with Don, no matter what he did. Can you see it was impossible for Don to send messages saying, "I love you. I support you. You matter to me"? Could Don be a successful husband even if he never made a single mistake?

No, he couldn't, because my inner belief, my deeply held story was, *no one* was there for me. To have a happier relationship where I felt loved and supported, I had to change the story. It was a vital step in creating the marriage I wanted to have.

When you find yourself at odds with what's happening in your life, it's wise to look for the story generating your emotions and your responses. These are your deeply held beliefs. When you rewrite them, you will impact your results for the better.

TIP 5—Track your thoughts

If thoughts are so powerful, we need to gain control over them in order to move closer to what we want and to stop getting more of what we don't want.

Once you're aware of a negative thought, you need to capture it—write it down. You might be thinking it's crazy to write down negative stuff, but I've lived this, and I know it works!

What's the value in writing your negative thoughts down?

- You get them out of your head!

- You begin to see patterns and cycles

- When you know what your weaknesses seem to be, you can counter them with the positive. Your weakness is actually your strength in embryo. Writing down the weakness and writing down the opposite allows you to begin to see a perceived weakness in a new light. April Hiatt has experienced this. She told me, "I'm so grateful you shared with me that I'm the opposite of my weaknesses. This truth has changed how I see my stumbling blocks and how I see and handle both of my sons as well." (from personal correspondence.)

- You get clarity on where you need to focus your growth. A mom once wrote me, "As I recorded my negative thoughts and wrote down the opposite, I began to see what was wrong. I realized I was 'Other' centered. I cared a great deal what others thought about me and how I thought they saw me. I was [making] many of my decisions from this viewpoint. This understanding made it possible for me to become more 'Christ' centered. This has made a huge difference in how I feel about myself, the decisions I make and the way I treat others and my family."

- You feel more in control of yourself and your feelings

- You make better choices

- You stop blaming

- You stop being a victim

So pay attention to your negative thoughts and write them down. Take control!

TIP 6—Teach others what you've learned

Teaching others what we're learning and experiencing is a powerful tool that helps us make even greater changes. As we teach others, we clarify it for ourselves. One of the best ways to learn a concept is to teach it. It helps motivate us to keep practicing the new skill.

> **"While we teach, we learn."**
>
> —Seneca, Roman philosopher

If we teach what we learn to our family, we'll be heartened as we see them making changes also, and our whole family will be blessed. We'll all be on board the same train, heading for happier days.

I have a friend who experienced the value and joy of teaching her son what she had learned. She told me the following:

I have a son who is particularly down on himself, frequently calling himself names and getting upset about small mistakes. One day when this started happening, I thought about what I had learned from [you].

I started celebrating his mistake and cheering with him, explaining to him it was a chance to learn. He thought I was a goofball, but it put a smile on his face and diffused a negative situation.

111

That situation could have been another proof to his subconscious that he is stupid/clumsy/fill-in-the-blank, but we were able to turn it around. I later heard him teach the same concept to his little sister. For me, knowing I'm breaking the cycle of negativity in the next generation is more exciting than learning these tools myself. (From personal correspondence.)

TIP 7—Keep practicing

You may never forget how to ride a bike once you've learned but trust this sixty-six-year-old—If you stop riding, you do get rusty and getting back on the bike can be a painful event.

Keep working at controlling your thoughts. This is something you need to do daily. There isn't a point when you're so good at it that you can stop working on it. Negative thoughts will come, and they'll need to be managed.

Lynne Nielsen discovered this for herself and so can you. After some practice controlling her thoughts, she told me, "I'm already noticing a change. It's becoming a little bit of a habit when I think a negative thought to follow it right up with thinking what the . . . positives are. It's very powerful and awesome! I'm glad I'm doing this and you're going to hold me accountable because . . . it would be easy to talk myself out of it and rationalize I had already gotten the good out of the exercise that I needed." (From personal correspondence.)

No matter what's troubling you, change is possible, and taking control of your thoughts is a great place to start.

IN SUMMARY

Take responsibility for your thoughts, the stories and emotions they create, and your responses. Stop blaming. Take responsibility for your words, which are your stories in concrete form.

You're in control of the stories you tell—stories about yourself, your family, your children, the world, the past, the present, and the future. Knowing this gives you *all* the power.

Let me end with a compelling example and a sweet story:

I met a woman at a retreat. She was crying, and we began talking. She felt all was lost in her life. She was in total despair, so we began working together.

At our first mentor session, she said, "When I first wake up in the morning, I lie there and think of all the things I'm doing wrong in my life. I think of stupid things I've said to people, things I should be doing but am not, and all the reasons people don't like me." And she is such a fabulous person too!

We began work on her thoughts and the subsequent stories she told herself. She started tracking her thoughts and writing down the opposite, which remember, is what is actually true no matter how it looks or feels.

By our fifth session, the despair was gone. She felt hopeful. She told me this story. "My mom called upset over a lost UPS package she had mailed to my sister because she had miswritten the house number. She was beating herself up and thinking all was lost. Because of what I've learned I knew all was not lost and how to handle the situation. I helped her through it and gave her hope. The package was found at the neighbor's house the following day."

In another session, the same woman said the relationship with her husband wasn't good. She felt like a single mom. He avoided being home because their relationship was so rocky. By session six, here's (in essence) what she had to say:

"I'm learning to see my relationships from a new perspective. I don't blame others when things go wrong. I can accept life happens and move on. I'm not holding grudges. My husband and I did get into a little spat the other night, and I woke up the next morning to a complete realization of my part in it, rather than being angry at him for his part."

When I first began helping this woman take back her power by stopping the blame, watching her thoughts and words and rewriting her stories, she felt despair and hopelessness.

At the end of our time together she said, "I feel light and grateful. I have tools to help me. I know I can succeed, and I have hope. I see my husband as a gift."

Three years later, I had the privilege of working with her again for a short time. She was a changed woman. Our conversations were entirely different, and she was able to resolve most of her concerns with very little help.

When you begin to manage your thoughts, you'll have better stories. As you do, you'll experience far better outcomes. You'll be able to check out less often and be Present more. Change your story, change your life.

Stories are powerful in determining our happiness level. My granddaughter, Mary, is six. She loves to watch the fish in our tank. We have a very sleek, silver catfish that swims fast and erratically whenever anyone stands in front of the tank. I believe the fish does this out of fear or because it has been disturbed.

One day Mary asked me, "Do you know why this fish swims so fast when I'm looking at him?" I replied, "No, why?" She responded with, "Because he likes me!" Mary, like all of us, gets to write the story, and her story makes her happy. And for all I know, her story may be as true as mine.

CHAPTER 6

DO the Simple Things

There came a time in my family when I recognized we didn't have what we wanted in terms of our family culture, and I knew we had to make changes. I felt passionate and I felt pressed.

I had the overwhelming feeling if I didn't get it taken care of *now* our whole family was going to end up on a garbage heap! I've worked with plenty of parents who have found themselves in this same position.

In addition to the family problems that put me in this overwhelmed and driven state of mind, reading books and attending classes on family management and parenting added to my frustrations.

Reading a book, attending a class, or going to a workshop can give you many ideas. You hurry home and begin tearing the fabric of your life apart to insert this system or that program or a new way of managing. *Wow*, it blows your family away. They often push against all the value you're trying to give them.

Then what happens? You know the story. In a couple of weeks or a month, maybe two, you've quit. You're back to being and doing what you did before. You're burnt out. You're family's burnt out.

I appreciate these words by Calvin Coolidge: "They criticize me for harping on the obvious; if all the folks in the United States would do the few simple things they know they ought to do, most of our big problems would take care of themselves" ("Quotations").

Doing the simple things we ought to do may have been needed in the good old days but it's also entirely true for families today.

BUSTING THE MYTH OF THE SILVER BULLET

Here's the crux of the matter. It's not the big, one-time things we try to implement that will help us get what we want. It's the small and simple things, done consistently over time, that create the biggest changes.

As you know from my introduction, raising our family wasn't always a bed of roses. We had children making poor choices. Those were hard years. That's when I felt we had to fix everything *now*.

In retrospect, I can see what I couldn't see during the heat of the battle. Don and I had already put in place many small and simple things. This made *all* the difference.

I asked my children recently, "What was the most consistent thing you can recall from your time as a child in our home?" My daughter Marie replied, "Dinner at the table, family prayer around your bed, and going to church."

Meals and Sundays in church, all lined up in a pew, were bonding times. These activities helped create a team that didn't fall apart when things got rough. They welded links between our children and us that kept them tethered to the family, despite the swirling waters of life attempting to tear them free and send them downstream to destruction.

And what of those early mornings when everyone was snoring through our family prayers? Well, our children knew without any question they were loved and that we had their back. So when things got rough, they came home for help, even though they knew we didn't approve of the choices they were making. They had a safe harbor from the storm they were choosing to sail.

I can think of many things my husband and I didn't do well. But the small and simple things we did do consistently, over time, when the chips were down, made all the difference. We didn't lose anyone. Our family stayed intact despite the odds. We all survived and went on to thrive.

There's a myth we occasionally buy into—when we want a significant change we need to implement something big. This big new thing will have the power to help us re-create ourselves or our family.

Rex D. Pinegar, in a speech given at Brigham Young University, said, "The achievement of true greatness is a long-term process . . . . It seems it always requires regular, consistent, small, and sometimes ordinary and mundane steps

> **"Small disciplines repeated with consistency every day lead to great achievements gained slowly over time."**
>
> —John C. Maxwell, author of *The 15 Invaluable Laws of Growth: Live Them and Reach Your Potential*

over a long period of time" (Pinegar, "The Small and Simple Things").

This principle—that consistency in small things, over time, brings *big* results—can be found in cultures all around the world and in most, if not all religions.

It's amazing we ever believe the silver bullet myth because the truth of small steps over time has been restated so often. But the myth is comforting. It's what we want to believe because the truth is harder to accept.

Why would we rather do one big thing to change our lives? Although the big thing may take a massive effort on our part, if we gave the effort, then the work would be done. But the truth is we have to decide to do it and then follow through—over and over and over and over . . . ! There is no one and done.

In her book *Daffodil Principle: One Woman, Two Hands, One Bulb at a Time,*

Jaroldeen Edwards recounts the day her daughter, Carolyn, drove her to Lake Arrowhead to visit a daffodil garden. It wasn't just any daffodil garden. It turned out to be five acres of beautiful golden flowers nodding in the breeze.

As Jaroldeen gasped in amazement, she asked the question that everyone who visited the garden asked, "Who did this?" On the porch of a small and neat A-frame house was a poster answering the question.

The first response to how many flowers there were was "fifty thousand bulbs." The second fact listed was, "One at a time, by one woman, two hands, two feet, and very little brain." The third was, "Began in 1958" (Edwards, *Daffodil Principle*).

> "A remarkable, glorious achievement is just what a long series of unremarkable, inglorious tasks looks like from far away."
>
> —Tim Urban, author of the blog *Wait But Why?*

When we multiply small amounts of time, with small increments of daily effort, consistently, we can accomplish magnificent things. We can change our part of the world.

Whenever you hear that a person has achieved an extraordinary goal, rarely, if ever, are you told the process they used—that is, the ordinary actions they took consistently. You only hear about the outcome.

We're led to believe extraordinary successes in business, home, or life are a result of significant actions, but they're not—they're a result of daily actions done consistently over time.

I enjoy the story of Naaman found in the King James Bible. Naaman was a captain for the king of Syria, "a great man with his master . . . because by him the Lord had given deliverance unto Syria: . . . a mighty man in valor, but . . . a leper" (2 Kings 5:1).

At the direction of his king, Naaman went to Elisha the prophet to be healed of his dreaded affliction. When Naaman got to Elisha's house, Elisha sent a messenger out to him who said, "Go and wash in Jordan seven times, and thy flesh shall come again to thee, and thou shalt be clean" (2 Kings 5:10).

Wow, Naaman wasn't even going to have to do the consistently, over time thing. He was only going to have to repeat the action a mere seven times. But Naaman was angry with Elisha. He felt the prophet should have come out of his house to see him and he should have done some *big* thing to take care of this *big* problem.

He said, "I thought, He will surely come out to me, and stand, and call on the name of the Lord his God, and strike his hand over the place, and recover the leper" (2 Kings 5:11).

Naaman was ready to go away in disgust at the simple instructions he received, but he had a wise servant who reminded him of the principle we've been discussing—simple things, done over time consistently, bring significant results. His servant said, "If the prophet had bid thee do some great thing, wouldest thou not have done it? How much rather then, when he saith to thee, Wash, and be clean?" (2 Kings 5:13).

Naaman came to his senses and he "dipped himself seven times in Jordan, according to the saying of the man of God: and his flesh came again like unto the flesh of a little child, and he was clean" (2 Kings 5:15).

As parents I think we are, at times, like Naaman. We know we have problems and issues, but we expect a significant or seemingly important thing to come along and bail us out of our affliction. In reality, it is truly the small and simple things we can do daily that, in the end, will make *all* the difference.

Understanding this is especially important in parenting because it nearly always takes until a child leaves home and creates their own life to see the results of our efforts.

While they're growing, it's tempting to let ourselves feel failure because we don't see our child as neat, quiet, mannerly and so forth. We often see a mud-covered child, a snitched cookie behind a back, spilled milk on the kitchen floor, or we hear voices' complaining that it's not their fault or "it's my turn."

Remaining Present while a child grows, not checking out because of feeling discouraged or overwhelmed, is dependent on doing simple things consistently rather than searching for a one-time fix to family issues.

THE 100% DEVIL VS. THE 1% PRINCIPLE

Over the years, while working with people, I've found there's one challenge that comes up over and over again. It's called the 100% devil.

This is the troublemaker who sits on your shoulder and tells you all your problems have to be fixed now; there's not enough time to make the necessary changes; you have to do it perfectly, or not at all; there's so much to do you'll never get it done.

His purpose is to make it difficult for you to begin, let alone stick with it long enough to effect change. And he's excellent at his job. He wants you to be aware of the fact you've been working on change for three months or three years, and it's not bearing fruit yet.

He makes sure you notice all the times you fail, fall off the wagon, or become inconsistent, as well as all the times your efforts are less than stellar. He's there on your shoulder to make certain you won't have success.

The 100% devil is the enemy of this true principle: small and simple things, done consistently over time bring *big* results.

> "You will never change your life until you change something you do daily."
>
> —John C. Maxwell, *The 15 Invaluable Laws of Growth: Live Them and Reach Your Potential*

I first learned of this little guy and the 1% principle from my daughter Jodie. Here's the story she told me:

> One day I was walking through the airport on my way to a business meeting. I felt impressed to stop by the airport bookstore. I walked in, and my eyes fell on a book written by one of the business greats, Peter Drucker. I bought it, put it under my arm, and proceeded to my gate.
>
> Settling down into my seat on the plane, I opened the book. Now, at this point, you need to know I was the leader of an organization that was in a lot of pain. In fact, we were on fire, getting ready to crash and burn. It's not a fun place to be. It hurts a lot to be the leader of that type of organization. I was hired to fix it, to heal it, and there was a lot to fix, a lot to heal, and it was all very urgent.
>
> As my plane sped down the jet way, I read these words: "What needs to be done almost always contains more than one urgent task, but effective executives don't splinter themselves; they concentrate on one task." I slammed the book shut as my plane left the runway and headed for the sky. "No way! There are too many things that are hurting. I can't focus on one of them. On that schedule, I'll never fix it all before we dissolve!" (Jodie Palmer, "Concentrate on one RIGHT thing for consistent improvement")

You probably understand her feelings. You may have the same struggle—your frustration with the number of things that need to be done or fixed in yourself or your family, and the urgency of all of them. But Jodie and I, and many others, have learned Drucker was right.

Effective executives, whether of a business or a family, don't splinter themselves. They focus on the one thing they feel will make the biggest difference right now, the best 1 percent.

You may be squirming in your seat a little at the thought of moving along 1 percentage at a time. At that rate, it feels like your kids will be grown and out of your home before you get it all together.

Understand the 1% principle doesn't work according to linear addition, 1 percent plus 1 percent. Rather, it works according to the law of exponentiality. In other words, when you work on the best 1 percent, other issues you weren't focusing on seem to miraculously resolve.

Trying to focus on everything at once ultimately maintains mediocrity at best and moves us backward in our goals at worst. This type of poor result is the goal of the 100% devil, but be assured that focusing on the best 1 percent will help you progress faster and more solidly than trying to do it all at once.

The 1% principle is another way of saying small and simple things done consistently over time bring *big* results.

MY 1% IMPROVEMENT

A couple of years ago I began anticipating the coming of the New Year. It was during September that I felt an urgent need to make changes in my way of being and in my life. I didn't want to enter the New Year in limbo. I wanted to know what one thing I could do to effect the biggest personal growth. I was serious. It wasn't a passing fancy motivated by a current problem. I wanted my life to feel different, better. I wanted to *be* better.

So I set out to discover the one thing that would give me the feeling of success I needed.

I approached the problem in the same way I approach most things: I began seriously pondering and praying. I have to admit the actual process of gaining the wisdom I sought reflected perfectly the principle we're discussing. The simple steps I took were to ponder or think diligently on the issue and to pray daily. I repeated this process for over three months.

But finally, Eureka, I struck gold. In December, a thought came clearly to my mind—Stop complaining. Now I hadn't considered myself a complaining person, so this was a bit of a shock. Nevertheless, I began monitoring my words, thoughts, and actions

> "You cannot change your destination overnight, but you can change your direction overnight."
>
> —Jim Rohn,
> American entrepreneur

over the next few weeks. I could see I had indeed struck gold.

It's been two years and I'm still working on this one thing. It's a toughie! But the changes I've experienced have been astonishing. I've grown in areas I didn't realize my complaining was affecting. My experience has been that 1 percent plus 1 percent certainly doesn't equal 2 percent, it equals far more.

SO HOW DO WE DO IT?

It isn't easy to pray and focus on one thing for three months when you're looking for an answer. You want the answer *now*. Doing the same actions over and over again for over two years isn't easy. We live in a quick-fix world. We want what we want now.

In many things, we can get it now. We have fast food, fast information, fast, fast, fast. But to live a successful life and have a successful family, we have to throw out the 100% devil, accept 1 percent improvements, and embrace the principle of small and simple things done consistently over time.

When I was a young mother, I was a yeller. It kept my family walking on egg shells because they never knew when I would explode.

It took a neighbor walking across my street and handing me a brochure on anger management to get me to look at what I was doing. It was a painful place to come to, and for a few months, I wouldn't even accept I was there.

But as I observed myself it became evident it was true. I was in the position Calvin Coolidge pointed out that I mentioned earlier. I needed to do the obvious and simple thing and stop losing my temper.

It may have been a simple thing, but it wasn't easy. It took over ten years for me to conquer that demon. But conquer it I did and I've been yelling much less for well over thirty years. It was worth all it took to make it happen.

So what kept me going? How was I able to persevere long enough to make it happen? How did I dash the 100% devil to the ground so I wasn't tempted to quit after a few months, two years, or nine years?

I learned a lot during the time I worked to conquer rage and anger. Here are the steps that worked for me. There may be other possible steps, but this list is more than enough to get you going and keep you going.

As you look through the list, remember it takes time to become a Present Parent just as it takes time to learn to control one's temper.

1. CONCENTRATE on the one thing you need to do right now

What's the one best thing you should work on first—the thing you *feel* you need to do? For one woman, it was to cover the mountain with daffodils. For me, it was to stop yelling and later to stop complaining. What is it for you?

Do you need to take a look at your current family culture and build a vision? Do you need to give up using technology when you're working with your kids? Do you need to listen more, yell less, play with your kids, have more mini-conversations, eat dinner together, or go to bed earlier? What is it for you?

2. COMMIT to being consistent for as long as it takes

The daffodil woman planted for over thirty years. It took ten years for me to stop yelling. I'm still working diligently on the complaining. Some of our family goals will take many years to come to fruition. So will many of our personal goals. Creating a family culture and sending well-adjusted, honest, loyal, and wise children out into the world takes years. Being a Present Parent is a lifetime work.

3. REMEMBER being consistent is not the same as being perfect.

James Clear reported in the magazine *Entrepreneur* that research shows, regardless of the habit you're working to build or change, the character trait you want to develop, or the family culture or tradition you're working on, missing a single day has no measurable impact on your long-term success.

> "There's a difference between interest and commitment. When you're interested in doing something, you do it only when it's convenient. When you're committed to something, you accept no excuses - only results."
>
> —Kenneth H. Blanchard, author and cofounder of The Ken Blanchard Companies

He wrote, "Daily failures are like red lights during a road trip. When you're driving a car, you'll come to a red light every now and then. But if you maintain a good average speed, you'll always make it to your destination despite the stops and delays along the way" (Clear, "Being Consistent Is Not the Same as Being Perfect").

Never let the 100% devil remain on your shoulder for long. Dash him to the ground. Don't believe his lies. Change takes time. Growth takes time. Perfect is not the goal; progress is!

4. BREAK what you want into smaller steps

If the goal is to stop yelling, how would that look?

- Accept that it's about you and not the behavior of others.

- Commit to your family you'll use a respectful voice—ask for support.

- Decide what you will do instead of yelling when times get tough.

- Get counseling if you need it.

- Practice, fail, practice, fail, practice . . . for as long as it takes.

If the goal is to learn to be a Present Parent, it might look like this:

- Determine one thing getting in the way of your being Present.

- Choose an action to help overcome that issue.

- Make a personal commitment to do it.

- Begin.

- Practice, fail, practice, fail, practice . . . for as long as it takes.

5. CREATE space

When I was working on controlling my temper, I had to create space for reflection, for getting help from others who had accomplished what I wanted to accomplish, and for nurturing myself as I did the work.

If you want to be Present, the process it isn't all that different from changing a habit of yelling to being able to control your temper. You have to begin by creating space for change. When talking about being Present as a family there are some steps you will want to consider as you think about creating space for Presence. You

1. Be committed to family time

2. Set the time aside

3. Consistently honor the time commitment

4. Continue to learn and practice what you learn

5. Clear out some of the good to make room for the best

1. To commit as a family unit to spending time together, you have to sell your family on what you want to do, get everyone on the same page. This is particularly important if you have pre-teens or teens in your family. It is rarely effective to make an announcement like "this family is going to change and get it together and this is what we are going to do!"

You can assist your family to take ownership of the idea of spending more Present time together by

- Making it sound special or exciting when you present the idea. What are the benefits for the individuals and the family? Make an emotional connection.

- Having a family discussion about hat the family wants to accomplish. Accept everyone's ideas. Honor feelings. Don't criticize each other's input.

- Keeping it fun and lighthearted when possible. Use words that tell what you want. Avoid stating what you don't want.

2. A commitment isn't any good unless you set an actual time for it to be accomplished. Otherwise it becomes a hope, or a wish. You may decide to spend more time as a family but if you don't talk about when you are going to do that, weeks can pass. Will you walk together after school on Monday, Wednesday, and Friday? Will you play ball each Saturday morning for an hour? Will you have a sit-down family meal at least three days a week? Will you read together every morning for twenty minutes? Decide what and when.

3. Once you commit as a family and set a time to make it happen, then you have to do it! For example: You all decide that you will spend at least two hours without TV, technology, or phone to play together. You decide that Monday evening will be when you will get together and that you will read together, maybe play a game, or go on a walk. Then every week you make sure that everyone honors those two hours and doesn't schedule anything else. It can be a challenge to do this for a busy family but consistency in small and simple things makes *all* the difference in the feeling you have in your family; that Present feeling.

4. Never quit working on what you want. Sometimes we are tempted to become discouraged because we aren't seeing the results we want in the time frame we want. But I cannot stress this enough—small and simple things done consistently over time is what is required for any real success. So don't quit. If what you are experimenting with isn't working take your family back to the drawing board and come up with a new experiment. Keep learning and keep practicing.

5. Stephen Covey, in his book *First Things First*, makes the argument that for most people the choice isn't between good and bad but between good and best. We have a great many things that are good, but in a family they can become distractions from what is best. It is good to get the dishes done. It may be best when we stand at the sink with a child and help them as we have a mini-conversation. It is good to watch a movie as a family but it may be better to read together. It is good to drive to McDonalds and let the kids play after they eat. It may be better to have a sit-down meal at home and have a mini-conversation and some laughter together. It is good to go to Disneyland. It may be even better to spend a weekend camping, talking, and connecting around the campfire. Each of us has to decide what is best. But when we take some time to determine good from best, our family outcomes will be better.

If you want to be a more Present parent, if you want your family to have more Present time together, then you must create space for that to happen. Wishing will not be enough!

6. KEEP your word

Do what you've decided to do. Be as consistent as possible. I had to keep taking the steps to control my temper for ten years. Don't quit.

In your family, keeping your word builds trust with your children. Trust pays dividends later when your kids need to talk. Your kids will know they can trust you because when you said you would do something as a family, you did it. You made space. You honored the commitment and that says to your children, "You can trust me!"

7. MAKE CERTAIN the steps you take are in your control

When I was overcoming yelling, I was careful my goals were in my control. I couldn't attach my success to someone else's behavior.

For example, if a mother wants to have the kids' chores done by nine, her actual goal might be to stay Present at chore time and move from child to child encouraging and helping them.

If she works with her children each day, supporting them, then she's successful and reaches the goal even if they're not completely finished with chores by nine. If success hinges on having it all done by nine, she has less chance of success because she doesn't have total control over what each child does.

Let's look at eating together as a family. If success hinges on having peaceful conversations at all of your meals, you've set yourself up for failure because you're not in control of your family's behavior or responses.

However, if your goal is to eat together and for you to remain calm, despite spills and childish arguments, you have far more control. You'll be more successful.

8. FOCUS on today—it's all you have to work with.

Ten years is a long time to work on one thing. But as I focused on one day at a time, I was able to persevere. Do your best today. If you don't do well today, then when tomorrow is today, begin again. Once today is yesterday, *let it go*! Don't quit!

9. BELIEVE the end result will be exponential growth.

Believe that 1 percent plus 1 percent will not equal 2 percent.

Remember my most recent 1 percent, to stop complaining? Here are a few of the things that changed in my life because I chose the one best thing to work on.

A. My relationship with my husband is better. I'm kinder to him. I hold my tongue more often. He isn't in trouble for not doing things my way as often. He likes that and is a happier man! Our relationship is more peaceful.

B. My small, emotional tantrums have decreased. Emotional tantrums are those moments when you fuss and fume because things aren't going your way.

I have stopped ranting and raving at other drivers, either verbally or in my mind because I'm not complaining anymore. (At least not most of the time) Now I mentally send them on their way with a prayer of safety.

I stopped fuming over the bad service at the market because I'm no longer complaining. I smile and give a kind, sincerely felt word of thanks to the bag boy who's doing his best to learn good public relations.

I don't speak harshly to the computer as often. It's just a machine and isn't out to get me!

I like having less emotional tantrums. It makes my days more peaceful, for me and others.

C. I feel more gratitude. There's a saying I've used so often that I worried my kids might have it engraved on my headstone— "How can I be so grateful and ungrateful at the same time!" Well, you can't. If you're complaining about it, any part of it, you aren't truly grateful.

> "The right choices and wrong choices you make at the moment will have little or no noticeable impact on how your day goes for you. Nor tomorrow, nor the next day. No applause, no cheers, no screams, no life-or-death results played out in Technicolor. But it is precisely those very same, undramatic, seemingly insignificant actions that, when compounded over time, will dramatically affect how your [family] life turns out."
>
> —Jeff Olson, *The Slight Edge*

Now that I've gotten a handle on my complaining, I'm significantly more grateful. More gratitude has upped my sense of happiness, contentment, and joy.

I could go on but I hope you see what I mean. When we adjust one significant thing in our lives, it adjusts other things and our happiness increases. We cease to live in a one plus one world and enter the realm of exponential growth. It's an exciting place to live!

IN SUMMARY

Real growth and change come from learning to move toward your goals and desires one step at a time, consistently, for as long as it takes. Planting one bulb, fifty thousand times, is what creates the miracle.

Having the family you want will take time. Becoming a Present Parent takes time. Raising kids takes time. It necessitates throwing out the 100 percent devil that confuses and discourages us. It requires accepting the 1% principle—small and simple things done consistently over time bring *big* results.

Remember what I said at the beginning of this chapter—it's a myth that there's one big thing, a silver bullet, so to speak, that can overhaul our life or our family. We believe it because we want to.

The myth is comforting because until we find the silver bullet, we can go on thinking it's not our fault things are "going to the garbage dump." After all, we're still diligently searching for the *big* thing, the silver bullet. It's what we want to believe because the truth is harder to accept.

It takes time and practice to make lasting change and to grow as a person or as a family. We must commit to it. We need to consistently do the work. We have to believe we can accomplish our heart's desire. In fact, it has to be our heart's desire.

We would rather do one big thing to change our lives. Although the big thing may take a massive effort on our part, if we gave the effort, it would be done. It would be easier—or so the myth tells us.

But it's not easier. It leads to discouragement and feelings of failure. Doing simple things, consistently over time, is what will ultimately give us the success we seek as individuals and as families. Real change over the long haul is the easier path.

CHAPTER 7

KNOW What You Want

One of the fundamental ways to check back in and be Present is to know what you want. How do you want your family to feel? How do you want family members to act? How do you expect to resolve problems? How do you and your spouse want to work together?

When you have a clear idea of what you want and a plan to make it happen, you have more motivation to stay Present. When you clearly articulate your plan to your family, they'll be more willing to be actively engaged in its accomplishment. This helps the family stay the course over the long haul.

WHY FLYING BY THE SEAT OF YOUR PANTS IS A POOR IDEA

My husband, Don, and I thought if we loved each other, were good people, brought kids into the world, and kept on living well, it would be enough. It wasn't.

What we learned through thirty-nine years of active, kids-in-the-home parenting is it's better to parent with a clear intention and to let your children in on your intention.

Intention, as defined by the Webster's Dictionary 1828, is a "design; purpose; the fixed direction of the mind to a particular object, or a determination to act in a given manner." It's the end or aim—the object you're trying to accomplish.

In short, an intention is when the mind, with great earnestness and by choice, fixes its view on an idea, considers it on every side, makes a plan for accomplishment, and is not diverted from the plan.

So what could Don and I have done that would have served our children and us better? We knew we wanted to raise children with good values, who would contribute to society and raise stable families of their own. We certainly had a purpose in mind. But we missed important aspects of the definition of intention.

1. Our minds were not fixed on our purpose daily.
We were often distracted and too busy. We would check out.

2. We had not, with earnestness, talked together,
expressing what we each wanted in our family. We made the assumption that because our upbringing, both spiritually and temporally, was similar we would have the same goals and would parent the same. We didn't consider questions such as discipline, spending time together, handling chores, maintaining peace, allocating money, how our children would understand and assimilate our values, and so on. We did all these things by default.

3. We did not, by choice, create a definite plan to
achieve the purpose we had in mind. What was our plan to accomplish our desires? What were the specifics of family management, tradition, and activity? We wrote nothing down; it wasn't ever in a concrete form we could refer to and share with our children.

> "A problem only exists if there is a difference between what is actually happening and what you desire to be happening."
>
> —Kenneth H. Blanchard, author and cofounder of The Ken Blanchard Companies

4. We were not always able to remain fixed in our determination because there
was no daily reminder. We had

not broken our lofty goal into smaller, manageable parts, nor did we have a particular method in place for its actualization.

It was easy to become discouraged or overwhelmed, to argue or check out because we needed a break.

Despite feeling frustration, Don and I desired to have a happy, well-adjusted family built on good core values and service. But good desires are not enough.

RUNNING A FAMILY IS LIKE RUNNING A BUSINESS

Running a family is somewhat like running a business or organization. Good desires will not make either one successful.

Warren Rustand is a lifelong entrepreneur and former NBA player. He's the father of seven children and sixteen grandchildren and has been married to the same woman for almost fifty years.

He said, "Families require leadership, in the same way businesses require leadership. . . . Yet as much effort as we apply to building our organizations, we rarely apply the same rules of engagement to our most important foundation: the family unit" (Rustand, as quoted in "What Is Your Family's Culture?").

There's a reason businesses and organizations have a written mission statement. It gives everyone in the company or organization a clear idea of where they're going as a unified group. It states the intention of what they're doing and why. It generates a *culture*.

When we look at the comment by Warren Rustand, we can see it takes more than wanting a company to be successful. It takes more than a vague idea of what success might entail. You have to lay out the purpose of the company and your plan to accomplish the purpose, and then you must lead. You must stay Present! This creates the company culture that leads to a successful outcome.

THE IMPORTANCE OF A FAMILY CULTURE

It's the same with a family. Most of us don't understand family culture. We think of culture as regarding countries and ethnic groups. Creating a family statement of intent forces you to envision, create, and put in a public place a written idea of what you really want so your family can internalize it. This is the process to create an intentional family culture.

Brett McKay stated: "A business culture . . . just doesn't happen. It takes a lot of work. As *Forbes* writer Mike Myatt argues, 'business culture is created either by design or by default'" ("Fathering With Intentionality").

If we allow the culture in our families to be created by default, we're going to have mediocre or possibly worse results. We won't get the outcome we're looking for because it's easy to let things go, to get distracted and to check out. If we want a better result, we must have a clear intention and do the work required.

Many family cultures, like Don's and mine, are created by default. Many parents believe the values they want to share and the close bond they want to have will happen over time, because they love each other and because they're doing good things and being good people. However, an intentional family culture will always be better than one created by default.

I love the article my daughter, Jodie, wrote for my blog a few years ago. Let me share the highlights:

> Sometimes, as a parent, we're handed opportunities for self-evaluation on a silver platter. I was given such a dish the other day when I caught my two-year-old son marching around the living room chanting, "Stop that! Now I have to take that away. Stop that! Now I have to take that away." Good grief!

I'm happy to contrast that little ditty with something he was muttering in my ear a few nights ago as I was putting him to sleep. "Daddy loves you, daddy loves you, daddy loves you."

It's a bit overwhelming to think how innocent my son is in his learning, how he soaks up everything that happens around him. . . .

In those two little exchanges my son confirmed how important it is that I not take lightly the obligation I have as a parent to lay a right and a solid foundation for him to build the rest of his life on. . . .

It's important to remember children learn more by what we are and the environment and feelings surrounding them than through what we're trying to teach with activities.

A statement of your intent breathes life into or inspires a family culture.

There's another important element a written statement brings to the table.

I've heard parents say "I'm not sure how much we need a statement of our intent. It seems the culture of our family is pretty good. We don't have a formal, articulated statement, but we talk about the things that might be in a statement a lot."

This is a model that works for many families. However, consider the particular model you're using to train your children in developing, managing, and leading their families.

For these parents, they were clear on the things they were regularly teaching to their children, which were influencing their family culture. But, were they also teaching their children how to do the same in their own homes? Are their children even aware there's a model to follow? Are they aware of the idea of culture, its purposeful creation, and the impact it has on the family?

Having a written statement of your family's intention is also a specific model of training for good family development, management, and leadership." (Palmer, "Family Mission Statement: Part I")

Wow, brings it all home, doesn't it? To intentionally create a family culture you have to know what it is you want to create. What does it look and feel like? You also need to be clear it's not for your home alone, but for the homes of your posterity.

HOW CAN WE KNOW WHAT WE WANT?

Don and I thought we knew what we wanted. But what did that look like? I don't think we knew. What could we have done to visualize what we wanted and make sure we got it?

FIRST, talk about what you want. Are your ideas the same? If they aren't, work them out until you come to a consensus on what they're going to be. Don and I ran into walls of difference over and over again. We would argue, or one or the other would back off and feel resentful. In my work I see this pattern in all kinds of families.

It would have served Don and me well if we had talked more about what we wanted our family to look and feel like. By doing so, we would have discovered our differences early on. We could have worked on them until we came to a consensus on managing our differences to accomplish the goal.

> "Culture is a way of working together toward common goals that have been followed so frequently and so successfully that people don't even think about trying to do things another way. If a culture has formed, people will autonomously do what they need to do to be successful."
>
> —Edgar Schein,
> MIT professor emeritus

To do this would have necessitated our understanding a detailed picture of the goal. Once we had the picture clearly in mind, we would have been better able to set our intention.

No matter where you are in your parenting life, it's never too late to come to a consensus on what you want, but you have to begin talking.

SECOND, ask yourself good questions:

- What are the values we want our family to embody?

- What's the feeling we want in our household?

- In what activities or items will we invest our time and money?

- What words will best describe our family?

- What words would we like our kids to use to describe our family? What words would they use to describe our family right now?

- What are our strengths as a family?

- What do we feel our family is called to do?

- What do we want our family legacy to be?

- What does our family stand for?

- What principles should guide decisions? Are they the same for both individuals and the family unit?

- How will religion or spirituality look in our family?

- What's our family economy?

This is a sampling of the many questions we, as parents, can ask ourselves to clearly define what our intention for our family is.

One family culture isn't necessarily better than another. There are as many family cultures as there are families. When we look at truly successful families, it's not the specifics of the culture that matter as much as the fact that parents have set an intention for what they want to accomplish; they've shared that intention with their children and they remain Present. In other words, they lead.

If parents value music, music will become a sustaining part of their family culture. They'll invest in instruments and lessons.

Some families will be traditional in their methods of problem solving and in managing daily life while others will be more creative and out of the box.

There are families who value together time at home playing cards, Risk, and the Wii, while others appreciate getting outdoors and being physically engaged.

Occasionally a family may value movies and entertainment. They'll buy equipment to pursue what they enjoy. There are other families who minimize technology in their homes and don't even own a television.

There are families whose focus is on education or travel or art. Each of these will color all aspects of their resulting family culture.

There are strict families and relaxed families, formal and informal families. There are those that eat together at a specified time in the dining room while others gather informally in the kitchen. Other families are in the family room, with TV trays and the television turned on.

Each of these choices reveals something of the family's culture and values. Each culture will have its rewards and its drawbacks. So knowing what you want is *key*.

Let's look in depth at a tool that can assist you in creating the family culture you wish to have.

A FAMILY STATEMENT OF INTENT

A family statement of intent goes by many names: Family Vision Statement, Family Mission Statement, Family Manifesto, Family Belief Board, and Family Statement of Purpose. The name doesn't matter, but your intention does. I'll be using the term Family Mission Statement or FMS for short.

No matter what the makeup of your family—newlyweds, empty-nesters, kids, no kids, extended family members living with you, and so on—creating a statement of intent helps you achieve what you want.

In times of difficulty, uncertainty, or a family crisis, family members can reference the FMS for clarity and security. It offers protection, establishes unity, clarifies behavior, and celebrates your family's uniqueness.

Here are the experiences of two families who have crafted and consistently used an FMS.

Family 1—Colleen Cubberley said, "We have found it helpful because there are phrases we refer to in our disciplining, or to encourage positive interactions between our children. It has become the 'why' for a lot of our parenting."

Family 2—Emily Frogley added, "We pull certain phrases out during the day to guide our actions, choices and to act as reminders to us of our goals as a family."

Once your family has created an FMS together, it's helpful to post it where it's readily visible. It can be framed or laminated. It can be simple or fancy. But it needs to be prominently displayed and easily used.

In an article by Sheila Seifert and Jeanne Gowen Dennis for *Focus on the Family*, they related the experience of two families.

Family A—Rhonda DeYoung shared when her children hear the phrase "Inward, outward, upward and onward," they know exactly what it means. She said, "When the kids were little, we used these words to encourage them to show who they were on the inside by being godly on the outside, through taking the high road upward and moving on from a situation—not being dragged down by it."

Family B—The Sanders family noticed they were already associated as a group by their last name in their community, as in a "Sanders haircut" or a "Sanders appetite." So they decided to let their last name determine their code of conduct, each letter standing for a value. The acrostic became their family mission statement (Seifert and Dennis, "Writing a Family Mission Statement").

I agree with what Bruce Feiler had to say in his article "Want to Give Your Family Value and Purpose? Write a Mission Statement," posted in *The Atlantic*.

> Every parent I know worries about teaching values to their children. How do we ensure that in today's ever-changing world they understand some beliefs are timeless? How do we actually know if they grasp the qualities that are most important to us?
>
> For a long time, my wife and I were so busy responding to the chaos around us in our family we never had a chance to address these questions. But when I set out a few years ago to try to find the qualities that united high-functioning families, I kept encountering a similar object in many homes. Some families call it a belief board, others a statement of purpose. (Feiler, "Want to Give Your Family Value and Purpose? Write a Mission Statement")

> **"A family mission statement is a combined, unified expression from all family members of what your family is all about, what it is you really want to do and be, and the principles you choose to govern your family life."**
>
> —Stephen R. Covey, 7 Habits of Highly Effective Families

And there you have it—Families who fly by the seat of their pants struggle more. They become enmeshed in the chaos naturally occurring with a house full of people.

When we take the time to get clarity on what we want, write it down, and let our children in on it, we can clear away some of the chaos. An FMS is a great way to define what's bedrock to your family and move toward creating the family culture you want to have.

WHY DOESN'T EVERYONE HAVE A FAMILY MISSION STATEMENT?

For many of you, developing an FMS may have been on your to-do list for a long time, but you've never gotten around to it. For others, maybe the idea is new and a bit daunting. My daughter Jodie wrote extensively about why family mission statements are important in a four-part series on my blog, "Home School Coach." With her permission, I will share many of her observations in this chapter.

Here are sabotaging beliefs and myths from real people on mission statement development.

1. My children are too young to get involved yet. Or, as one mom put it, "I don't want my four-year-old influencing our mission statement."

Even though children might not be able to articulate it, it matters a lot how their family feels to them. The family is a child's world, and they can, even at young ages, make valuable contributions to the discussion of what matters to the family. Even if children are too young to participate, it's never too early to begin consciously creating the culture of your home through the development of an FMS. Their contribution might be joining in the daily reciting of the mission statement.

My daughter Jodie wrote,

> In our home we have a disabled, non-verbal four-year-old, a very busy two-year-old, and a five-month-old. Our children were too young to have participated in the actual development of our family mission statement. But they actively participate in the daily reciting of our statement. Our two-year-old loves to say the first line, "The Joyful Palmers are a team! Yeah!" Our disabled daughter

engages with a huge smile and the five-month-old soaks in the feeling of it all. (Palmer, "Family Mission Statement: Part II")

2. My children are too old. I don't think my children will accept it.

Older children may reject what challenges the current family status quo or comes down from the powers that be. Working with older children requires that we pay particular attention to *doing the dance* of inspiring. We want them to buy in or to take ownership of the family statement.

Primarily, an FMS should not come down as an edict from parents when you have older children. No matter how fabulous your statement might sound, it must be created by a joint effort to have any real investment by everyone.

Consider engaging your older youth and young adults in a way that gives an air of anticipation and excitement to the development of this statement. In fact, be prepared to invest in the process.

For example, consider taking a special family retreat. Or perhaps your children would respond to private, preparatory one-on-one talking. Avoid creating it yourself and announcing it to the family as the new thing. Make it fun; involve food and activities your family enjoys.

3. I'm not creative enough. Mission statements don't require creativity; they require truth. There are dozens of examples on the Internet that will help you get an idea of what your family might want. However, every family is different, so don't shortcut the process of writing your own by copying someone else.

4. A mission statement has to be short. We can't fit all that's important to us in a short statement. But an FMS doesn't have to be short. Here's an example of a long family mission statement.

Habits of Our Home

We tell the truth.

We consider one another's interest ahead of our own.

We don't hurt each other with unkind words or deeds.

We speak quietly and respectfully to one another.

When someone is sorry, we forgive him.

When someone is happy, we rejoice with him.

When someone is sad, we comfort him.

When someone needs correction, we correct him in love.

We take good care of everything God has given us.

When we have work to do, we do it without complaining.

When we open something, we close it.

When we turn something on, we turn it off.

When we don't know what to do, we ask.

When we take something out, we put it away.

When we make a mess, we clean it up.

We arrive on time.

We do what we say.

We finish what we start.

We say please and thank you.

When we go out, we act as if we're in this house.

When necessary, we accept discipline and instruction.

We love, honor, and pray for each other.

5. A mission statement has to be long.

Here's an example of a short and sweet family mission statement.

Our Family Mission

To encourage others to become like Christ through loving relationships, healthy lifestyles, and stimulating experiences.

6. I'm not sure we need a family mission statement.

We seem to be doing fine without one. A fair evaluation if *fine* is your standard. But wouldn't you like to work toward great? Great family relationships will trump "fine" every time.

THE BASICS OF GETTING STARTED

Hopefully, your myths are put to rest and you can get going. Here are ideas for writing your own family statement, family manifesto, family belief board, family statement of purpose, or family mission statement. It doesn't matter what you call it; it matters that you do it.

Here's the basic process in a nutshell. Don't worry at its brevity. As we go through the chapter you'll get the details you need to follow through.

- The parents talk among themselves and decide what's important to them. Work out any differences. Have a united front.

- The parents tell their children about these values.

- The entire family discusses the values so everyone understands them.

- Help family members buy into or take ownership for the statement. You can do this by
  - Making it sound special or exciting when you present the idea. (What are the benefits? Make an emotional connection. "Kids, we're going to get this family in order . . . " isn't going to cut it.)

- Have a family discussion to come up with great ideas on writing and displaying your FMS.
- Don't edit or criticize each other's input.
- Keep your meetings about your FMS at a reasonable length for the age of children that you have. Don't turn its creation into a chore. This may take you a few gatherings and then you will need time to rewrite and refine. Take all the time you need. There isn't any hurry.
- Keep it fun and lighthearted when possible. Use words that tell what you want. Avoid stating what you don't want.

- Parents make the final decisions. You know what's best. Children can contribute their ideas, which should be treated as valuable, but you make the final decisions.

- Make changes as they're needed until it's what you want. This takes time. As you recite it, you'll feel if anything needs to be adjusted.

> **"The goal is to create a clear, compelling vision of what you and your family are all about."**
> —Stephen R. Covey, *7 Habits of Highly Effective Families*

THE PROCESS—FLESH IT OUT, GET KIDS INVOLVED, GET IT DONE

1. THINK

Start your family statement experience by thinking of ways to involve your family. Before you jump into the writing portion, spend time getting your family engaged with the idea of what an FMS is and what it contains. Use activities allowing each member to privately consider what he or she thinks should be part of the family culture. Here are ways to get ideas flowing and help everyone feel involved.

A. The Core Values Box

Core values are simply people, activities, beliefs, skills, or things that matter most to us. Core values range from concepts like love and acceptance to material things like a home. Other examples include caring for animals, honesty, entrepreneurialism, freedom, wise money management, education, and so on.

As a family, decorate a Core Values box and put it in a prominent location in your home—your dining table for example. You could decorate it with a collage of pictures identifying things your family values. One or two children can each take a side to decorate however they wish. The idea is to get the whole family engaged with the Core Values box.

During your activity and throughout the week family members can put ideas in the box as ideas come to them. During your family statement development activity, you'll open this box and use the ideas inside to create your first draft.

B. Core Values Collages

Gather magazines and other materials that can be used to create collages. Each person will make their own, depicting words and images highlighting the feeling and the core values they want to become part of the family's culture. Hang these pictures up in a prominent area of your home so they can be pondered throughout the week.

During your mission statement development activity let each person describe the meaning of the items on their collage. Have a person write down all of the ideas, which will help create your first draft.

C. Core Values Artwork

If you have younger children, it can be more effective to create drawings or paintings that help your children describe their feelings.

Again, put these pictures in an area where they can be seen, and ask your children often to describe the things they have drawn.

2. DISCUSSION

After you've taken the time to think of ways to engage your family and family members have about thought what they want in their family culture, it's time to start asking the right questions. Questions will help deepen the articulation of the things your family values.

Gather your family together for a question and answer activity. You can have each member write down their answers or have an open discussion with one family member assigned as scribe to capture each person's ideas.

Below is a list of various questions. Choose those that best fit your family, or make up your own. If you have young children, make your questions age appropriate.

- What makes you happy? What things in life put a smile on your face and get you through your difficult days?

- What makes us fulfilled? What are those things in life that bring us the most satisfaction and leave us with the feeling of completeness?

- What do we want for ourselves and our family? What are our hopes, dreams, and aspirations, not only for our family but ourselves as well?

- What's most important to you about our family?

- What are our collective goals?

- When do we feel most connected to one another?

- How would you like to relate to one another?

- What are some of our family's strengths?

- How would we want our family described in five years . . . ten years . . . fifteen years?

- What do we value? (For example, relationships, faith, independence, wealth, hard work, generosity.)

- What do we love to do together?

- In what ways can we help each other more?

- How can we serve others outside of our family?

- How do we want our family to feel on ordinary days?

3. ORGANIZE YOUR THOUGHTS

Finally, it's time to start organizing your ideas into a concrete form. Don't allow this family activity to break down over "word-smithing" details. Later you'll assign a family member, usually Mom or Dad, the job of designing the final draft to bring back to the family for approval.

The easiest way to begin getting your FMS down is to choose a design formula that feels right for your family. Mom and Dad should select the formula before this activity begins.

Although there are many different forms mission statements can take, here are three basic types you could choose from.

Formula #1

Gather together all of the core values you've identified as a family. Decrease these by two, and then decrease by two again until you have one final core value. Keep track of your final four to six subsequent core values and insert them into the formula below.

"To (insert Central Core Value here) by [or through] (insert three to five Subsequent Core Values here)."

Example—To encourage others to become well rounded through loving relationships, healthy lifestyles, and stimulating experiences.

Formula #2

To . . . . (Do something)

In such a way that . . . .. (Quality of action)

So that . . . . (We gain these results or benefits)

Example—To realize our dreams, goals, and aspirations as a family and as individuals in a way that stretches our intellect, enriches our faith, strengthens our character, and enriches our family life; so that we're fulfilled, happy, confident, and always close.

Formula #3

Create a big list of the things that matter to you. Use verbs suggesting *now* (such as "are" and "is") rather than terms suggesting *will be* (such as "want" or "will").

Example—

- We celebrate our family's faith, heritage, and traditions.

- We show our love for one another in word and deed; we pray for each other.

- We're courteous, caring, positive, supportive, and considerate.

- We live a healthy lifestyle and maintain order and cleanliness in the home.

- We raise up children in the way they should go, making learning together an integral part of daily life with books and enriching experiences.

- We optimize the competing forces in our lives for good: health, wealth, aesthetics, rest, exercise, recreation, work, skills, and knowledge.

- We enjoy life today and live it fully.

- We're wise in the way we use our time, talents, and money; we establish good habits and help others.

- We contribute something of worth to the community— maintain the environment; mankind's institutions; and religious, political, cultural, social, and individual freedoms.

4. THE FINAL DRAFT

Don't try to make the final draft as a family. It has the potential of creating too much contention. Once you've got the core ideas down, give someone the task of editing and making it sound good. Then bring it back to the family for the final unveiling.

Once you have your FMS ready to go, it's helpful to have ideas on using it in your family. Here are five possibilities and you may come up with more of your own.

IDEAS FOR USING YOUR FAMILY MISSION STATEMENT

- Recite it daily. Determine a time when your family's generally together. When your FMS is memorized and reviewed daily it will begin to come to mind when you need it most, for example, during a teaching or a disciplining moment. Jodie Palmer said, "Lines of our family mission statement often come to mind when I feel tempted to speak or act in ways contrary to the specific culture we're trying to nurture in our home" (Palmer, "Family Mission Statement: Part IV").

- Use it to help make big decisions. Is your decision in line with the objectives of your FMS?

- Use it to help regain focus and realignment with what matters most to your family.

- Use it to guide your family's educational plan. The specific values your FMS mentions can inform your educational opportunities, ideas, and materials (money management, entrepreneurialism, freedom, honesty, or service).

- Have fun with it. Have your children create artwork or collages reflecting your final mission statement. Display this art in a prominent place in your home. Develop a family cheer, motto, flag, or T-shirt inspired by your mission statement. At sixteen months old, Mary Palmer could recite the final word of their family cheer—"The joyful Palmers are a team. **Yeah**!" (Palmer, "Family Mission Statement: Part II")

Using your mission statement consistently is what turns words on paper into the culture of your home.

DOES IT WORK?

Colleen Cubberley wrote to me and said,

My family has had a family mission statement for four years now. I know some create their statements together as a family, but the one we have was created by me. At the time, I created it my kids were three, four, and seven. It was mostly me reading it to them, but now they're all able to recite it and discuss it.

We've repeated it daily since 2011, but we've also adapted it over time.

The beginning starts, We the C. family, love and support one another. We are patient and kind . . . .

The first line has undergone the most changes . . . [It was] recently [changed due to] a new need/focus in our family. It [now] reads love and serve one another.

We pull certain phrases out during the day to guide our actions, choices and to act as reminders to us of our goals as a family.

There are days I wonder if changing it up would be good and having a new mission statement that we all create together, but I also feel this one is fairly comprehensive. After ten plus years, my children will look back as adults and after having repeated the same thing for so many times it will be a cherished childhood memory.

It will inspire them to continue the habit and create their own family mission statements. More important, here and now, we have a guiding sense of family culture and what we're about in this life.

ASSIGNMENTS TO GET YOU STARTED

Assignment #1: Begin by evaluating your family's current culture. Consider the daily environment and feelings in your home. Talk to your spouse. Are your family environment, the atmosphere, and culture what you want? Now, try a brainstorming exercise by asking yourself: What are the core things I want my child to do or know? Put your list where you can add to it when things come to your mind.

Assignment #2: What roadblocks, if any, have been keeping your family from creating your family mission statement? Are these barriers real or excuses? If they're real, write them down. Now begin considering solutions to these roadblocks. If you need help, reach out to someone you know who uses an FMS or do research on the Internet. This may help you to begin seeing opportunities and solutions.

Assignment #3: Make a plan for which activities you'll use to prime your family's pump of creativity, which questions you'll ask, and the form you want your mission statement to take. Determine your time line. As you develop your plan, give particular attention to making these activities fun and memorable. Include food, outings, or whatever will make the event special for your family.

Remember your FMS is a tool; it's not an end in itself. Your FMS is designed to serve your family and not for the family to serve it. It's only useful inasmuch as it assists you in fulfilling your purpose—to get what you want for your family, and to help you lead by being Present.

IN SUMMARY

Flying by the seat of your pants is an uncomfortable way to travel as a family! It's more helpful to know what you want and what can help you reach your goals.

Flying by the seat of your pants can lead to discouragement, feelings of being overwhelmed, and the desire to check out more often. Having a vision of what you want can lessen the chaos and help you choose to be Present with your family.

Parent with intention! When you plan how you'll parent and why you're parenting a particular way, you'll have a more favorable outcome. You'll be able to lead your family and remain Present.

CHAPTER 8

MAKE It about Them

Part of a Present mind-set is to make what you're doing about your child and not about you. This isn't always easy to do. However, if we make a shift in how we think with two truths, it will become easier.

In this chapter we'll explore how to shift our thinking by

- Recognizing that adults and kids are different.

- Understanding that our motives impact our ability to be Present.

OUTCOME VS. PROCESS

Kids and adults are different. Adults are outcome (product) driven while children are process driven. This difference can get in the way of being Present.

Let me illustrate:

My friend, Victoria, has three, busy, excitable, and creative girls. One day I decided I was going to help them make a batch of yummy peanut butter cookies, and I had the perfect recipe.

On the appointed day I arrived at their home with my large stainless steel bowl filled to the brim with everything we needed to do the job. I began by explaining how to use a recipe. We would each take a turn putting an ingredient in the bowl and then stirring, rolling, flattening, and so on.

I had a vision in my mind of talking about measurements, the history of peanut butter, and so forth. The cookies were going to be beautiful and delicious. My expectations were high.

I've been working with children for many years, and I don't know what I was thinking! These were busy girls aged three to eight. They were all over the place. It took all I had to maintain some semblance of order and keep the majority of the ingredients in their original containers.

As the girls measured and mixed, I knew the teaspoons were not level, the one cup wasn't quite accurate, and the half cup was closer to three-quarters. Sugar and flour dusted the chairs and floor. Peanut butter dotted the tabletop.

> **"Cooking with children does not have to be stressful. It can actually bring excitement and create an opportunity for bonding and communication building. My best advice to my clients: it is about the process, not the end result!"**
>
> —Clancy Harrison, fieldsofflavor.com

Despite my experience in helping children cook, I was frazzled by the end. As the pan of cookies slid into the oven, the girls all dispersed into other parts of the house, and I dropped wearily into a chair. *These cookies are never going to turn out*, I thought.

When the timer went off, the girls descended on the kitchen. It was as I feared. We had large crumbs. Oh, those cookies looked all right in the pan but when you picked one up, it fell into three or four crumbly pieces.

Despite this, here's what the girls said. "*Wow,* look at those great cookies!" They were happy and excited to eat them just as they were.

They pronounced them delicious and felt the whole project was a roaring success.

They had measured, stirred, and produced these delicious crumbs almost by themselves, and they were ecstatic about it. The energy was high and the feeling of accomplishment equal to it.

I had a picture in my mind of how this project was going to turn out. That isn't the outcome I got and I felt a twinge of disappointment.

The girls had a far different vision. They saw themselves as super cooks, measuring, stirring, laughing, tasting, and experimenting. They were into the process of creation. They had a magnificent and satisfactory experience.

We were all doing the same project but the girls had far more enjoyment than I did. Rather than being energized as they were, I felt disappointment.

Remembering children are process driven while adults are outcome driven is crucial because it makes an enormous difference in the amount of enjoyment you and your family experience when you're working or playing together.

Author Debbie Clement humorously describes the difference between the process (child) and the product/outcome (adult):

Process

It's all about the engagement, the exploration, the experiment. The joie-de-vivre.

The moment at hand. The immediate feedback. Process, by its very definition is an *open-ended* experience. It's you and the media, and there are no right or wrong answers. It's literally: go with the flow + see what happens.

It's quite possibly messy. Even *totally* messy! It's very often exciting. It's inherently personal process. It's a moment-by-moment, *play-by-play* (get it?) unfolding with the material, the medium, the moment.

Outcome

It's all about the parents, the grandparents, the refrigerator. It's typically cute and gets the response, "Oh, you made a _____." There's a preconceived idea. There's a pattern. We need to march along and get the steps in order.

Teacher has counted out the parts. Teacher has pre-cut the tricky bits. First this. Then that. This goes here. That goes there. Add some of these. Teacher adds a magnet. Voila. It's usually pretty difficult to tell yours from your friends. Sometimes impossible in fact. (Clement, "Children's Art: Process VERSUS Product")

THE DIFFERENCE IN WORKING WITH ADULTS AND CHILDREN

The product or outcome is about us. It's tied up with our expectations and personal needs—our motives. This sets us up for feelings of frustration, disappointment, and sometimes anger when things don't go as we planned. When we make family activities or work about our kids, we're actually making it about the relationship. We begin to care less about how something turns out and care more how it feels to our children.

I've had a lot of joy teaching thousands of children. I've also had the opportunity to teach adults for many years. This has given me an opportunity to experience the difference in how children and adults approach a project.

Here's why kids are so fun to teach, especially when you, as the adult helper, have learned to allow the *process* to be king, rather than the *outcome*.

- They love learning new things. They feel excitement at the prospect and very little trepidation.

- They aren't intimidated that they don't already know how to do something. They're excited to experience this new thing.

- Because the process is what counts most, they want to experiment, to see what happens if they do something different.

- They're easy to please.

- If they're allowed to see the end product through their eyes rather than adult eyes, they rarely feel disappointment, rather genuine pleasure and satisfaction.

Adults, on the other hand, are almost the exact opposite. Here's an example:

I've taught many people to make a pie, and I want to avoid as much frustration as possible, especially when I'm working with adults. I want my new pie makers to go home feeling they've accomplished something magnificent, to know they've made the pie of the century and their families are going to be thrilled.

When I'm working with kids, I don't have to prepare them very much. They mix and roll and pat and piece until they have a pie, of sorts. They're always happy with their pie.

But when I'm working with adults, I prepare them. I remind them, "You're learning a new skill. It's like riding a bike; it won't be perfect right off the bat. Your crust might not fit the pan perfectly; it might even crack. Just piece it back together.

"You're making this pie because you love your family, and they're going to be blessed to have it. Remember it's going to taste delicious and that's what counts, not how it looks. You're going to have fun making this pie."

In one class of adults, a mother brought her eleven-year-old daughter and they worked together.

> "Make it accessible to them, create alongside them, and don't be worried about the final product. The process that got you to the end (exploring, imagining, creating) is the part that matters."
>
> —Kristen, comment on tinkerlab.com

The pies were turning out as you would expect beginners' pies to look. Everyone had taken my counsel and was feeling satisfied except Rosemary, the older half of the mother-daughter team. She wanted her pie to be perfect; she wanted to be able to do it better on the first try.

She was fretting and stewing because their dough was a tad dry and it broke into pieces as they put it into the pan. Her daughter, Ariel, was busy piecing away, having a wonderful time, but Rosemary kept fussing.

Finally, Ariel looked at her mom and said, "Remember Mom, the taste's what counts, not how it looks."

Rosemary was outcome-driven. She wanted her pie to look as if she'd been making them for years. Her daughter was process-driven. Ariel was enjoying creating her first pie far more than her mom.

MAKE THE MENTAL SHIFT FROM OUTCOME TO PROCESS

As an adult the outcome is always going to matter to you, but when you're with your child, make the mental shift from outcome to process. If you can keep your mind on the child and the joy they're experiencing, you'll have a far different experience. This is true in organizing, playing, working, taking a hike, going on vacation, shopping, whatever. For kids, it's all about the process. They want to experience it.

I love this comment by the motivational speaker Dan Clark: "Begin with the why in mind rather than the end in mind."

I love his comment because when adults adopt this attitude, we and our kids have more fun and satisfaction in just about everything we do together.

Remember *why* you're going for a family drive, why you're letting the kids help you paint, why you're making cookies. If it isn't clear in your mind yet let me state it once again. The purpose for just about everything you do in your family is to build relationships.

Stop worrying about how the cookies taste, how the painting looks, whether there's a mess, or how long the project takes. Keep your mind focused on relationship building and your child. Let it be about them and not about you.

MOTIVES IMPACT A MAKE-IT-ABOUT-THEM MIND-SET

Our motives color the experiences we have with our children and can make it challenging to focus on the relationship rather than the outcome. Let me share an experience and the motive that drove me.

For over forty years I've been going into homes, churches, and schools helping children make gingerbread houses. I would carefully explain all the rules so we wouldn't have a mess, and so the project would be orderly.

I would go around the room monitoring candy use, covering imperfect seams, and removing doors and windows from roofs. I was careful no one overused the frosting. In short, I meddled with everyone's creation. I wanted each house to fit my idea of what they should look like.

Why are we, as adults, so concerned with the outcome? Why did it matter that the candy was evenly distributed or doors were in the correct spot? It was all about my motive. It was, frankly, all about me. The kids had fun but it wasn't the same as if I had allowed them the freedom to create in their own way.

Don't misunderstand. I love kids and I wanted to share something that I enjoy with them, but I also had a motive that impacted the experience the children had. I wanted those houses to turn out well because it was a reflection of me.

The better the result, the better I looked. My motive is what drove how I presented the project and my willingness to allow the children to create and experiment or not.

As I got older and wiser, my motive for doing the project changed. It stopped being about me looking good to other adults. It switched to watching the joy children experience when they're free to explore something new.

A couple of years ago I drove to Colorado to help my grandchildren and their school classes do the whole gingerbread thing. I met with the teachers ahead and counseled them to allow children to do their houses as they wanted to.

I told them seams would be left bare. Some children would put *all* their candy on one side of the roof and nowhere else. I let them know an occasional door would find its way to the roof. I also shared the fact that some children would feel compelled to squeeze every last ounce of frosting from their bag even if they didn't need it anywhere.

On the day of the project, I gave about a quarter of the instructions to the children than I had given in the past. We stayed together as a group to put the actual house together and then it was a free for all of candy, frosting, and experimenting. The teachers and I didn't *help* anyone by taking the frosting bag and putting a bit here and there to finish out a seam or restick a candy.

Watching those one hundred plus children was pure delight: the faces, the joy, the occasional laughter, the intense concentration, and the pure bliss of experimenting with frosting, squeezing, messing, and eating. It was energizing.

I experienced a great deal of joy doing this project because I didn't care what anyone else thought. I wasn't concerned with cleaning up a mess. I had ceased to need such rigid order. I cared about the happiness generated by allowing kids to create freely and enjoy themselves. I cared about the relationship I was forging with my grandkids and their friends.

Our motives make an enormous difference in the level of enjoyment we and our children have. Our motives impact our ability to be Present, to see and hear.

Let's take a look at some of the motives that can keep us outcome driven rather than process driven—into management and out of relationship. What you're going to notice is that these same things have come up before in other chapters. I hope you'll see how important it is to make a mental shift.

MOTIVE 1—We want the experience and the outcome to match our expectations

Leah, a friend of mine, took her three boys (ages nine, six, and three), on a road trip. They were finishing up a year's study of minerals and rocks as a family. This trip was going to cap it all off perfectly. Leah had it all planned out in her mind.

A few weeks later she gave me a call. I asked her how the trip went, and she said, "Well, it was okay, but it didn't turn out as well as I'd hoped." I asked her what went wrong, and she told me all the things they hadn't done.

I asked her to tell me what they did do. They went on a dinosaur dig and had a fun day. They sang a ton of songs in their van as they traveled. They had interesting conversations about the creation of the earth and what outer space would be like. They dug for gems one afternoon. They visited museums and other cool places. They had a lot of fun and laughter. Her boys learned new things to add to their growing store of knowledge about rocks and gems.

"My goodness," I replied, "there are parents out there who would give anything for a week like that with their kids." There was a pause on the other end of the line and then she said, "You're right. I guess it was a pretty good trip after all. I hadn't thought about it that way."

Leah let her expectations get in the way of enjoying what was. When you're doing something with your child, it's not about you; it's about the relationship you want to forge and the enjoyment you have together. It's about being Present. It may not turn out as planned. Too often our satisfaction is tied to how well an activity matches our expectations.

If that's the case, then working with kids will be less enjoyable because someone will do it incorrectly. Another may not listen to directions. Yet another will do it their way. There will probably be a mess. There may be an argument. It won't meet *our* expectations.

Children don't do things in a balanced manner. They aren't even aware that all the glue, glitter, or frosting is on one side of the project. They don't see the way we do. This is also evident in how they do chores. They pick up the middle of the floor and think it's done. They forget corners, or clothes hanging out of drawers. They just don't see all that we see, so they take care of what they do see.

Youth have ideas, and they want to experiment with them. You may want it done one way and they have an entirely different idea. If it's not illegal, dangerous, or unkind, let them experiment. Failure's a marvelous teacher, and it's useful to fail in safe ways.

Link your satisfaction to your ability to enjoy *what is* with your family even when it falls short of your expectations.

MOTIVE 2—We want a reward

In our world, we get rewards for getting stuff done. If the job's *right*, we get bigger rewards. Rewards are what we're used to.

In school, children get a reward if they get the work done. There isn't praise for the process they went through to get the work done, especially if the outcome is incorrect. There's no praise for the experience. The praise goes to the child who can efficiently, correctly, and, I might add, neatly get stuff done in the way the teacher or parent wants it done.

Working adults experience this same thing. Finishing the job, in a prescribed manner, is what gets the paycheck.

In our families, the reward isn't a paycheck but a sense of accomplishment and a feeling of happiness. Frequently, we withhold this reward if what we're doing as a family doesn't turn out right, in other words, if it didn't meet our expectations. We don't give ourselves the reward for simply engaging with our family and solidifying relationships.

In our homes we have the freedom to set the rules, to determine the feeling. Let's decide to experience more satisfaction and happiness in the process of living and working with our children. Let's resolve to stop worrying so much about what gets done, how well it gets done or how perfect projects and activities turn out. Let's enjoy the experience more and let our children do the same.

Here is the rest of Dan Clark's comment that he made in his class "The Twelve Steps of A.R.T.," which I attended. He said, "Begin with the why in mind rather than the end in mind. This allows us to reward effort rather than results."

Let's reward our kids for swishing and dripping paint, ragged cutting, imperfect folding, splotchy dusting, or whatever it is. Let's celebrate that we all got in the car together and went somewhere, even if it wasn't all we hoped it would be.

Let's reward ourselves by allowing our family to experience a sense of satisfaction and happiness even if we fall short of our expectation. Let's focus on relationship building.

MOTIVE 3—We don't want a mess

This has come up before! I never understand why we, as adults, think kids can do anything in a neat, orderly, and clean way. Good grief!

Our experience living with them should quickly show us that the natural state of children is messiness. They have a sense of abandon that keeps them totally focused on the joy of what they're doing, the process. They're completely into experiencing whatever they're doing, which makes it difficult to notice mess.

How can a five-year-old think about the blue paint that's dripping on the floor when he's completely mesmerized by the fact that when the red paint meets the blue paint something magical happens: it turns purple?

It's hard to see and hear our children when we're busy managing everything so there won't be a mess.

To assist us with this whole messiness issue we can put systems into place: paint cups that scrape paint from brushes, child-friendly glue containers, shoes that can handle mud

> "'Process' means allowing children to explore art materials with freedom without the pressure to copy a model or stay in the lines. Process is experimenting with paints, watching the mixing colors, and feeling the textures of more or less. Process is gluing various sizes, shapes, and colors of paper together to create a collage. Process is freedom to experiment and enjoy the feeling of creating without being concerned with the outcome or the product. Process is creating something that is uniquely yours and not a copy of someone else's."
>
> — Kathy Hardy, contributor to The Alliance for Early Childhood

puddles. These things are helpful, but it's more helpful to mentally prepare for messiness.

Recently I took my granddaughter on a trip with me. I've taken grandchildren on many trips, and I had a lot of experience with this with my own kids. I know cars are a mess at the end of a trip. I keep my car clean. I like it that way, but I knew if I traveled with my five-year-old granddaughter, I would have messes in my car.

We stopped at a fruit stand and I bought apricots. She wanted to know what she could do with the pits. She was sitting in the back seat of the van with a large empty space between her and me. I wasn't as prepared as I should have been and I didn't have a bag or anything for her pits and we couldn't reach each other. So I said, "When you finish with your apricots, drop the pits on the floor, and we can pick them up when we stop next."

At our next stop, I remembered to clean up the pits. There in the middle of the floor was a half eaten, squashed apricot. It had been too ripe for my granddaughter's taste and so after taking a bite she had followed my directions and dropped it on the floor, where it splattered into a gooey puddle. I was able to remain calm because before the trip, I had mentally prepared for messiness. I also have to admit I couldn't help laughing at how literal children are!

MOTIVE 4—We want it to look good

My youngest daughter made her handprint in white plaster of paris at school. She wrote her name and added the date. When she brought it home, I was thrilled. I planned on hanging it on the wall.

Later that day she brought it to me and was so proud because she'd painted the fingernails. I can still remember my response. I was not happy. I asked her why she painted the nails. I'm confident she felt sad I didn't think it was as perfectly beautiful as it was in her eyes.

I have to confess I didn't hang her handprint. The fingers were messy because she was seven and her ability to paint in the nails was a bit shaky. It's embarrassing to confess, but we all do this sort of thing.

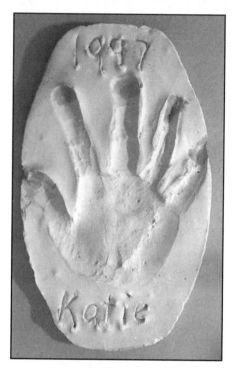

I want you to know I did come to my senses years later. Kate's sweet little handprint hangs above the sink in my bathroom today, reminding all that clean hands are beautiful. I look at it with great fondness, and I wonder what in the world I was thinking way back when. Those fingernails are perfect!

I've seen a child look at their creation or a chore they've completed with great satisfaction. Then a parent or teacher points out what they didn't do correctly using phrases such as these:

- Next time . . .

- Why didn't you . . .

- It would look good if . . .

- Why don't you . . .

I've seen a child's pride turn to disappointment because they didn't do it quite right. That's what Kate felt. This feeling of not having measured up can happen when children do chores, make something, or participate in a family activity.

If children are worried about the result, it's often because they've been taught to worry by observation or because we remind them their efforts are less than acceptable. Resist the temptation. Choose the relationship over the look of the finished product or outcome. As much as you can, make it about them and not you.

MOTIVE 5—We want others to think well of us

My example of making gingerbread houses with kids demonstrated this motive well. I wanted teachers, parents, and others in the community to see what a great parent/teacher I was, to think well of me. I believed the better those houses looked and the more orderly the instruction, the more favorably others would think of me. It was about me, not the kids.

Since I learned to let what I do with kids be about them and not about me, they're freer to enjoy the process, and so am I!

MOTIVE 6—We don't want supplies/materials wasted

My children were creative so we've used lots of paste, glue, rubber bands, construction paper, paper tubes, egg cartons, and so on. We've used thousands of crayons, gone through a few dozen pairs of scissors, innumerable pencils and pens, not to mention compasses, rulers, and other drawing devices. We've used rolls of paper and tape and gallons of paint and brushes. We've used pounds of flour, butter, and sugar. I can't even imagine the number of eggs we've used. We've used lots of gas going from place to place to do this and that. In short, we've consumed a lot of resources.

Thinking about this makes me happy. Let me share two experiences I've had with children that demonstrate why I'm happy when children use resources and how I know whether they were well used or wasted.

Experience 1—When my youngest daughter was seven we purchased an item in a large wooden crate. Of course a large wooden crate's a magnet for kids. She and her friends were all over that crate.

One day Kate came and asked for paint and brushes. When I questioned what she wanted them for she said it was to paint the boat. So I gave her lots of poster paint. I never went to see what was happening. I knew they were painting the wooden crate and now it was a boat. They hadn't asked for my help, and I was pretty sure they didn't want it either.

Next, she came and asked me for a piece of material to make a sail. I got a sheet for her. She asked if I could help her figure out how to get the sail to stay up. I went out to the boat, gave her directions, and she and her friends went to work. Throughout the day, they came in and asked me for this and that and I got whatever they needed.

I didn't go out to the boat again until they came to say they had finished and for me to come and see. Wow! It was an amazing boat for a bunch of seven-year-olds to have created. They played with the boat for a long time. I think they loved it even more because they had made it themselves.

They had used a lot of paint and glue, material, and other items. The boat didn't last more than a month or so, but I can tell you they played with it daily, and it brought a great deal of pleasure to those seven-year-olds.

Experience 2—A few summers ago, Jack, my then six-year-old grandson, came in and asked me for a couple of empty paper towel tubes and glue, real sticky glue. That meant my good tacky glue. I asked Jack what he was making, and he said, "A robot." I gave him the glue.

Later in the day, I went upstairs and out to the car. As I went out the back door, there was Jack busily working on his robot. It was a square piece of plywood lying flat on the ground. He had used half a jar of the real sticky glue to adhere two round balls on the board and a length of broken necklace. He had used half a roll of tin foil to cover things, robot style. Hmm, what in the heck was that? When I went back downstairs I told my husband Jack wasn't making a robot, he was gluing stuff to a piece of board.

> "Children instinctively understand that process is more important than product. The stacking of blocks is more important than the tower. The smooshing and squooshing of finger paint on paper is more important than the painting. The singing is more important than the song."
>
> —Kimberli Pelo Robison, "A Dangerous Woman"

The next day as I left for work I stopped dead in my tracks because right there, at the bottom of the back steps, was a perfect robot.

Jack had envisioned a robot from a square piece of board and over the course of half a day had assembled all the materials he needed, and he had created it.

I was amazed. It had looked like a junky piece of board covered with glue and odds and ends the day before, but Jack knew what he was doing. There it was—a perfect robot.

The robot lay at the bottom of the back steps for four days until it rained. Then the pieces were gathered up, and it went to the junkyard in the sky. Jack's robot couldn't be played with or hung on the wall.

So the question I ask is, "Was it a waste of materials for Jack to build the robot?" My answer would be a resounding "*No!*"

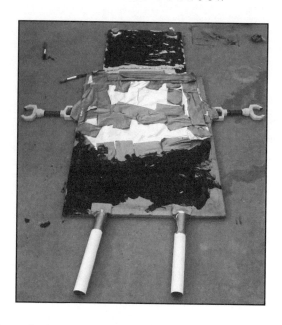

The boat had an obvious use, but the robot seemed useless. However, in both cases, the child had to conceive an idea. They had to determine what materials they needed to bring their idea to fruition. Next they had to take the initiative to gather the materials and organize them in order to bring their vision to life.

In both cases, since I was somewhat involved and observed the process, those kids had to problem solve to make things work out. They worked independently, for the most part, trusting they could figure it out and get the job done. At the same time, they had to determine when they needed to ask for help, and exactly what help they needed.

In Jack's case, he had to figure out how to get the job done with two smaller siblings getting in the way. Yelling or hitting wasn't an option. He had to use diplomacy.

In both cases, the child was able to look at the finished product and beam from ear to ear because they knew they had done a spectacular job. They both felt proud for many days. Their belief in themselves was stronger and their ability to *do* increased.

When I look at the results from the use of the materials in both cases, I think those materials were used perfectly. They accomplished what paint, glue, junk, brushes, rubber bands, scissors, pencil, pen,s and all the rest were designed for—to help people problem solve and create. The use of the materials assisted these children in feeling more capable and able than when they began; to feel the pride of having done something that mattered to them.

If I'd been more involved, or if I'd been worried how the materials were used, we could have saved paint, glue, tape, and so on, and we would have had less mess. But I hope you can see what the children experienced would have been far different.

As adults, we do have to pay attention to the use of supplies because children need some guidance, but we should worry less about waste. Think instead of what they gain by creating on their own:

- Increased vision

- Initiative

- The ability to bring the vision to life

- The ability to gather together what's needed

- The ability to problem solve

- The ability to work independently

- Learning when to ask for help and what help they need

- Learning to work well with others

- Developing leadership skills and attitudes

- Learning to use diplomacy

If you decide to see your children's projects differently—how they feel to your child and what the process of creating is teaching them— you can better evaluate the right use of materials. You'll be able to let it be about them and not you.

Couldn't we use a few more adults who aren't afraid to turn their dreams into reality because they spent their childhood doing it?

MOTIVE 7—We like doing it ourselves

When Maggie was almost four, Jack was two, and Mary was brand new. I was babysitting them on what happened to be their mother's birthday, and I had planned on making a cake. I wanted to make the cake myself and I wanted it to turn out the way I envisioned it. It was an important birthday.

But, it was their mother's birthday and the kids wanted to help. They were all little, and Maggie has cerebral palsy. She's sharp as a whip but working her arms and legs is a challenge. I knew the whole project was going to feel and be different if the kids were helping me. I just wanted to do it myself!

If I had held onto my desire to do the cake by myself, but let the kids help anyway, it would have remained about me. I would have over-managed. I would have fussed about the mess. I would have opted to do much of it myself anyway.

But I decided I would let them have the experience. I would be Present and let it be about them.

Because of Maggie's condition, she has a special chair she sits in. It isn't high enough to reach the table, and so I put her and the chair on the table. Jack, of course, took his position on one of the kitchen chairs. I opened the cake mix bag and allowed each one to pour half of the contents into the bowl. Some made its way to the tabletop and some to the floor.

I filled a cup with water. I helped Maggie get hold of the large cup and pour it into the bowl. Because this wasn't the first time I'd cooked with them, I wanted to see if Jack could pour the cup himself, so I said, "Pour it in, Jack." He took hold of the one-third cup and gently tipped it to one side onto the table. Okay . . . I could see he still needed help. So I refilled the one-third cup, and he poured it into the bowl, with help.

Next, I showed Jack and Maggie how to break an egg and how to get the contents out. Woohoo! Whacking eggs suited Jack just fine. He gave it a whack and voila! Egg all over the table. Not to worry. We picked out the egg shells and scraped the egg into the bowl.

> "Go ahead and let them make a mess (but have them clean it up, too). Let them create an experiment just to see what happens (but keep it safe!). Let them play and have fun...Let them ask questions for which you may not know the answer."
>
> —Vince Harriman, "What Can Kids Learn from a Failed Science Project? Everything!"

Then I helped Maggie get hold of her egg and smack it against the bowl edge. This was necessary to make it pliable enough for her to squeeze the contents out of it and squeeze she did. Egg was dripping down the front of her shirt; there was a small stream running down her knee, and the rest was oozing out her fingers. We did get all the egg out of the shell; the shell was pried out of her little fist and hands wiped clean. Whew!

As I turned to get a cloth to wipe up the egg mess, Maggie, who was desperate to do it herself, plunged her arm into the batter up to her elbow. I turned around at the same moment. It was perfect! I took hold of the bowl and said, "Stir Maggie, stir."

She had a tremendous time mixing batter with her arm and fist. It's challenging for her to hold a spoon and she needs help. For a four-year-old that's so lame. But stirring on your own, now that's living! I would never have come up with the solution she found.

Of course, being unable to control her limbs, her hand and arm went in and out of the batter a couple of times and so we had cake mix on her, me, Jack, and the table.

After the cake was baked, we frosted it. Maggie loved this part of the process. She held the cake knife in her hand, with help, and slapped frosting all over the cake. That's exactly what the process felt like, slapping frosting all over the cake! I have a photo of her sitting in her special chair cooking. :)

Jack enjoyed squeezing the frosting out of the decorating bag. As he made the borders, the frosting strip would be on the cake and at times it would be on the table.

Does reading this tire you out a bit? It tired me out a bit. There was a mess. It took a lot more time. We found a shell or two in the finished product. The cake didn't look the same as it would have if I'd done it myself.

I know why we all want to do it ourselves. It's easier. It's faster. We get a better result. And often, without the chaos children can bring, it feels more enjoyable. Even when we let our kids participate, if in our mind we still want to do it ourselves, we limit what they can do, get upset, frustrated, and even angry when things aren't smooth, neat, or how we pictured it.

When we lay aside the need to do it ourselves, we're better able to let it be about them and not us, to allow our children to create and enjoy the process. If they aren't allowed to enjoy the process, it doesn't fill their need because for kids, process is what counts. And it's a bonus when they know we're enjoying ourselves too.

MOTIVE 8—We want to get it done quickly

If you're like me, you have a lot on your plate. When you do anything with children, it's going to take T-I-M-E. Time is a resource parents frequently feel is in short supply. This feeling of needing to move on as quickly as possible makes it very hard to be Present.

Benny, my two-year-old grandson, caught me cooking and he was desperate to help. I was making gingerbread men, a Christmas tradition. When I'm cooking alone I can do it in no time because I've been making these men for a long time. But when you put a two-year-old into the mix, the whole equation changes!

I had lots of gingerbread men to make, and I had carved out a certain amount of time to do it in. I didn't want Benny's help! I wanted to get the job done in the allotted amount of time. It was Christmas, and there was a lot to do!

It would have been easy to say, "Benny, Grandma's busy. Run upstairs and I'll let you know when I finish." I was sorely tempted. I wanted to send him away. But here's what I did instead. I watched him for a few minutes as I kneaded my ball of dough. I got Present so I could see and hear him.

I saw his sheer delight in doing something new. I observed as he floured the counter and the floor so his men wouldn't stick. I listened to his laughter as he rearranged my utensil drawer. And guess what . . . I loved watching him. It was fun. He made the whole project worthwhile. The process became the focus and not the outcome.

My motive changed mid-stream. It changed from getting another thing off my list in as short an amount of time as possible to creating a memory with Benny and adding to our relationship.

When I stopped worrying about time and my endless to-do list I was able to see and hear this delightful two-year-old. Love is spelled T-I-M-E. When we give our children our time, we let them know loud and clear they're on our list, in fact, at the top of our list.

IN SUMMARY

Adults want things to turn out well. Often our interpretation of what *turning out well* means matters a great deal in the level of satisfaction and happiness we experience as a family. However, ultimately success is not determined by the outcome but is determined by strengthened relationships and the level of engagement and enjoyment we have with our children. When relationships are strengthened and we enjoy our family, it has turned out well.

"Is it about us or them?" is a good question to ask ourselves each time we engage with our children. At times it needs to be about us, but if we're interested in giving our children an enjoyable experience and building a solid, loving relationship with them, we need to check our motives. As we do this and let it be about them more often, we'll be better able to be Present. When we're Present it always sends the message, "I see you, I hear you, I love you. You matter to me."

Real success in any family endeavor can be measured by how people feel during and after an activity together. Is the family energized? Did you have fun? Did you feel happy being with one another? Was there a sense of satisfaction or accomplishment? Was individual esteem strengthened? Are relationships better? Is the family feeling still strong? We can answer yes more often if we make it about them and not about us.

I'm *not* saying we shouldn't ever take care of what we need. Sometimes we do need to say no. We do need to hurry or have less mess. Sometimes that's what has to happen. What I *am* saying is that when we're working with our children, it will be easier to build a relationship and enjoy the experience if we make it about them and not us. When we're Present, it's much easier to do.

As we practice being Present and keep our focus on the child, our families will be happier, and we'll personally experience more satisfaction in our parenting.

That's the reward for allowing children to enjoy the process: more satisfaction in our parenting. The outcome that matters most in family activities, events, and projects should always be relationship and memory! As often as you can, make it about them and not you.

CHAPTER 9

ADJUST Your Approach

Let me share a humorous story. It may be a bit off track, but you'll get a kick out of it and I'll get us back on track, I promise.

Don and I've been married over forty-five years. It's been a good marriage, and we've raised a fine family, but we've been married a long time!

One day I mentioned that we needed a little romance. We'd had plenty of romance in our marriage, just not lately. I felt the need for romance.

A few days later Don was home and spent a couple of hours in the kitchen making a terrific casserole for lunch. It was nice and we had an interesting conversation. We both enjoyed it. The food tasted great and I appreciated not having to cook it. As we were finishing he looked at me and said, "This is how I'm romancing you." Hmmmm. I just smiled and didn't say anything.

A few days later the romance topic came up again. Don said, "Gee, honey, I made you a casserole."

"Don, a casserole is not romance. It's nice, it's kind, and it's serving, but it isn't romance. I think you've been married too long and need to look romance up in the dictionary."

With a smile, he said, "Then I don't get any points for romance, right?"

"Right, no points."

Now, I was not mad at Don. I love him very much, but I wasn't getting what I needed, which was romance. Used as a verb, it means to court. A casserole and lunch at home did not feel like courting to me, and he was disappointed because he took two hours, was nice, and still didn't get points for romance.

MANAGEMENT VS. RELATIONSHIP

Parents find themselves in this same situation, getting no points when they think they're filling a child's need.

Didn't you rush home from work to be with your kids? Didn't you cook and serve a tasty meal? Didn't you take them clear across town to their ballet lessons and don't you do that weekly? Didn't you wash the clothes and hang your daughter's favorite dress in the closet so she could have it for the party tonight? Didn't you orchestrate an amazing birthday party for your fourteen-year-old? Didn't you repair the rain gutters so no one has to be embarrassed about the outside of the house anymore?

Because you've invested so much time in managing and caring for your family, you equate it with being Present, just as Don thought making a casserole equated to romance. But you may not actually be Present. You're kind, you're nice, you're taking care of business, and you're serving but *it isn't the same as being Present.*

> **"Kids will remember less what we did for them and more how we spoke and reacted to them."**
>
> —Roma Khetarpal, *The "Perfect" Parent: 5 Tools for Using Your Inner Perfection to Connect with Your Kids*

These are the things we DO to manage our home and family. They have to be done. Good mothers and fathers take care of the physical needs of their home and children. They cook, clean, teach, admonish, and model appropriate behavior.

Being Present happens when we stop long enough to actually see and hear our child. What do they need? Not, "what do we think their needs are?" but "what do they need?" Remember my daughter, Marie? She didn't need a drink or food or help with anything. She needed me to see her. When I took the thirty seconds required, she was satisfied, and I got points.

MAKE BEING PRESENT YOUR GOAL

What would happen if being Present with our children was our ultimate goal rather than ticking things off our list?

Let's take chores for example. Part of our job is to keep our home clean, as well as teaching our children to be responsible. So we assign duties. One of the most common chores for kids is cleaning their bedroom. So there's the weekly ritual of saying to children, "Go clean your room." We spend the next few hours cajoling and possibly yelling in an effort to get our kids to behave in a responsible way and also get the room cleaned. We're deeply into home and family management.

The bedrooms do need to be cleaned—your children do need to clean them—but are you invested in having a Present relationship with your kids, rather than just getting the room cleaned? How can we get chores done—the management part—and keep being Present as the end goal?

Here's how:

You send your children off to clean their rooms. After ten or fifteen minutes you go into a bedroom and say, "How's it going, John?" John may be stretched out on his bed reading a magazine. He rolls his eyes at you or makes an excuse as to why he isn't cleaning his room. You respond with, "Let me help you clean under your bed, clean out the closet, or pick up your dirty clothes," and so on.

While you're flat on your stomach with John, pulling stuff from under his bed, smile and have a mini-conversation. "Wow, this sock really stinks. It must have been under here for weeks!" John replies, "Well, dad's socks stink too." You answer, "Yes they do. Maybe that's where you get it from. Did you know there is a cheese that smells like stinky socks?" And so the conversation goes until you've pulled everything out from under the bed.

You put one or two things away, pat his shoulder, look him in the eye, smile and say, "I'll be back to check on you." Just stay three to five minutes, talking, listening, and helping. Now go do your own work or visit another bedroom. Return in fifteen to twenty minutes and repeat.

Doing this may seem like a waste of your time when John should just clean his own room and allow you to do your work, but it pays dividends. Your kids' rooms will get cleaned, you won't yell, and you may have an interesting conversation and a laugh. You will have been Present, and you will get points. It replaces management with relationship.

APPLYING THE 1% PRINCIPLE

Let's look at applying the 1% principle from chapter 6. You're the CEO of your family. Michael Gerber, in *The E-Myth*, states most businesses fail because the boss spends all of his/her time working *in* the business, meaning always focusing on the day-to-day tasks necessary to keep the business going. The boss never spends any time working *on* the business, usually because they don't have the time. He calls this getting stuck in the "doin' it, doin' it, doin' it" cycle (Gerber, *The E-Myth*). Don't you often feel like you're just "doin' it, doin' it, doin' it?"

Using the 1% principle helps us step out of the day-to-day management of our family and look at working on the family. Ask yourself, "What's the one thing I could do that would make the most difference now?" Focus your efforts on making that one thing happen.

Of course, we're still responsible for running a family! However, we've now focused our vision on the one thing we're going to work on improving while we manage our home and family. In the bedroom cleaning example, the 1 percent was being Present, working on parent-child relationships while getting chores done.

What would your relationship with your children look and feel like if you did this one thing consistently for a year? A good question to ponder!

As a parent running a household, you have a million things to think about and manage. You have all of the physical tasks required to maintain the home both inside and out. You have all of the jobs that keep the people in your home cared for—meals, clothes, housekeeping, and chauffeuring people from place to place. Managing all of this is a *big* job. However, this is the "doin' it, doin' it, doin' it."

To be successful in creating your family culture, you need to stop "doin' it" all the time and put more effort into working on your family. That's the relationship part of the job. That's the "cleaning under the bed with John" part.

You can't successfully tackle everything at once. Why not, for now, let your 1 percent be learning to be Present while managing your family. There are *big* pay offs for letting go of the less important tasks occasionally so that you can be Present with your children more often.

THE PAY OFF OF REPLACING MANAGEMENT WITH RELATIONSHIP

PAY OFF 1—Reduced Stress and Increased Energy

Being Present isn't just to help your kids know they matter. It's also a prescription for stress reduction in your own life.

Kids are like batteries. They're filled with energy and light. The younger the child, the truer this is. When I'm stressed, I work at remembering to *stop* and just grab my grandchild in a big hug as I say, "I love you!"

For example, when I'm writing and a grandchild keeps coming over to me and standing by my side waiting for me to notice them, I remember to *stop* rather than getting frustrated. I do this because, as I hold them and look into their eyes, the stress drains out of me for a moment and I'm renewed rather than annoyed.

> "The next time you're feeling out of sorts, stressed to the max, pulled in a million directions, take five minutes to sit down, reach out, and create an essential connection with your child. Open your hearts to each other again. And sooner rather than later you will feel renewed and ready to face life again."
>
> —Sharon Silver, founder of Proactive Parenting

If you're down, you can get up by accessing your child's energy. They're up more often and are far more energetic than you are. It is a gift of being young. Even children who live in poverty can be seen smiling, playing, running, jumping, and experiencing joy. If the body of a child is not in distress through starvation or debilitating illness, it's full of energy.

When I thought about swatting my daughter Marie because she kept coming in the sewing room and bugging me, it was because I was *stressed out*. I am glad I didn't swat her because how do you think I felt after the thirty seconds I held her? I was far less stressed. In fact, I glowed. I felt renewed and successful as a mom.

Sharon Silver has expressed this perfectly: "Focusing on love and creating a connection causes unseen properties to magically eat up stress. It's as if stress and love can't exist in the same space. When a stressed-out parent takes a few minutes to sit and lovingly reconnect to their child, heart to heart, it's like a key has been inserted and the stress begins to dissolve" (Silver, "4 Minute Way to De-Stress").

PAY OFF 2—Extended Patience

When we *stop* managing things and look at our child, when we see them and hear them, our patience level increases. Remember one of those moments when you felt angry or frustrated but stopped and reached out to your child lovingly, and you felt the negative feelings dissipate? It may not happen often but I'm sure it has happened.

When you're Present with your child, anger and frustration evaporate. You feel a moment of loving compassion. You become more patient. It feels great and helps you feel successful as a parent. These moments of extended patience help you stay in control when things are heating up in your life.

PAY OFF 3—Reduce the Need for Consequences

When you're Present, it reduces the need for consequences. It diffuses situations that push moms and dads to the breaking point, causing them to lose control and act like children.

I was frustrated by my daughter Marie when I was sewing. I felt she was naughty and needed a consequence. However, when I gave her thirty seconds of Presence, the need for a consequence disappeared. She went away and didn't bother me again. She never was being naughty; she was just making her need known.

When I finally stopped to hear and see her, I got the message and I responded.

Marie could have ended up crying. I would have felt like a crummy mom and I would have still been stressed out. Instead, I have a sweet memory and Marie went away firm in the knowledge that she mattered. The need for a consequence evaporated.

I have a friend who had nine children living with her, all under the age of eleven. She was distracted, interrupted, and overly busy one day. As the day wore on, the children became awful; they were fighting, noisy, and making messes. It was constant chaos. My friend felt she was going to explode any minute.

Finally, as she was cooking dinner and things were escalating in the living room, she *stopped*. She turned dinner off and gathered them all in the living room and began to read. Eventually, they calmed down and listened. It got relatively quiet and as peaceful as it can get with ten people all together in the same space.

She didn't give it a significant amount of time—about thirty minutes. She said it made a difference in the rest of the evening. Things were more peaceful. They enjoyed eating together and being with each other. The feeling of chaos was significantly reduced. She didn't explode and she didn't dole out consequences.

> "To have influence in a person's life, we must start with a relationship."
> —Andy Stanley, pastor

Later, she asked me an interesting question. She wondered if stopping in the middle of her dinner preparation was the right thing to do. Was she giving in to their naughtiness? I responded, "Often it isn't a case of naughtiness, but an issue of need. They needed and wanted your Presence." When she gave it to them, it ended the need for consequences.

PAY OFF 4—Children Who Know They Matter

As adults, we're end product driven, and it can become a challenge to be Present. We tend to focus on the job at hand, how it should be done and how it turns out in the end. We talked about this in chapter 8. This keeps us in management mode and out of relationship mode.

Here's a true story I read in one of my favorite magazines. A father was painting the outside of his home. His five-year-old son wanted to help. So this good father let him. They both went to work on the door, dad painting the top and son painting the bottom. It just happened to be the door to the main entrance of their home.

Because of his age and size, the young boy wasn't able to spread the paint evenly and consequently the paint was beading up. That wasn't how the father envisioned his front door. So each time the five-year-old bent down to get more paint the father would hastily smooth out the paint on the bottom panel.

As the father thought over the situation and his redoing of his son's work, he decided working with his son trumped a first class paint job. He realized his son was doing mighty fine work for a five-year-old. The relationship being forged over the painting of a door was more significant than the appearance of the door. He stopped smoothing out his son's work.

Later, when the father approached the front door and saw its distinctive style of decoration, he remembered what's really important. Despite wanting the door to look good, this dad had eventually *seen* his son. He responded to the real need of his son—to be allowed to participate in helping the family at the level a five-year-old can—to help his dad. When the father accepted this offer, he was Present, and his son felt he mattered more than the door.

This same father spoke of his experience with his own dad. His dad had a workshop where he made beautiful things. He said,

> I would wander into this workshop and watch him. Just to be in his presence was a thrill for me. He invited me to help him by passing a hammer, a screwdriver, or other tool. I was convinced my help was necessary and that without me he would not be able to complete his task.
>
> As I look back and reflect upon those wonderful memories, I realize my contribution was not necessary for my father to

complete the work he was engaged in. I was the beneficiary, as through these experiences I came to know him and to love him. (Johnson, "We All Have a Father in Whom We Can Trust," 30)

This boy felt he mattered to his dad because his dad let him help him. His dad didn't let what he wanted to accomplish get in the way of allowing himself to be Present with his son. The fathers in both stories took the time to be Present, not worrying about the outcome or time.

Parents can care too much about the outcome and too little about the relationship. When we take the time to be Present with our children, we give them the opportunity to know and love us, and we let them know they matter more than whatever job or task is at hand.

PAY OFF 5—Enjoyable Relationships

I have a friend who was 111 years old in 2015. You read that right, 111! She lives with her daughter who's 87. She's in good health. She can get around with her walker. She bathes herself, feeds herself, and is as sharp as a tack. Her name is Anna.

It's been fun watching Anna. I've learned a lot. It's like watching a movie in slow motion. Anna conserves her energy. She does everything slowly and with great thought. I guess in 111 years you figure out there's no need to hurry. There's time for anything that truly matters.

She also conserves her energy when a conversation's going on. She listens a great deal. If you ask her a question, her answer's short and to the point. I guess in 111 years you learn you can get more from listening than from talking and that most things don't need to be said.

It's also been fascinating watching the interaction between Anna and her daughter, Marie. Now remember Marie is 87 and she's responsible for her mother who is 111. A fair percentage of their conversations sound like this:

- Mom, please take your shower and don't mess up the bathroom.

- Mom, stop slurping your food. You're going to choke.

- Mom, why did you do that?

- Mom, wake up. You can't sleep at the table.

- For goodness sake, get dressed. It's already 10:00.

- Mom, you're wearing me out.

To me she might say,

- Mom has really been naughty this week.

- I'll tell you, I'm so worn out.

- I think Mom's having a pity party. She just wants attention.

- Sometimes I think she pushes my buttons on purpose.

Does this sound familiar to you? Of course, it does. It sounds as if she's talking to or about a three-year-old, a nine-year-old, a twelve-year-old, or an eighteen-year-old. It's been fascinating to see that when you're in the position of custodial care for another person, regardless of age, you spend a lot of your time in management and only a fraction in relationship building.

Anna's daughter loves her mother, but let's face it, when you're in charge of the health and well-being of another person, you feel a great weight of responsibility. It doesn't matter if you're twenty years old and have a one-year-old, thirty-five with seven children, or eighty-seven with a mother who's well over a hundred.

The days Marie and Anna have remaining are growing fewer, and when her mother passes away it won't be how well she managed their home that will bring peace to Marie's heart. It will be all the times she and her mother connected in those last years.

To have fulfilling and enjoyable relationships with those in our care, our children, we need to *stop* managing so much and give more time to building the relationship. We can do this with small increments of time as we consistently practice being Present. Relationship is everything, and ultimately it depends on you!

PAY OFF 6—The burden of Parenting is Lightened

Not much feels better than laughing with your child or getting a sloppy kiss and hug when you're feeling frazzled. It's sublime hearing the words "you're the best Mom/Dad." There's a feeling of renewal and peace as you rock quietly, holding a child.

In the end, relationship will surpass just about everything else in its ability to bring happiness, peace, and satisfaction to your family. It makes the job of parenting lighter.

WHAT YOU WILL TREASURE MOST

One of the pivotal moments in my life happened when I was sixteen. I was in the play "Our Town" by Thorton Wilder. I played Emily Gibbs, a young woman on the threshold of a beautiful life. Then suddenly and tragically, life was over for her.

> **"It's so easy to get lost in the responsibilities of parenting that we forget to actually enjoy the journey!"**
>
> —Sumitha Bhandarkar, founder of A Fine Parent

In the play, we meet her in the spirit world and she desperately wants to go back, just for a day. Those who are older and wiser advise her not to go. But back she goes, to the happiest day of her life—her twelfth birthday.

BECOMING A PRESENT PARENT

It's painful because she quickly realizes those she loves best can't see one another because they're so stuck in the doin' it, doin' it, doin' it. They're busy doing all the things they think matter so much: laundry, cooking, education, church duties, work, making money, changing the world.

At the tender age of sixteen, I could feel the pain Emily experienced because she couldn't get her mother to turn away from her work and look at her—just see her, for one moment. That's what Emily wanted more than anything else.

She had returned to what she considered her happiest day while on earth, but now she was no longer among the living and could see with new eyes. She realized that although the party was nice and the gifts were exciting, what mattered most would have been just one moment of real connection, one moment of Presence from her mother. It was painful for her to realize how little they had actually connected during their lives, even though her mom had so efficiently taken care of all the management needed for a large family.

When we make connecting with our kids a priority and do it consistently over time, it says, "I see you, I hear you, I love you, you matter to me," more clearly and loudly than any words we say. It gets us those important relationship points we think we're garnering with all the things we do for our kids. When all is said and done, the relationship we have with our children is what we're going to treasure the most.

IN SUMMARY

It takes thought and effort to be Present, but when we're Present we'll find it energizes us and makes us feel more alive. This additional output on our part pays us in a greater sense of family well-being.

Ninety percent of people on their deathbed say their biggest regret is they didn't get closer to the people in their lives and almost all parents whose children are grown say they wish they'd spent more time with their kids—truly Present time.

It takes more thought to be Present than it does time. We need to think on it daily as we take care of the management of our family. We need to watch for moments when we can disengage from management and engage in building relationships.

Make this a practice. Let it become how you are with your children. When you're engaged with your child, be right there, right now. You won't be able to do it all the time but if you do it every day for a bit, you'll find yourself doing it more and more. We don't have all the time in the world. We just have now—today. That's all. It's all we've ever had—just today. We can fill it with busy or we can simplify and make room for relationships. It's a choice you make.

One day you'll be older. Your kids will be gone from your home. You won't care how clean your house was, how spectacular the yard, if you homeschooled or public schooled. You won't value the amount of money you made, how often you went to Disneyland, what college they went to, or if your kids got a new bike yearly. You won't care if they're carpenters or lawyers. You won't care if you impacted thousands of people. What you will think about more than anything else is the condition of the relationships within your family. That, my friends, is what you're going to treasure most. Take time now to make them sweet.

CHAPTER 10

REMEMBER Less Is More

I did some digging on the Internet to see what people were saying kids need to be happy. There are certainly a lot of articles out there. Each had a list of five to ten ideas for raising happy children. They didn't all agree but here's the one thing that was on most lists: Connected kids are happy kids.

And connected kids are kids who have parents that have learned to be Present. In this chapter, I want to explore two ways of thinking and behaving that impact an adult's ability to be Present with their children: what we perceive as the cost of raising children vs. the real cost and how our belongings and our emotional baggage affect our ability to be Present.

1—THE REAL *COST* OF RAISING KIDS

Think back to your favorite memories as a child. What were they? Who or what are the most distinct elements of those memories? Let me share one of mine with you.

When I was five, my family lived in sunny California. My mother loved to take drives. She and my dad would put us all in the car on a Saturday morning and head down the road with no particular place in mind; we would just drive. My father expected us to be quiet and not cause any disturbance, and he didn't like to stop. So that meant what seemed like an eternity in the car being regularly shushed and needing to pee badly.

On this particular drive, we were far out in the country when we came to a field entirely filled with California Poppies. Oh my gosh! I can still see that place in my mind. It was immense or seemed so to me; it was a blanket of yellow-gold. Did I mention that I love flowers?

I loved flowers with all my little girl heart, and these flowers were particularly mesmerizing because there were so many of them and because they were so vibrantly yellow-gold. My sisters and I began hollering, "Stop. Stop. Dad, stop!"

Here's the memory: My father stopped the car. He let my sisters and me out, and we ran through that field until we were completely worn out. We touched, smelled, picked, and thrilled at the beauty of those poppies. He never once said, "Girls, we have to go." Not once. He let us explore and enjoy until we had gotten our fill.

I know there was a cost to this for my dad, but it wasn't money. What it cost him was T-I-M-E and putting his desires on hold long enough to let us fill ours. Remember, my dad didn't like to stop. He wasn't particularly patient when it came to the use of time. His whole purpose of those outings was to show my mother the countryside from a speeding car. But on this day, my dad *stopped* and let three little girls make a precious memory.

The real cost of raising children isn't money—it's time and Presence. It's taking the time to see and hear and respond to another person, even when it's inconvenient and not on our to-do list.

WHAT MAKES A GREAT MEMORY?

The world is filled with things we can buy for our kids—toys, technology, clothes, and gadgets. There are many places that we can take them—theme parks, water parks, grand vacations. We live in a world influenced by media, which says that really good parents give their kids _____ .

There isn't anything wrong with taking our children on cool trips or buying them a special toy or piece of clothing, but in the final analysis, no matter what we think, it won't be any of those things that our children will remember with the most fondness. What they'll remember is whatever created that family feeling: whatever let them know they mattered, that they were on our list, in fact at the top of our list. This feeling is not created by things or by just being together. It's created when we're Present while we're with them.

My children are grown adults, aged twenty-five to forty-four. Recently I asked them and their spouses what their fondest memories were from childhood. Here are a few responses:

Jenny—"Camping trips in Yellowstone Park. Spending summers in Logan at Grandma and Grandpa's. Playing with the big jar of buttons!"

Marie—"I remember you used a fridge box and turned it into a little store. I remember Seth being the clerk inside the box and us buying things. I remember the frozen chocolate covered bananas you made and the frozen rattlesnake you scared anyone you could with. (Yes, I, a sane mother, had a frozen rattlesnake in a chocolate box!)

"I remember the fourth of July at the park having a picnic. I also remember loving to look at your sticker books. I remember the night we pretended we didn't have electricity and had to use our food storage stuff. It was so fun camping in the back yard."

"A friend took his young family on a series of summer vacation trips, including visits to memorable historic sites. At the end of the summer, he asked his teenage son which of these good summer activities he enjoyed most. 'The thing I liked best this summer,' the boy replied, 'was the night you and I laid on the lawn and looked at the stars and talked.'"

—Dallin H. Oaks, "Good, Better, Best"

Barry—"I loved our Christmases at different cabins (We rented Forest Service cabins for five dollars a night). I loved how much food we had on Thanksgiving and how tasty it was. I loved eating the tops of the cakes you cut off when baking. Canning, sewing, and cross country skiing in Red Lodge and to school were all enjoyable for me! I loved all the camping that we did and sitting in the dark with the Christmas lights on in the living room."

Seth—"I loved New Year's Eve and the cheese and meat tray that we ate while sitting on the floor watching a movie. I remember sitting on the front porch when it rained and smelling the rain and the lilacs (This is still his favorite scent). I remember our walks together and stopping by that beautiful yard, smelling the flowers.

"I loved it when dad let me sit on his lap and drive on the rolling road outside of Bozeman, MT when he took me on business trips with him and watching man movies while traveling with dad. I liked going hunting with dad, and I remember shooting a deer uphill on the first shot. And remember that yellow bird that got stuck in our grill while we were traveling?"

Jodie—"I loved going to the park for the Fourth of July and eating watermelon. My most cherished memories are of the Thanksgiving and Christmas season. I loved all of the little traditions we had, from the way we decorated, to making gingerbread houses, to what we ate."

Kate—"I remember you and me sitting under the table reading a chapter of *Katie John* together. She painted her face with lipstick on picture day and it wouldn't come off. We laughed and laughed together. I remember gardening with you and finding that HUGE spider.

"I remember you sitting with me while I wrote that tough poem for school. I loved you teaching us to make snow candy, homemade noodles, sugar eggs, pillows filled with milkweed fluff and quilting. I loved the whole family lying on their backs on sleeping bags watching fireworks together. I remember when you stood up, not saying a word when I fell during a cheer contest. I knew you were silently saying, 'Get up. You can do it.'"

Andrew—"I remember dad letting me sit on his lap and drive when I went on business trips with him. I also remember working with him in the crawl space. I don't think either of us actually liked going down there, but we did like working together."

Kendra (Andrew's wife)—"My fondest memories of my childhood were the times spent at my grandmother's house. She would always wake up early and go to her garden if it was nice or her sewing room if it was cold and stormy. As soon as I woke I would look for her. Once I found her I would sneak up and try to scare her. It would always result in a tickle fest. It was so simple but something I loved and will always remember!

"Another thing I loved at grandma's house was learning new things. She was a patient woman and would always take the time to teach my cousins and me how to do things on our own. If we were baking she would let us crack the eggs, hold the hand mixer, and so on, making a HUGE mess, but she never showed us if she was getting frustrated. She would push through and teach us how to do it correctly for next time. The same was true for sewing, crocheting, gardening . . . just about everything."

I also put the question of fond memories to my siblings, cousins, nieces and nephews. Here are a few of their responses:

Cindy (a sister)—"I remember mom reading us a chapter each night from *Old Yeller*. I loved the inflections in her voice, that undivided time with her, and the comfort of our warm bed."

Deidra (a niece)—"My mom used to sell Avon, and she would keep all the big boxes her orders came in. We used the boxes to makes houses to play in. It was so fun!"

Dianna (a cousin)—"Going horseback riding while we were camping."

Nanette (a sister)—"Mom helped me sew a dress for 4H. It was so cool and had pom poms on the hem. I was constantly breaking the sewing machine, and she would always get it working again. I won 1st place and went to state. To this day, I sew because she taught me."

Are you getting the picture? Can you see that the most memorable memories of the respondents to my question cost very little or nothing in money but cost a parent time, patience, and Presence? It's also interesting to note that the majority of these happy and pleasant memories are of events that happened in the course of daily living.

Not one respondent mentioned a fancy toy, a fancy vacation to a memorable place fabulous name brand clothes, a cool car the family had, the size of their home, or where their home was. No one mentioned the great lessons or classes they took. No one said Little League or other teams they played on. Not one. The majority of the memories centered on being with family. They all mentioned when their parents and grandparents were kind, helped them in some way, were patient while they learned, were good examples to them, and gave them time.

Time is truly the greatest gift we give another person, and when coupled with real Presence, it's of inestimable value!

THE NUMBER ONE ELEMENT TO HAPPINESS

In a study of thirteen to twenty-four-year-olds conducted by the Associated Press and MTV, more than a hundred questions were asked of 1,280 young people. The questions were all centered on determining what made these youth happy.

Can you guess the number one answer? Spending time with family! Yup, that's right, spending time with family. These kids and young adults were ages thirteen to twenty-four (Associated Press, "Youth Happiness Study," 2). Does this surprise you?

In our world, there's an erroneous belief spread by an unenlightened little elf that youth and young adults prefer their peers over family; that they're selfish and self-centered. That what makes them happy are designer clothes, fancy toys, money, or a car. Here's the truth—although all that stuff piques their interest and few would turn it down, what they want is that family feeling. They want to belong to a family that's connected. They want to matter!

Edward Hallowell, MD, child psychiatrist and author of *The Childhood Roots of Adult Happiness* pointed to the National Longitudinal Study of Adolescent Health, which included ninety thousand teens, as evidence that "'connectedness'—a feeling of being loved, understood, wanted, acknowledged—is by far the biggest protector against emotional distress, suicidal thoughts, and risky behaviors including smoking, drinking, and using drugs" (Lamb, "7 Secrets to Raising a Happy Child").

So what were second and third on the list in the Associated Press and MTV study? Spending time with friends and time with a significant other (Associated Press, "Youth Happiness Study," 2). Isn't it enlightening to note that the top three answers dealt with relationships—T-I-M-E spent with people they love and trust?

And even better, in the AP-MTV study, nearly three-quarters of those youth and young adults said that their relationship with their parents made them happy (Associated Press, "Youth Happiness Study"). What kids and youth want is *you*! They want a relationship with *you*.

When asked to name their heroes, nearly half of respondents in the study said one or both of their parents (Associated Press, "Youth Happiness Study"). Kids want *you*! They want your Presence.

My favorite response to my question about memories that mattered came from my sweet daughter-in-law Kendra. She said,

> "What better way to show your love for your kids than to give them your time. It's a tangible expression of how worth it they are in your eyes."
>
> —Hannah Goodwyn, "Make Memories With Your Kids"

"Another thing I'll always cherish from my childhood was the time my parents spent with me outdoors, going to the beach, hiking, fishing, swimming, and letting me be a kid. It was something we often did because it didn't cost much but to me it was the greatest thing ever. In fact, one time my dad took me to Disneyland and I asked him if we could leave and go to the beach. I look back on that now and think that must have both surprised him and probably made him wish he had saved all that money. I'm so grateful my parents taught me to cherish experiences and nature over money and things."

Spending money doesn't build relationships. Giving your kids all the *in* stuff doesn't build relationships. Leagues and classes, lessons and even educating a child at home don't necessarily build relationships. These things may help your child as they grow. They may better equip them to succeed in the world financially. There isn't anything wrong with providing these things.

However, relationships are built when we learn to be Present with another human being. It requires that we hear and see our children. It requires T-I-M-E. In the final analysis, a good relationship with trusted adults is one of the key elements of happy children and youth.

WHAT ELSE MAKES KIDS AND FAMILIES HAPPY?

Many elements go into helping families and children be happy. I'm not going to make an exhaustive list, just those items that relate to the topic at hand—becoming a Present parent, the real cost of raising happy kids.

1. Love—Love helps children develop self-worth, esteem, and confidence. It helps them learn to love others. It shores them up so that in tough times, and there will be tough times, they can thrive. Love is most effectively shown when we hear, see, and respond to our children on a consistent basis.

2. Time—Whether you have money in your bank account or not, you have something your children need: T-I-M-E. Children need both quantity and quality time with you. Part of your job as a parent is to order your life so that you create space for your family. It's one of the most important things you can do.

When we turn away from technology, we create space. When we simplify our calendars and life, we create space. When we worry less about home management, we create space. When we utilize the touchpoints that occur daily, we create space.

The most valuable resource you have is your time. When you give your time to a child it says, *"You matter!"* loud and clear. And isn't it thrilling to know you can often give that time in small increments of five minutes or less as you create space for your family?

3. Humor—The old saying that laughter is the best medicine turns out to be true. The more we laugh, the happier we are! It changes our body chemistry. And did you know that smiling makes us happier, even when we force it? The feedback from your face lets you know you're happy and improves your mood. So when you feel like yelling, storming away, or engaging in a bit of contention, smile instead.

To find humor in the chaos of family life requires us to be Present with ourselves and our children.

One day my son-in-law Doug was giving Mary and Jack a bath. He gathered up the PJ's and brought them back into the bathroom. When he came back in, everything in the room that wasn't nailed down was in the tub: scale, towels, dirty diapers, toothbrushes, soap, shampoo bottles—everything.

As Doug began fishing all the stuff out of the tub while trying to control his temper, this is what he heard, "Hey Dad, you're ruining my island." How's that for funny. I laughed and laughed. Even Doug had to laugh.

Another day I was preparing to attend an event with my then eleven-year-old daughter. The dress was Sunday best. We were running a bit late, and lateness was not an option for me. So the stress was on to get there on time!

As we walked out to the car, I stepped off the curb into a pool of water up to my ankle. I was instantly mad. My shoe was full of water, and there wasn't time to change.

As I drove down the road I was fussing about the cussed water, the inconsideration of people who let their sprinklers run all over the place, the foolishness of having the event at this time of day, and on and on. You can hear it, can't you?

We had driven six blocks when I visualized myself stepping off the curb and into that gutter. I saw my shoe fill up with water and saw the shocked look on my face. It was such a funny picture. I began to laugh. My poor daughter who had sat silently through the so recent tirade stared at me. Then she began to laugh. When I finally got control of myself, I said, "That was so funny!"

In her sweet way she replied, "Mom, I wish you had known it was funny when it happened." That wise statement from my youngest daughter sent me on an adventure of change. Now, I don't always see the funny side of what happens in an ordinary day or in an ordinary family, but I can tell you this, I work to laugh more than I cry or complain or yell.

I've discovered that this is a funny life. Children are funny even at what seems to be their worst, most messy, frustrating moments, and we can laugh with them if we decide to enjoy our family and take control of our stories. Take the time to practice seeing *the funny* in life. Funny is generally free.

4. Hugs and kisses—As many as possible and as often as possible! Use random touches all day, every day. Let physical touch be part of how you are with your children. This doesn't cost you a dime, just a small measure of time.

5. Spirituality—Close to half of the thirteen- to twenty-four-year-olds in the AP_MTV study said religion and spirituality were very important to them (Associated Press, "Youth Happiness Study"). Almost half! I think this will be a surprise to many people.

One of my daughters listed the fact that we were faithful to our spiritual beliefs as one of her fondest memories. She mentioned going to church as a family, praying as a family, and serving others as a family.

The spirituality in our home was about staying together emotionally and physically. Despite all of our ups and down, spiritually being Present on a regular basis felt good; it felt safe while we navigated some pretty rough water.

6. Encouragement/Affirmation—Often one simple word of appreciation can change an entire life. I've seen this play out with my children. When we're Present we're more apt to notice the good in our kids and take the time to let them know. Parents who are deep into their technology or family management miss many opportunities to confirm to their children that they're wonderful, worthwhile beings and that they're proud of them.

7. Happy Parents—A recent study showed when parents are unhappy or depressed, they have children who are less happy. It also mentioned unhappy parents are less effective parents. That's right, one of the ways you can help your kids and family be happier is for you to be happy!

I mentor people who are unhappy. They're unhappy for a multitude of reasons. They're unhappy with their parenting, how their marriage is working out, how their finances look, how busy they are, how overwhelmed they feel, or how their kids behave.

A parent will set up a meeting to share what's bothering them. They usually want to know how to "fix" their spouse or kids because then they'll be happier. Guess what we work on most of the time: the parent.

When we find our own happiness, it resolves a multitude of problems. Much of what we need to do to be happier won't cost much money. What it will require is your T-I-M-E and an understanding that you're responsible for how your life looks and feels. The return you get for the effort you make to become happier will be a happier family. Did you notice each item on the list of what makes for happy kids and families is tied to being Present? Did you notice that none of them required much money? These activities and attitudes are money-free. What they require are our Presence and time, and that we create space so they can happen.

TO BE HAPPIER, BE PRESENT

If you ask moms and dads what they want for their kids, they'll often respond, "for them to be happy."

In her book *Raising Happiness: 10 Simple Steps for More Joyful Kids and Happier Parents,* Christine Carter said, "The well-being of children is more important to adults than just about anything else— health care, the well-being of seniors, the cost of living, terrorism, and the war in Iraq. More than two-thirds of adults say they're 'extremely concerned' about the well-being of children, and this concern cuts across gender, income, ethnicity, age, and political affiliation."

If happy kids are our aim as parents, learning to be Present becomes all the more important. That's what makes this conversation we're having about money valuable. It's vital we let go of what we can't give our children and instead focus on what we can give them: our time, our Presence. It's vital to understand that even if we can afford to give them everything it won't be enough, because what they need is our Presence.

It makes no difference what your financial situation is, the size of your home, the car you drive, or whether your kids ever get to the Grand Canyon or Gettysburg. It doesn't matter if they play the piano, are star pitchers in Little League or wear the latest styles. It isn't imperative they have the most recent toy sensation. It's not a "make it or break it deal" whether they're in private, public, or home school.

The true cost of raising happy children is not measured in money. What it ultimately requires is your time and Presence.

> "It is amazing to me that most things I remember from my childhood make me smile and happy, considering that we had really little money, a lot of empty stomachs and much reason to pray for help. I had a wonderful childhood, not because of the things we had but because we had each other."
>
> —Desirée Campbell, "Ten Things Children Will Always Remember"

When your relationships are strong you'll be better able to teach, correct, comfort, and help your children. It's not enough to merely possess a deep love for your children; they have to feel it!

2—KEEPING IT SIMPLE = GREATER PRESENCE

In a book titled *Life at Home in the Twenty-First Century*, researchers at UCLA observed thirty-two middle-class Los Angeles families and found all of the mothers' stress hormones spiked during the time they spent dealing with their household paraphernalia (Arnold, et al, *Life at Home in the Twenty-First Century*).

I'm not surprised by this. Each item we own requires some of our energy. The more belongings we have, the more emotional energy, as well as physical energy, is needed to maintain it.

I want you to visualize something. Close your eyes and imagine you have threads of energy attached to your shoulders and these threads connect to every item you have in your possession. Every item—each dish, cup, and pan; pictures in the photo album, DVDs, and hammer; each nail, sock, book, magazine, sweater, car, guitar pick, and even your computer files. It's one energy thread per item.

Now envision wherever you go you energetically drag all your possessions with you. You drag them via the connecting threads of emotional energy. How much are you dragging?

What if you eliminated a quarter of your belongings? How much lighter would you feel? Would you even miss any of the things you discarded or gave away? Through my experience, the answer is surprising: not really.

I lived in Montana in the same house for over twenty-one years. I bet you can imagine the amount of stuff we accumulated!

We frequently had to organize the garage. One whole end of the garage was a special room dedicated to storing stuff. Hours of time went to cleaning out closets, drawers, and toy boxes. I can recall the time required to sort, launder, store, and fold all of the clothes we managed to accumulate.

Eventually, we decided to move. I was ready! I began cleaning out the house. I held numerous garage sales. I wanted to let it all go. My husband felt stressed when he left for work because he wasn't there to monitor what was being sold. He was worried about what we were going to have to replace.

Here's what happened. We left Montana with one van load and one small U-haul trailer, the smallest we could get. After over thirty years of living together and raising seven children, we pared it all down to one small U-haul and a van.

Would you be surprised to know in all the years since, we haven't replaced a single item?

When we first moved to Utah, we lived with our thirty-three-year-old daughter because we were assisting her to buy a home. After a couple of years, she found her sweetheart and they married. We moved a few blocks away into a very large and roomy three-bedroom apartment. We were required to downsize our possessions again. We lived there for seven years and we never missed anything, and we didn't replace anything.

A couple of years ago we made the most drastic move of all. As previously mentioned, one of our granddaughters has severe cerebral palsy. She requires a great deal of care. Don and I moved a few blocks away, so we were able to come at a moment's notice to help out or to babysit.

When our daughter decided to move thirty minutes away, we thought long and hard about what moving again—to stay close to them—would mean for us. We finally decided we were going with them. For the last two years, we've lived in the basement apartment of their home.

Here's the downside: it's a three-room apartment. Our living room, office, and kitchen are one room, the length of the house. We had to seriously downsize again.

Here's the upside: Have we replaced anything? No. Have we missed anything? Don hasn't. I've missed two things: an enormous stack of printable writing paper and my large bottle of buttons. That's all. It feels lighter, freer. It's easier to manage. There's less to clean, less to order, and less to organize. It leaves me more time for relationships. I have more energy.

WHEN WE SIMPLIFY, WE FREE UP TIME AND ENERGY

I'm not suggesting we should all move to three-room apartments. What I am suggesting is that we generally accumulate too much stuff, which has to be maintained, managed, cleaned, organized, kept safe, stored, repaired, safe-guarded . . . it all requires our mental energy and our physical time. All this sucks away the time and energy we could be giving to enjoying our family, to doing things together that bring us happiness.

I'm a believer that part of the reason we're so overwhelmed is that we're using so much of our energy and mental space managing stuff. And it's not only our physical belongings sapping our energy. It's our endless to-do list and our overflowing calendars. It's our stored hurts and wounds. No wonder we go to bed weary and wake up tired! It's challenging to be Present when you're overwhelmed and weary.

I promise you can increase your energy, free up mental space, and reduce what you're tolerating in your life as you reduce the events on your calendar, shave your to-do list, get rid of stuff, and forgive and heal. When you do this, you open up space for your family and for being Present.

The word *simplify* means to make simpler or easier to do or understand. To simplify is a principle wise men and women have espoused throughout the ages, and with good reason.

When we simplify our lives, we manage them better. We can spend more time, both mental and physical, where it matters, and less time in activities that in the long run are not going to matter. We open up time to think. We stop spending so much time putting out fires. When we simplify our lives we can tune into our children, our spouse, our God.

When we can't find time to eat a meal together, when mothers spend great amounts of time in their cars chauffeuring, when we're so exhausted we can't have a conversation with a child, when we aren't doing the things we know will create a *great* family culture, then we're too busy because we have too much stuff in our lives.

WHY WE HANG ON TO STUFF

1. We bought it and we don't want to waste our money

Let me share two stories about how hanging onto stuff we aren't using wastes more money than letting it go.

Story 1—When we made the *big* move from Montana to Utah, I had a couple of large boxes in my garage filled with unfinished craft /sewing projects. As I went through the boxes, I remembered my grand plans for each item. It was tempting to pack them up again because I had spent good money on that stuff and I was going to get to it, some day!

But I am happy to say I made the wise and only slightly painful decision to drive those boxes to the neighborhood Goodwill. I realized those items sitting in a box in my garage for years weren't blessing anyone. It was a waste of my money! As I drove away from the Goodwill, I visualized all the happy women who would now finish those projects.

Story 2—When Don and I had been married for fifteen years, his dad gave us all the camping equipment he had stored in his basement for over thirty years. We were excited because we loved camping and had taken our kids a lot. But we had substandard gear. To our dismay, we found most of what Dad gave us was no longer useful. It was falling into disrepair or not working from lack of use because it had been stored for so long. What a waste! We could have benefited so much from that stuff while raising our young family.

Both Don's dad and I had been so careful not to waste our money, but we ended up wasting it anyway. I came to my senses soon enough to let my expenditure bless others before

> "It is the preoccupation with possession more than anything else, that prevents man from living freely and nobly."
>
> —Bertrand Russell, philosopher

the contents of those boxes turned to dust. So let belongings that you're no longer using go. Let them bless someone else now!

2. We may need it later

While I was raising my children, I stored clothes they had outgrown, a few more pricey toys, and baby supplies. This was wise because from 1972 to 1990 we had babies coming and children growing, but then it stopped.

However, the items stayed stored in the garage because I thought we might need it or our kids might need it. Eventually, a friend of my son's asked me if I had any baby gear she could have. She was young and newly married and in need. After a moment of trepidation, I opened the gates and began letting it go.

I didn't need any of it later. I never had another baby. My kids never wanted it for their new babies. My garage was emptier. Others were well served and I freed up space and energy in my life.

3. It all has memories—It's part of who I am

We all have mementos that fill our hearts with joy when we look at them. However, lots of our cherished stuff is just that: stuff.

When my grandparents died, my dad got a lot of stuff. When my dad died, I got the stuff. Recently, I've been going through all of this stuff and sending it to those to whom it belongs. I sent cards written in childlike script to the adults who had written them. I returned letters, pictures, and so forth. You can't imagine the responses. People were glad to see what they had said and made all those years ago. A few of the people will hang on to the items. Others enjoyed seeing it again for a few days and then let it go. After all, those memories are in their minds and hearts, and they take up far less space there.

Over the last ten years, I've also been giving some of the family relics to my grandkids. Oh, I know they're still small, and not all of the items will survive their handling, but I've seen how much joy they derive from owning a piece of history and thinking of the grandma or grandpa who it belonged to. I know the ancients are smiling in heaven. Stuff is only of value when it's used.

My brother, who had been estranged from our family for many years, was thrilled with photos of himself and old letters he had sent to Mom and Dad. In a recent conversation, he said to me, "Most people have this kind of stuff stored in a box somewhere, but you're doing the right thing and getting it out there for people to enjoy." Enough said!

4. It was a gift; I have to keep it

In our family, we've come to a conclusion concerning this. We've decided, as a group, to be regifters. I know you may think this is tacky, but it has served us well. If we get it, and we can't use it, we regift it. The person who gets it can do the same. No one has any hurt feelings. We're all about simplifying our lives, and it's working out well!

5. I like to buy stuff

Recently the husband of one of my clients told me they were adding an addition to their home. He said they needed more closet space. After all, he confessed, he had twenty-eight golf shirts. Let me say as crazy as this sounds it isn't the exception. We're a consuming society. We frankly buy too much stuff!

> "Everything we possess that is not necessary for life or happiness becomes a burden, and scarcely a day passes that we do not add to it."
>
> —Robert Brault, author

The Self Storage Association reports that Americans spend twenty-four billion dollars each year to store their stuff in self-storage units. The National Association of Professional Organizers reports that organizing consultants and products has grown into a one-billion-dollar industry (Johnson, "The Real Cost of Your Shopping Habits").

We as a society buy lots of books on tidying up stuff and how to most effectively store stuff, not to mention books on how to get rid of stuff.

Here's what helps me buy less stuff and get rid of the excess stuff I already have: I continually picture myself strapped to my belongings via the energy threads attached to my shoulders. That does it for me. I want to be free.

It's not helpful to have three sets of dishware and forty-five plastic cups in the cupboard. It isn't useful to have five hammers and a box of fifteen screw drivers unless you're a professional. It's not necessary to have twenty-eight golf shirts.

So stop buying, no matter how attractive or interesting it is. If you can't stop buying, do what my friend Laurie does. If you buy a new blouse, you have to give a blouse away. If you buy a knickknack, you have to give one away. If you purchase a new hammer or drill, you give the old one away. It's working for her.

WHAT ABOUT THE NON-PHYSICAL STUFF?

As problematic as the physical stuff we accumulate is, our emotional stuff and our activity stuff can also keep us from being Present.

This book isn't about fixing your heart and mind. However, each unforgiven hurt, old wound, hard feeling, unresolved and hurtful event takes space in your heart and mind. It requires energy to manage or hide. If you have enough of this inside of you, there's less room left to be Present. I was in this place for years and had to do some serious work.

There are many avenues for cleaning your emotional house and I counsel you to do the work to make it happen. Get a mentor who's been where you are and is now where you want to be. Attend a class, listen to a speaker, or read a book. Pray. Ponder. Think deeply and reflect on your life. Forgive. Clean out your emotional house.

Finally, take a look at your calendar. Ask the hard questions. Why are you doing what you're doing? What ties you to each activity? And while you're asking the hard questions, be honest.

Are your kids taking piano lessons because they're sufficiently interested or because you think good parents provide piano lessons or because you always wanted to take piano lessons and didn't get to?

Are your children playing Little League or soccer because they love the game or because you want them to play sports because you like sports? Are you serving at the senior center because you care deeply for the people or because you didn't know how to say no? Ask the hard questions and be honest.

One of my past mentors said something very profound to me. It's changed the way I make decisions about spending my time and my family's time. She said, "Every yes is a no to something else!"

Let's make sure that what we're saying yes to will, in the long run, bring us true happiness and solid family relationships.

Each person and family has only twenty-four hours a day. There isn't any way to increase the allotment of time you have. So if your time container's bulging at the seams, you have a few choices.

1. Continue to be overwhelmed with all you have to do and struggle to be Present.

2. Continue to believe somehow you can stuff more activities into your twenty-four hours.

3. Empty stuff out of the container.

I suggest the best choice of the three is to empty out the time container. Begin today to notice what you're putting into your twenty-four hours.

How much time do you allot for technology? How often do you shop? How many hours are you spending in the car and are you going places that matter? How much time is required to keep your closets and drawers in order? What are your commitments? What are your kid's commitments? How often do thoughts about past hurts surface? How frequently do you feel resentment?

I'm not old by any means, but I've been on the planet for a while. My kids are grown, and my husband and I are moving quickly along time's path. I have a clearer vision of what matters than I did when I was younger.

So here's what I can suggest from my perspective—take time and begin sorting out your stuff: your physical possessions, your emotional baggage, and your time commitments. Regret is often the result of letting what really matters slip through the cracks.

Stop using your T-I-M-E for managing stuff. Spend more of this valuable commodity on your family relationships. Make space for your children. Make space for conversation and touch. Make space.

IN SUMMARY

The things of the heart always trump the things of the pocket book. A trip to Disneyland cannot be measured against a mom or dad who tucks you in at night and gives you three minutes of hugging, mini-conversation, and real Presence.

Money cannot buy Presence. Presence is a gift freely given. No matter what your financial circumstances, you can choose to be Present.

Physical belongings require energy to manage. Holding onto hurts and old wounds takes energy to nurse or hide. Over-filled calendars steal your T-I-M-E.

When you clear out stuff, heal your heart, and empty your calendar, you'll be less overwhelmed and have more energy. You'll be able to give more to your family. This investment in simplifying will free you up and your life and family will be happier. I promise. Remember, less is more!

CHAPTER 11

TURN Away from Technology

I f you recall from chapter one, technology is a primary way parents check out.

As a review: in the Highlight Magazine 2014 survey, kids said they know their parents are really listening when parents look at them (56 percent), respond (28 percent), and stop doing everything else (11 percent) ("National Survey Reveals 62% of Kids Think Parents Are Too Distracted to Listen").

We can't do any of these things unless we're willing to turn away from our technology for a few moments.

I know a mom who has children under the age of twelve and she loves them. She takes care of them and they do fun things. However, she feels stressed by her children. It's hard to keep up with them. They make messes and get into things. Often they don't mind her. They seem *naughty*.

I've noticed this mother posts to Facebook many times a day. I calculated once how much time she spends posting. She probably doesn't realize how much it is.

Her social media time has set up an unsettling cycle in her family. She checks out with technology because she feels overwhelmed. Her children are running amuck because they want and need her

Presence. This heightens her feeling of being overwhelmed, and the need to check out increases. She thinks the question that needs an answer is, How can I get my kids to _____? But that's not the most useful question.

A far better question would be, How can I manage technology so it doesn't negatively impact my home and family?

WHY IT'S HARD TO TURN AWAY FROM TECHNOLOGY

There's a reason it's hard to turn away from technology. It's not because we're bad parents or even overwhelmed and need a break.

In the '30s and '40s, psychologist B. F. Skinner experimented on rats in a maze. He discovered if a pellet of food were delivered to the rat when it accidentally bumped a lever, the rat would eventually learn to push the lever on purpose to get the treat. The rat would do this over and over again in a process called positive reinforcement.

Here's something else Skinner discovered. If he randomized the treats and didn't give the rat one every time it pushed the lever, the rat would press the lever more often and with greater anticipation. The rats became addicted to the process of pushing the lever even if there wasn't always a pay off (McLeod, "Skinner—Operant Conditioning").

This is a bit like our need for technology. How often in the day do you have the urge to check a social media site in case something interesting or important might be there? How compelled do you feel to answer your phone if it rings or to check a text the minute it comes even if it's not someone you need to respond to now? How often do you want to slump in a comfortable chair and watch television when there's not anything good on? How diligent are you at finding moments when you can work on reaching another game level even if it's not your favorite game?

You, like the rat, have learned to push the lever even if there isn't a treat.

Ken Knapton, an Internet safety expert, proposes a second reason it's easy to overuse technology. Jan Pinborough summarized his comments: "[Technology lacks] the kind of natural boundaries that help us moderate other activities. A child [or adult] stops playing softball when his or her arm gets tired or when it gets too dark to see the ball. It's much easier to ignore the subtle cues that tell us when it's time to stop watching funny animal videos, looking at friends' Facebook photos, or beating the next game level" (Pinborough, "Keeping Safe and Balanced in a Google-YouTube-Twitter-Facebook-iEverything World").

THE TECHNOLOGY PICKLE

Technology can be addictive, and I realized I was becoming addicted. If you're honest, you may find you are too.

As I pondered this technology pickle I found myself in, I decided to look for an answer. I pondered the situation and prayed. It didn't take long to have a thought, but I felt a bit of trepidation. Here was the thought—unsubscribe from most things. Turn off all notifications on Facebook except for your family. Determine a set time for email.

I'll be honest; I had to ruminate on this for a couple of weeks. What would happen? How would I stay abreast? Would I be forgotten? What about my business? It was a tough decision to make. Warily, I began unsubscribing and turned off a few notifications a day. It didn't take long to begin feeling a sense of freedom. I also determined not to look at email, social media, or websites on my computer for the first two hours

> "Technology . . . is a queer thing. It brings you great gifts with one hand, and it stabs you in the back with the other."
> —C.P. Snow, *New York Times*, March 15, 1971

223

of each day. I reserved those hours for things I knew would help me be fruitful and feel successful—prayer, study, thinking, exercise, and so on.

What was the result of this radical move? Well, for one thing, this book. I finally had time to write it. For another, more Present time with my grandchildren, both those close and far away. My husband and I are talking more. We've had a few more dates and have taken short trips.

When I work with parents who are having time issues, I have them track their technology use. They're usually amazed at how much time they give to it. They also usually admit this loss of time is taking its toll on their family life and peace of mind.

Let's look at a few of the ways technology can negatively impact your family.

HOW TECHNOLOGY IMPACTS A FAMILY

1—Technology Makes You Grouchy!

A study done by the Boston Medical Center revealed that parents who get absorbed by email, games, or other apps have more negative interactions with their children.

We all know what this looks like. You're working your way through a pile of email and your three-year-old comes to you, pulls on your shirt, and says, "Daddy, Daddy!" You respond with "Just a minute." The three-year-old pulls on your shirt again, repeating "Daddy, Daddy!" This may occur a few times. You finally turn your head and say "*What!?*" You may yell the word or you use a tone that says, "You're bothering me."

The best of us have done this. We're swimming in technology and well, when we're interrupted, we get cranky!

The Boston Medical Center study was conducted by Dr. Jenny Radesky, a fellow in developmental-and-behavioral pediatrics. Because she's an expert on children's behavior, she was curious as to how the allure of smartphones might affect the quality of time parents and their children spend together.

In the study, she and two other researchers spent one summer observing fifty-five different groups of parents and young children eating at fast food restaurants.

Many of the caregivers pulled out a mobile device right away. Dr. Radesky said, "They looked at it, scrolled on it and typed for most of the meal, only putting it down intermittently" (Radesky, "Patterns of Mobile Device Use by Caregivers and Children During Meals in Fast Food Restaurants").

Radesky points out this wasn't a scientific study, just observation with field notes. Nevertheless, it netted interesting information. Forty of the fifty-five parents used a mobile device during the meal, and many were more absorbed in the device than in the kids.

Radesky and her team reported there were "a lot of instances where there was very little interaction, harsh interaction or negative interaction" between the adults and the children.

Catherine Steiner-Adair is a psychologist and the author of *The Big Disconnect: Protecting Childhood and Family Relationships in the Digital Age*. She commented on the Radesky study:

When you're plugged into your screen the part of your brain that lights up is the to-do list. Everything feels urgent—everything feels a little exciting. We get a little dopamine hit when we accomplish another email—check this, check that. And when a

> **"[Using the phone] is not recommended at the dinner table—a time that we think is valuable to fostering cohesion."**
>
> —Dr. Wendy Sue Swanson, Seattle Children's Hospital

child's waiting by or comes into your room . . . [i]t's very hard as a grown-up to disengage and give them your attention with the [same] warmth that you give them . . . when you're scrambling eggs. (Henn, "When Parents Are The Ones Too Distracted By Devices")

When we're totally engrossed in our technology, it's more difficult to be pleasant and Present.

2—Contributes to Losing the Ability to Relate to Others

Dr. Wendy Sue Swanson of Seattle Children's Hospital commented, "My concern is that if the device use becomes really excessive, and it replaces our day-to-day interactions, then kids won't get much practice with having conversations, reading social cues and responding sensitively to something that the other person expresses" ("Don't Text While Parenting—It Will Make You Cranky").

Kids are little sponges. They absorb what they see and experience from their parents. If parents are fully involved with their digital devices and other technology, kids begin to lose their social role models. What we could get is a generation who texts each other while eating dinner, plays online games while on a date, or talks via text to someone in the same room.

These scenarios aren't so far-fetched. In chapter 1, I related my experience of watching a group of youth sitting together and texting one another. For over ten minutes, not a single word was spoken. No one looked up from their phones to even look at each other.

I was at a restaurant recently, and you cannot imagine how many couples I saw using their phones while eating. The conversations among them were few! Is this how we want the next generation to interact?

Here's an example of the model that's informing kids on how to interact with others. Dr. Radesky remembered a mother placing her phone in the stroller between herself and the baby. Radesky observed, "The baby was making faces and smiling at the mom, and the mom wasn't picking up any of it; she was watching a YouTube video" (Neighmond, "For the Children's Sake, Put Down That Smartphone").

According to Radesky, that type of behavior is a big mistake because the main way children learn is through face-to-face interaction.

"They learn language; they learn about their own emotions, they learn how to regulate them. . . . They learn by watching us how to have a conversation, how to read other people's facial expressions. And if that's not happening, children are missing out on important development milestones" (Neighmond, "For the Children's Sake").

A *Wall Street Journal* article describes "silent fluency" as "the ability to read cues like tone, body language, and facial expressions. E-mail and texts don't convey empathy, tone or subtext the way face-to-face or phone conversations do. We have to learn those things by interacting with real people" (Bauerlein, "Why Gen-Y Johnny Can't Read Nonverbal Cues").

> "Technology: the knack of so arranging the world that we don't have to experience it."
>
> —Max Frisch, novelist

Larry Rosen, a well-known psychologist who has studied the psychology of Facebook interaction, wrote, "Our study showed that real-world empathy is more important for feeling as though you have solid social support" (Larry Rosen, "Why Would Kids Who Spend More Time On Facebook Display More Empathy Online and In Real Life?").

Isn't that what we want in our families? Don't we want our children to feel solidly supported? Don't we want them to be able to support each other? Of course we do. Most of us want this feeling in our family culture but we won't move as easily or effectively in the correct direction unless we model interactions between real people more often than we model interactions with technology.

3—Emotional Distance and Loneliness

Responding to email or scanning Facebook while your kids are attempting to get your attention or are waiting for you to respond can, and often does, change the nature of your relationship with them. This is because they don't feel as important as the device. Who wants to be in second place to the most important people/thing in your world?

That's what happens to kids when parents focus on their digital world first—ahead of their children. There can be deep emotional consequences for the child. There's a feeling of emotional distance and loneliness.

Again from psychologist Catherine Steiner-Adair, "We're behaving in ways that certainly tell children they don't matter, they're not interesting to us, they're not as compelling as anybody, anything, any ping that may interrupt our time with them" (Steiner-Adair, "For The Children's Sake, Put Down That Smartphone").

Steiner-Adair interviewed one thousand children between the ages of four and eighteen to find out about their parents' use of their mobile devices and how the kids felt about it. The words they used over and over again were "sad, mad, angry and lonely" (Neighmond, "For The Children's Sake, Put Down That Smartphone").

A four-year-old called his dad's smartphone a "stupid phone." Children admitted to throwing their parent's phone into the toilet, putting it into the oven, or hiding it. One child said, "I feel like I'm just boring. I'm boring my dad because he'll take any text, any call, anytime—even on the ski lift!" (Neighmond, "For The Children's Sake, Put Down That Smartphone")

Steiner-Adair commented, "One of the many things that absolutely knocked my socks off, was the consistency with which children—whether they were four, eight, or eighteen—talked about feeling exhausted and frustrated and sad or mad trying to get their parents' attention, competing with computer screens or iPhone screens or any kind of technology" (Henn, "When Parents Are the Ones Too Distracted By Devices").

There isn't much research on how these mini-moments of disconnect between a parent and child affects the child long term, but I can make some assumptions based on work I've done with parents who've checked out.

- Kids seem naughty in their attempt to get parents attention

- Kids stop listening and they become harder to motivate or to get to cooperate

- Kids begin to veg out on technology themselves

- Less conversation between parent and child and what conversation there is generally concerns family management

- The number of hugs, kisses, and other types of touch decrease

In short, kids and parents begin to experience an emotional disconnect. This can prove to be problematic as children grow and experience more challenging things, because who can they talk to? It won't be those with whom they feel little connection or trust.

Turning away from technology and getting Present with your children is going to pay huge dividends when they become youth and young adults. In fact, it will impact your long term adult relationship as well.

There's also a sense of isolation and loneliness when technology is too prevalent in a home.

Recently I visited a friend on a Sunday afternoon. Both Mom and Dad had been using their computers before I arrived, one in the study and one at the kitchen table. Their older son was in the family room playing a video game on the TV.

Two young children were lying on their stomachs on the floor, each with an iPad. Their older daughter was in her room talking and texting on her cell phone. Now this is a normal, ordinary family, but these Sunday afternoon activities were isolating, lonely, and de-energizing.

This wouldn't be a problem if it happened on one afternoon, but it is a problem for families if it occurs three or more days a week. We begin to lose our sense of family, the connectedness that gives a child a feeling of stability and support, a sense of belonging and safety.

What if I'd found them reading together or playing soccer in the backyard or watching a movie together? Even if no one spoke a word during the movie, at least they would have been together; possibly sitting on the couch by one another, cuddled in a parent's lap or sitting by a sibling. There would have at least been a sense that this was a family, that they liked each other and enjoyed being together.

Turning away from technology a bit more, and engaging in those things that help us be Present with our children, ramps up the sense of family. It creates a place of belonging and safety; a place where we can go to feel connected and supported.

4—Naughty Children and Weary Parents

A number of children in Radesky's study accepted the lack of engagement from their parents and entertained themselves during the fast food meal, but others acted out in a bid for attention.

This brings me to some unscientific research of my own. I asked the people who read my blog what they would ask if they were sitting at my kitchen table. How could I help them? The responses were all very different but, nevertheless, carried a familiar refrain:

"I'm just trying to figure out how to take care of my family (I have five children) and still be sane and relaxed myself. Maybe you can help me with that."

A joking response came from a dad—"If we could ask you one question, it would be one of the following:

- Can I take a nap?

- [Will] you [come and] stay forever?

- [Will] you take my kids with you when you leave?

- What's wrong with me?

- What's wrong with my kids?

- [Will] you bake me some cookies?

- Is there any ice cream?

We hope this made you laugh as much as it did us. We continue to need help with keeping the anger at bay."

"What can I do to help my kids remember rules and manners . . . there are too many for me to post them on the walls . . . Having to say [the rules] over and over and knowing they know better and yet choose to be rude or disrespectful makes me lose my temper. I'll yell at times. I need to know how to get the rules to stick in their brains! I think if they cared or had the respect they should have then this wouldn't be an issue. What can I do? I've tried so many different things."

"I feel like I need a personal assistant to help me do everything that needs to be done while I watch and correct and teach all of my children."

"The younger set of kids [don't] feel as much responsibility to help, and it requires a LOT of energy from me to get them to do their chores, and so on, and it's not done as well as the older kids learned to do it, because they don't seem to care as much, ugh. Help me fix this."

Despite the difference in each parent's need, here's what stood out to me—All these parents, although they love their kids, are hanging on by a thread.

They're trying to be calm and loving and not yell so much. They feel overwhelmed and a bit angry because their children aren't better behaved, helping more, being obedient, and so on. I have to tell you this is what I hear when I work one-on-one with parents. But listen to this:

When Radesky looked at the patterns in what she and the other researchers were observing, she found kids with parents who were the most absorbed in their devices were more likely to act out to get their parents' attention.

She tells of one group of three boys and their father: "The father was on his cell phone, and the boys were singing a song repetitively and acting silly. When the boys got too loud, the father looked up from his phone and shouted at them to stop. But that only made the boys sing louder and act sillier" (Radesky, "Patterns of Mobile Device Use by Caregivers and Children During Meals in Fast Food Restaurants").

> "Want to be a great parent? Want to raise a happy, healthy, well-behaved kid? Want to live in a home where discipline becomes unnecessary? The secret is to create a closer connection with your child."
>
> —Aha!Parenting.com

I've repeatedly said when you're Present, your children will respond more positively. There will be less need for discipline and consequences. I've observed this when working with families and through watching my children and grandchildren. When parents turn away from technology, and children feel seen and heard, the contention and acting out goes down in the home. I've even seen this happen in troubled relationships between youth and their parents.

Let me share an experience I had over fifty years ago. I was fourteen. I had a sister aged thirteen and another aged twelve. There were five other siblings and we were all crammed into an old station wagon with our mother.

There were no computers, no cell phones, no in-car televisions, no iPads. In this case, the car was the technology absorbing our mother's focus. This story will be a slight stretch, as far as technology goes, but it's a great illustration of the principle I'm trying to teach.

We were moving from Idaho to Utah. Our dad had gone ahead with a big load. Mom had a toddler and an infant in the front seat with her. There were no infant or child seats in those days, and we were all loosey goosey in the car. Are you getting a picture of how distracted our mom would have been?

We three oldest were lying down in the back of the station wagon and had been cramped there for hours. We began teasing one another. Soon the teasing turned into an all out battle with hitting, yelling, and probably a bit of kicking thrown in.

My mom, of course, was yelling from the front seat for us to knock it off. Weren't we old enough to behave ourselves? It didn't do any good. Finally, she pulled off the highway, marched to the back of the car, flipped up the back window and reached in to grab whoever she could catch.

We, of course, were crammed up against the back seat by this time and she couldn't reach any of us. "You girls stop this right now. We have a long way to go and I can't be stopping the car to referee you. For goodness sakes, act your age!"

I'll never forget what happened when she began driving again. Never! It's as clear today as it was over fifty years ago. I looked at Cindy, she looked at me. We both looked at Shirley. Then we smiled and went at it again! Yes, you heard correctly. We deliberately misbehaved!

We were tired. We were bored. Our mother was totally engrossed in driving the car. She was too far up front to have a conversation. There were a bunch of little kids between us and her. We wanted her to pay attention to us, and negative attention was better than no attention.

I'm sharing this story because I want to impress upon your minds that children don't think like adults. They think like kids. It can be so maddening. What in the world was our mother to do anyway? There she was somewhere between Idaho and Utah with a car full of kids and no help. My mom's brain was fully engaged in the to-do portion, and the to-do was getting to where we were going as safely and as quickly as possible. You're probably thinking; "You little brats!"

But we weren't brats. We were good kids. What we needed, whether it was convenient or easy for our mom, was for her to be Present. We wanted to talk with her. We wanted to rest. We wanted to be out of the car. If our mom had been able to let go of the to-do and be Present, she would have seen and heard what we needed.

Possibly she would have stopped in the nearest town and located the city park. The little kids could have run off energy. While feeding the baby, our mom could have talked to us. After all, we were moving and my sisters and I were teens. It was a big deal.

> "Dad showed me that I was important enough to listen to by turning off the television when I wanted to talk. Actions speak much louder than words, especially in the eyes of a child. So, act out your love to your little ones (no matter their age)."
>
> —Hannah Goodwyn, producer

Even if mom had given us fifteen minutes, I know it would have made the final leg of our trip more bearable because of personal experience; my husband was a master at this. It didn't matter where we were going, he had stops planned along the way. If it was warm weather it was a city park; if it was cold, a McDonalds.

When our kids would begin to act out, needing our attention and a break from the trip, he was able to tell them when we'd stop next. When we stopped, he played, hugged, held, and listened. He was a master at *On the Road Presence*. He let our kids know that what mattered wasn't the getting there. What mattered was our family and the fun we could have as we traveled together.

It wasn't convenient to do what he did. He was far wiser, far earlier than I. The whole thing irritated me. Why couldn't we get in the car and get where we were going? Why couldn't our kids behave and act as if they had manners and knew what's what? Why couldn't they?

But my Present husband got it. When you take the time to be Present, it goes a long way to quieting contention, naughtiness, and other problems. When we take the time, despite the inconvenience or frustration, and tune in long enough to hear and see a child, we can sense what the real issue is. It's more often than not something other than the urge to be naughty. When we see what the real issue is behind a behavior, we can determine how to meet the need.

When we're Present we calm contention and help children settle down and behave differently. Turning away from technology to be Present can change a naughty child to a loving child and can ease the weariness of parenting.

KEEPING TECHNOLOGY IN ITS PLACE

With the release of each innovation, there's much to think about. As we embrace new devices, we may not know the toll they're taking on our mental, emotional, and physical health or on our family's sense of connectedness.

What can we do?

Take control of how you spend your time. Take control of your outside interruptions. Make it part of your family dialogue. When will you, your spouse, or the kids be on the computer? How much TV will any of you watch? What family times call for silencing cell phones? Who can use cell phones and where and when? How much Wii or other electronic games will you play? Decide how and when you want to be connected and where and when you want to be interrupted. Make it a choice.

> **"Talk openly about the two-edged sword of innovation."**
>
> —Kerry Patterson, author

Technology boundaries are important in a family. It's helpful for our kids and for us. When we're accountable, it keeps technology in its proper place, and that's never before the people in our family.

Here are suggestions to help you and your family cut back on your technology time.

1. Have a set time when you answer email. I know a mom who realized checking her computer first thing in the morning was messing up her day. She made a decision to turn the computer off each night before bed and leave it off until after noon the next day. It's made a world of difference.

2. Have a time limit when you use email and social media sites. Not only have a scheduled time to view them but give yourself a time limit. I've found the time limit helpful.

3. Be brave. Unsubscribe from a few sites and turn off some notifications. I've discovered I'm not as out of the loop as I feared and no one has forgotten me.

4. Unplug! Have a day, a few times a week, each month, or each year when you completely unplug. At the end of this chapter, I share how one family goes screen-free once a month each year. Yup, a whole month! Unplugging gives your mind a break. It re-energizes you. It puts you back in control.

5. Connect on a personal level. At least once a day, when you feel like sending a text, make a phone call instead. At least a couple of times a month, when you feel like sending an email, send a letter or card. I do this and it's brought me a great deal of satisfaction and it's brought joy to others.

6. Decide on technology-free time. Which regular activities will be technology-free? During those times, turn off all technology, including land line phones as well as cell phones. There are many possibilities—meal time, family reading time, car time, bedtime, and family meeting/activity nights to name a few.

7. Practice being Present at least once a day by putting down your phone, turning away from the computer, or turning off the television when a child needs you.

SIGNS YOU MAY HAVE TROUBLE WITH TECHNOLOGY

In her article "Keeping Safe and Balanced in a Google-YouTube-Twitter-Facebook-iEverything World," Jan Pinborough shared common signs that people have trouble with technology. I adapted her list. Here are questions to ask yourself:

1. Do you leave activities with other people to check your email and other social networking sites? Count all your extra trips to the bathroom!

2. Do you visit the same sites repeatedly in short periods of time?

3. Do you and your family spend most of your time indoors?

4. Do you find it difficult to finish projects or work without stopping to check email or visit other sites?

5. Do you spend more time texting or emailing than spending time in face-to-face interactions with friends?

6. Do you use technology to check out when you're sad, upset, or when you want to avoid an unpleasant task?

7. How often do you find your family members in separate rooms looking at a screen?

8. How often do you find yourself using digital devices to entertain your children rather than engaging with them?

9. Do you check your email first thing in the morning or do you get up in the middle of the night to use your digital devices?

10. Do you spend long periods of time surfing or viewing content that's inappropriate or borderline?

THE SCREEN-FREE EXPERIMENT

What if you went screen-free, as a family, for a *whole month*? Do you think you could do it? Would your family go nuts? Would everyone crack up? Would the fighting increase? Yikes! A whole month!

> "Remember that you alone control your entrance and exit from the world of media and communication technology. Do not let the distractions convince you otherwise."
>
> —Josh Misner, PhD

I know a family that goes screen-free once a year. I got all the details from Courtney, the mom, and I want to share them with you. I think you'll be so impressed that you might consider making this a tradition in your home.

So what is screen-free? No TV, no movies on TV, no computer time, no games on the phone, no screens.

HOW DOES IT WORK?

1. Prepare your kids ahead of time. This particular family goes screen-free in June. They usually begin talking and making plans a month in advance.

2. Presentation is everything. They talk it up. They talk about all the great things they're going to do as a family, how much fun they're going to have together, and the family's reward at the end of the month.

3. Get kids to buy in. As Courtney was telling me how they get their kids to cooperate I said, "Oh, you get them to buy in." She smiled and said, "Well I didn't have a term for it but, yup that's what we do."

They get their kids to buy in by allowing them to pick a reward to have at the end of the month. It has to be a fun family activity. It might be swimming, camping, eating out, going to the movie theater, visiting grandparents, a road trip, whatever the parents want to throw out there. When the kids pick it, plan it, and talk about it—they're *in*.

Here's their one caveat—They don't use screen time as the reward. They don't want to reward *no screen time* with screen time.

4. Parents have to be honest! It's not the kids who struggle the most; it's the parents. They do have to commit. Courtney told me the hard part for her was at lunch. She usually has lunch when the big kids are at school, and her little one is taking a nap. She enjoys reading Facebook, watching a show, and catching up on the news as she eats lunch. It's a challenge to read or call a friend instead.

It's also been challenging for her and her husband in the evening when kids are in bed. They usually veg out a bit in front of the TV but . . . it's screen-free month. She told me they've learned to play games or read to each other. It's become fun.

The one caveat—They do occasionally check email, pay bills online, or prepare church lessons, but no screens for entertainment purposes. The operative word here is *occasionally*.

5. Plan ahead. Get the games out. Check books out of the library. Stock up on popcorn. Know in your mind what you're going to say to your kids. How are you going to direct them when they come and ask to watch TV or a movie? Get prepared.

This family goes screen-free in the summer months because they feel in the winter you're shut in, and it's more difficult to disengage from TV, videos, games, and so on. In the summer, you can get out, walk, go swimming, go to the mountains, and so forth.

THE RESULTS

Courtney said it's a bit hard the first few days because it's a serious transition, but then they settle in. They have a lot of fun. They play together, they talk, and they laugh. She said it's something they look forward to each year.

They feel more connected at the end of their screen-free month. It takes a while for screen time to become important to them again. The break feels good—after the first few days.

In fact, Courtney shared this with me, "Last time we went screen-free our kids wanted to continue for more than a month! And they hardly ever asked when it would be over."

So why not consider it and give it a try? You might find out how much your family enjoys reading, playing games, hiking, or swimming. You might find out how much you like each other, and being Present will have become much easier.

IN SUMMARY

Technology is a boon and a danger. It can bless our family or bring harm. As parents, we have the charge to use technology wisely and to model responsible use to our children. As a family, we need to be accountable to one another so technology stays in its proper place in our home.

Remember, it's not an all-or-nothing proposition. You're not required to take a vow of digital celibacy. You don't have to chuck your devices; you just have to control them so they don't control you.

When you make wise decisions concerning technology use, you free up time for your family. When you turn away from technology to hear, see, and respond to your children, you send the powerful message that they matter. When you manage the technology in your life wisely, your ability to be Present increases. Increased Presence will boost your personal and family happiness level.

CHAPTER 12

CARING for Self = Better Presence

I s self-care and having children mutually exclusive? We often think of taking care of ourselves as being child-free, away from home, in quiet. But if that's the definition of self-care, most moms and dads are going to get precious little of it.

Self-care is crucial for parents because it helps them maintain calm for longer periods of time. Self-care facilitates patience and staves off taking our frustrations out on our children. Self-care helps us remain freer of resentment, exhaustion, or feeling depleted. It keeps us healthier.

Self-care helps us tune into the joy and satisfaction of having children, even during overly busy or chaotic days. It makes it possible for us to remember to be Present, to want to be Present, and then to actually be Present.

Self-care benefits not only us but also our whole family. It's an investment in our family relationships, rather than a selfish indulgence.

We let our children know they matter when we're Present, and being Present requires small amounts of time. This can feel like a big problem if you're a parent who already finds your time limited. Where in the world could you get time for self-care?

> "Self-care is never a selfish act – it is simply good stewardship of the only gift I have, the gift I was put on earth to offer to others."
>
> —Parker Palmer, author, educator, and activist

We're all guilty of using the time excuse as our reason to neglect ourselves, but we've talked about the need to take full responsibility for how our lives look—to stop blaming other people, circumstances, money, or time. Self-care is a choice.

In this chapter, I want to look at self-care differently (rather than just getting away from it all). I want to help you understand how you can care for yourself while in the thick of parenting. We'll look at seven areas of self-care. You won't see some of them on standard lists but they work. They apply to both moms and dads.

SEVEN WAYS TO CARE FOR SELF

1—TALK NICELY TO YOURSELF

Think and talk nicely to and about yourself. We would rarely speak to others, even those who are messing up, the way we talk to ourselves. Pay attention to what you say and how you say it. I cannot express the importance of this one step. It will change everything! It's magic when it comes to helping you parent well and be Present.

As Carol M. Colvin, life coach, stated, "When we say things like 'I'm such a loser,' 'I'm an awful mother or father,' 'I'm so fat,' or 'I'm just not good enough,' we do devastating damage to our souls. If we continue to think and speak negatively about ourselves over time, we'll find that we've eroded our self-esteem and extinguished our inner light."

> "Lighten up on yourself. No one is perfect. Gently accept your humanness."
>
> —Deborah Day, author of *Be Happy Now*

You need to be your own best friend, no matter *how* you're

doing presently. Best friends speak kindly to each other and are honest and support one another, even if one of them is floundering. It's self-care when you treat yourself like your own best friend.

I make it a habit to rephrase any negative words or thoughts immediately. For example—if I say, "I'm so impatient," I immediately rephrase and say out loud, "I work to be patient and I'm making progress." It won't always feel true. Rephrase anyway. The most powerful voice in the world is your own, so rephrase out loud.

I made myself a "Who I Am" poster. I copied a drawing of a woman from the Internet. I picked a drawing that looked like the kind of woman I felt I wasn't but wanted to be—perky and cute. Next, I did some free writing. I wrote all the things I wished I was inside the body of the woman. I wrote exactly what came to my mind without judging the thoughts.

Each day I would stand in front of my poster, strike the pose of the woman, and repeat all of those amazing qualities. It felt so weird at first! After all, it was clear I didn't currently exhibit many of these qualities, but I was also fully willing to accept that these were my actual strengths in embryo.

I did this little exercise for well over a year. It felt better and better. Those qualities felt truer and truer. But here's when this little exercise in self-care was the most powerful:

When I messed up, I would march myself to my poster, take that perky, happy pose, and recite all those qualities that were mine, even those in embryo. With tears streaming down my face or anger in my heart or dislike of self coursing through me, I would repeat them loudly and with conviction.

As I repeated the attributes, I accepted that this is who I am despite my weaknesses and my errors in judgment or my occasional poor choices and behavior. By the time I was done reciting, I would feel better. I would be able to do whatever I needed to do to make the situation right. Apologize. Forgive. Pray for a better solution, whatever the need.

I still have that poster in my office where I see it daily. Whether I'm doing well or poorly, I'm reminded of who I am! These are the thoughts that I want to hang on to each day as I work toward becoming the best person I can be. Those attributes are what I replace my negative thoughts with.

There are few things that you can do that will help you care for yourself as powerfully as speaking kindly and with respect to yourself and about yourself, even when, in your mind, you least deserve it.

2—PUT DOWN EMOTIONAL WEIGHT

A young lady confidently walked around the room while explaining stress management to an audience. With a raised glass of water everyone knew she was going to ask the ultimate question, *half empty or half full?* Well, she fooled them all.

"How heavy is this glass of water?" she inquired with a smile. The answers called out ranged from eight ounces to twenty ounces. The young woman replied, "The absolute weight doesn't matter. It depends on how long I hold it. If I hold it for a minute, that's not a problem. If I hold it for an hour, I'll have an ache in my right arm. If I hold it for a day, you'll have to call an ambulance. In each case, it's the same weight, but the longer I hold it, the heavier it becomes."

What was being demonstrated is called emotional weight. Emotional weight is what we generate when we have things we know we should do, but we put them off.

When we carry a lot of emotional weight we tend to feel weary, overwhelmed, and resentful. It can manifest as anger. This anger frequently spills onto our children when the pot gets too full.

Here are four short stories to help you *see* emotional weight.

Story 1—A few months ago there were things in my business I needed to do but they took skills I felt I didn't have. I was intimidated to learn these skills. I felt it was going to take too much time. So even though I knew I needed these skills, I put it off, day after day. I did other things instead that filled the time and felt like real work but didn't move my business forward. Like the glass of water example, the burden of this emotional weight got heavier and heavier.

Eventually I made myself start. I picked one small thing and moved forward. It wasn't as hard as I thought. In fact, part of it was enjoyable. I've had a fair amount of success. I haven't done a perfect job but I am getting better. I feel happy with myself. Walking into my office has ceased to feel burdensome and overwhelming.

Story 2—I hadn't cleaned my bathroom for a long time. Although I knew it needed to be cleaned, I kept putting it off, choosing to do other things I felt were more important.

One day, as I prepared for a shower, I thought again, "Man, you need to get this bathroom clean!" I observed hair in all the corners, grunge on the sink, the stain around the base of the toilet.

I stepped into the shower and I noticed the bottom fourth of the shower curtain was orange. I'd been watching this colony of bacteria grow and each time I took a shower I would say to myself, "You have got to clean this bathroom!" Then I remembered all the things I had to do (what it was going to take to get it done), and the slight sense of being overwhelmed would descend. I would put it off.

However, on this day I took one small step to lay down the emotional weight of the dirty bathroom. I stepped out of the shower dripping wet, grabbed the spray cleaner, which sits behind the toilet, and I sprayed the heck out of the bottom fourth of my shower curtain. I didn't need to clean the whole bathroom to get a feeling of satisfaction. For now this one step was enough.

The next morning I saw a perfectly white curtain. The colony was gone! The room wasn't clean but there was improvement. I had picked one thing I knew would make a difference and I did it. The burden was gone and I felt much lighter.

Story 3—Recently, I attended a women's conference. I listened to amazing speakers. I took lots of notes. I starred ideas that would bless my family, business, and myself.

> "Sometimes you don't feel the weight of something you've been carrying until you feel the weight of its release."
>
> —Unknown

When I got home, I put the notes on my desk and there they sat. I wanted to follow through on the things I knew would make a difference, but there were so many items with stars by them. It felt overwhelming because after being gone for a couple of days I had catching up to do. I had picked up a new emotional weight.

Eventually, I chose one thing from the list and did it. It was the easiest and quickest thing on the list. Since then I've been able to check other items off the list. I still have a number of things to do but I've made headway. The emotional weight is gone.

Story 4—I have a sister who's two years younger than me and we have a sister between us. We were all born in February. Although we're now in our sixties, my sister Shirley is still bothered by how she remembered us celebrating our birthdays. She remembered Cindy and I had our own birthdays but she had to celebrate hers, which fell later in the month, with us. This was her memory and she has carried the weight of feeling left out and unnoticed for over sixty years.

She knew she needed to work it out but she hung on to the story. This year she took a step towards laying down that emotional weight. She asked her five sisters what their experiences were.

I remembered having two great parties. All the rest were family dinners. Cindy remembered one party. The younger girls remember mostly family dinner celebrations. Shirley was amazed at how different her memories were from what the rest of us experienced.

After she got feedback from all of us, she finally worked out her feelings. She let it go. She lay down the emotional weight.

When we care about ourselves, we look at the things that are causing us pain, and we do what needs to be done to put the weight of them down. Putting down emotional weight is a healing form of self-care.

THE COST OF EMOTIONAL WEIGHT

- It steals your feelings of happiness
- It depletes your energy
- It feels heavy, both physically and mentally
- It creates a feeling of being overwhelmed
- It builds stress

- It causes illness
- It breeds feelings of anger, which are often taken out on others
- It causes weight gain

These are a few of the possible outcomes of carrying emotional weight. Here are six steps to help you put down emotional weight.

SIX STEPS TO PUT DOWN EMOTIONAL WEIGHT

A—Begin! Commit to one action you can take immediately. Exercise your power of choice over the situation, whatever it is. Choose to get things moving right now.

This is the key to taking care of all the *big* issues in life. It doesn't matter if it's maintaining our relationships, working out our money problems, finding the need for more education, learning to care for ourselves, getting control of our thoughts and emotions, overcoming an addiction, cleaning our house, or being Present . . . it doesn't matter. The process works. You have to choose to begin.

> **"The way to get started is to quit talking and begin doing."**
>
> —Walt Disney

You might have to make adjustments. It might take a bit more time than you want it to, but I assure you the relief you'll feel from starting is fantastic. There will be a sense of satisfaction.

B—Break it into smaller steps. You don't have to clean the whole room for it to appear, feel, and be cleaner. You don't have to implement all your new ideas or learn everything required for a task to feel satisfaction. You don't have to clean out your whole emotional house to begin feeling better and lighter.

The first step doesn't have to be the biggest thing in your messy room, just something that will make a difference, help you feel better, and give you hope that yes, in time, you'll have the whole room clean.

The first small step might be admitting we do have enough time, or that we're strong enough. We aren't victims and we have the power to choose our response to what happens in our lives.

C—Be consistent and don't quit. If you mess up, keep going. Don't beat yourself up. It's counterproductive. Let it go and begin again. It doesn't matter how often you must begin again. Just do it and don't quit!

D—Accept the time line. You can't always fix or do everything at once. Understand how real progress happens. Real progress comes from building on a solid, consistent, 1 percent improvement or movement, over time. However, we tend to live with and accept the 100% devil, who says if we aren't doing it all right now, in just the right way, we're not going to get a good result. That's a lie! Pick one thing on your list that feels weighty, break it down, and work on it. Take one step. Then take another.

Time and consistency are required to take care of most things. Commit to giving any issue time and be consistent. Don't allow discouragement and don't quit! **Time doesn't equal failure. It equals eventual success.**

E—Celebrate! Fill yourself with recognition for any accomplishment, of any kind, at any level—acknowledge your successes, however small! After I sprayed the shower curtain I danced into the bedroom. I went to sleep with a smile on my face. I felt terrific!

There are amazing results from laying down emotional weight. You'll feel overwhelmed less often, and things will no longer look dim and dark. Rather, life will be bright again; you'll experience a sense of inner expansion.

Can you see how nurturing it is to get rid of the emotional weight you're carrying? When we take responsibility for how our life looks, we open ourselves up to putting down emotional weight.

3—AVOID THE SUCKER'S CHOICE

Have you ever wondered how you could resolve issues in your home more creatively so everyone was happy? It often seems in order to get what we need, someone else has to give up what they need, and often it's the parent.

The Sucker's Choice is a choice between two alternatives, with the false premise that they're the only options available. Often both options seem bad. Don't be sucked in and pick one of them. There's *always* a third alternative, and you can find it with a little creative problem-solving. Remember, holding positive stories in our mind tends to open up our ability to see options.

HOW TO AVOID MAKING THE SUCKER'S CHOICE

A. Work on you first. You're likely to benefit by improving your own approach and you're the only person you can work on anyway. I use prayer to figure out where I might need to adjust my perspective, my response, or my behavior. Pondering and meditation are also helpful.

B. Get your heart in the right place. Treat other people as people and not as problems that need to be solved. Have a desire to have a win-win rather than an I-win-you-lose outcome!

C. Stay focused on the matter at hand. Don't get lost in past experiences, behaviors, or problems.

D. Avoid settling for either/or. Ask the hard questions.

- "What do I really want?"
- "What do I want for the other person?"
- "What do I want for the relationship?"
- "How would I behave if I truly wanted these results?"

From the book *Crucial Conversations* we learn, "When we present our brain with a demanding question, our body sends precious blood to the parts of our brain that help us think, and away from the parts of our body that make us want to fight" (Patterson et al, *Crucial Conversations*).

However, when we're presented with a Sucker's Choice, a situation where a problem seems to have only two solutions, our brain restricts blood flow, which makes it hard to think creatively. The Sucker's Choice keeps us stuck in ineffective strategies.

Let me share an example:

My daughter had her fourth baby a few years ago and suffered postpartum depression. To combat the effects, she decided to exercise by taking a brisk walk in the morning. She has four children, so how do you think that went?

Here's an example of a walk I took with them. Jack and Mary took off running! *This walk will be fast*, I thought.

Soon they reached our neighbor's home with a ramp. It was up the ramp and down the ramp at a full run.

Next was the cement retaining wall. It had to be climbed on and carefully followed by little feet. If anyone fell off, they felt they had to go back to the beginning and start again.

Next was the yard with all the kids. Stop and chat. Let's see what they're doing. Let's join in!

And dogs! Every dog had to be spoken to and if it was a happy dog, petted. *Every* dog! I never realized how many dogs we have in our neighborhood!

Then there were the treasures. A walk is all about the treasures, which have to be picked up, examined, and stowed in the stroller to be carried home—stones, sticks, leaves, gum wrappers, and so forth.

Halfway around the block, Mary's little legs began to wear out. Remember, they covered the first half at a full run (disregarding all the stops) and she was only two. So it was into the stroller. The key to knowing when she wanted in the stroller was the phrase, "*Wait, wait, wait!*"

We would press on for two minutes (I do not exaggerate here) and she would need to get out. The key phrase to know when she needed to get out was a clear, *"Stop, stop, stop!"*

> **"Your life is a result of the choices you make. If you don't like your life it is time to start making better choices."**
>
> —Inspirational Quotes, November 23, 2015

Did you get the timing on this little exercise that lasted for the second half of our walk: into the stroller for 2 minutes or less, out of the stroller for two minutes or less.

Can you see how frustrating this walk would be to my daughter who needed sustained exercise?

She had a couple of obvious choices:

- Don't take a walk
- Be frustrated and get angry with the kids and make them stay in the stroller.

In the first case, Jodie loses. In the second, the kids lose. So how did she solve the situation she was facing?

First she asked, "What do I want?" She did need and want to exercise so she could return to good health, and she did not want to be frustrated.

Next she asked, "What do I want for my kids?" She knew she didn't want to be yelling at them. She wanted them to enjoy the walk. She realized she wanted to avoid jeopardizing the relationship she has with her children by being angry with them for natural, childlike behaviors.

She knew if these were things she wanted, she would need to find a way to help her children understand her need for a sustained walk. She would also need to allow them to take a walk the way a child walks.

She asked the rest of the pivotal questions posed above and set her brain working to come up with at least a third alternative. She made a list:

- Get a babysitter
- Trade exercise days with another mom who also wanted a sustained walk
- Walk when her husband got home and could watch the children
- Get up before the children and walk. (They were up at 5:30 a.m. sometimes!)

None of these options appealed to her because they were not realistic for her family situation for many reasons. So she kept thinking and pondering what she wanted and didn't want, and here's what she finally came up with—Mom's Walk and Kid's Walk.

If it was a Mom's Walk, kids stayed in the stroller and Mom would walk fast. If it was a Kid's Walk, kids could get in and out of the stroller and they would go slow. Even her two-year-old could understand and accept this.

Here's how it played out at her home. Each morning was Mom's Walk. If they walked in the afternoon, which they did at least twice a week, it was Kid's Walk.

Her children were happy with the arrangement. She's wasn't frustrated and her health and outlook improved significantly. Relationships were strengthened. They experienced happiness.

As you work on recognizing when you're facing a Sucker's Choice and working at creative solutions to your family's problems,

- Don't expect perfection.
- Aim for progress.
- Celebrate successes—When you come up with a successful solution, celebrate.
- Cast out discouragement—Take pleasure in knowing you and your family are improving.
- Keep trying!

Can you see how the Sucker's Choice can be hard on family relationships? Can you see how learning to avoid the Sucker's Choice would feel nurturing? When we want to nurture ourselves, we do what will bring us happiness and peace. We take steps to keep harmony in our lives. We make better choices. Avoiding the Sucker's Choice helps us achieve those things.

4—CARVE OUT ALONE TIME AT HOME

Most of us aren't going to get away from home often. It can be challenging to take a few days away with a spouse. Babysitters aren't cheap. Even going shopping alone can be tricky. So how can your bedroom, your bathroom, or the far end of your house help you get quality free time away from your kids?

When I work with parents, I ask them to come up with experiments in order to get specific outcomes. I use the term experiment because it attaches nothing to the result. An experiment is just that, an experiment. You do it to see if you can get the outcome you want. If you don't, instead of beating yourself up for having another failure, you try a new experiment.

Here are three examples of experiments that had great results. They're about moms but this applies equally well to dads.

Experiment 1—Deon was feeling burnt out and needed a way to have space away from her family when she felt over the top. In one of our conversations, she told me about her bedroom. It had a lovely window seat that looked out onto a green field. The problem was it was the messiest room in her home. So together we came up with a list of things that she could easily do to make it an inviting space.

She cleared all the stuff off of the window seat and got a basket for her husband to put his stuff in—so it would stay cleaned off. She made changes in how they managed the laundry, so it wasn't always piled on her bed. She painted a wall. She added her favorite books to the window seat.

Deon talked with her family. She told them that when it became difficult to react the way she wanted, she was going to her room to regroup for five minutes. She asked for their support in allowing her to do this when she needed to. They all agreed to help her out. (Yes, she does have a couple of small children.)

When Deon is on the verge of exploding or ceasing to be the adult, she retreats to her bedroom. She sits in the window seat and looks out on the field. She breathes deeply; she may read one or two paragraphs in her book. Then she heads back out into the fray. She's managing better, her kids are happier, and her husband is relieved. This experiment has had a positive impact on all of them.

Experiment 2—Amy has multiple health issues that tax her strength and resources for parenting. She expressed her desire for alone time each week so she could paint and write, feel better, and get a handle on her health.

Finding time wasn't her only issue. She also has a child with serious health problems. Amy worried that if she took time away from her family, something might come up with her ill child and her husband wouldn't be able to handle it.

Nevertheless, she was willing to try an experiment. She asked her husband if he would take over for two hours a week, in the evening, so she could write or paint. He was open to the idea.

Amy chose a room at the other end of the house, away from the family room where her husband and children would spend their time. That way she could have her quiet time and be close at hand in case of an emergency.

The first week was a grand success. Amy was frankly impressed with her husband and was surprised that he managed so well without her. She was equally surprised that her kids managed without her.

She's been doing this for a while now. It's given her husband an opportunity to be with the kids, and she's been able to fulfill her need to write, paint, and have time to herself. The whole family is happier.

Experiment 3—Melanie has a large family, and her husband is often gone.

She wants time to be by herself and read. She asked me how I find time to read, because I raised a large family and now my grand-kids live upstairs.

I mentioned to her that my bathroom was my retreat. That surprised her; I mean really, the bathroom for your retreat? Who does that?

In my home, it's the only practical place. I live in a one-bedroom apartment. The living room, office, and kitchen run the length of the house and are, for all intents and purposes, one room. The bedroom's right off that part of the house, and you can hear the TV. The way the bathroom is situated makes it a perfect alone space. When I was raising my children, it was also the only practical place. Kids were in all the other rooms!

I shared the simple things I've done to make it a sanctuary. A beautiful picture hangs on the wall. My favorite colors are in the shower curtain and rugs. A vase of flowers and candles sits on the tub for decoration. Most important, there's a basket of fabulous books.

When I go into the bathroom, which is at least three times a day, I read one to three paragraphs. Occasionally I'm lucky and get a whole page. You'd be amazed at how much you can read in a year, one to three paragraphs at a time.

Melanie decided to give it a try. One of her worries was that her bathroom was always so messy because of the kids. When she began putting it to rights, she discovered that almost all of the clutter was hers. She devised simple systems to keep her stuff corralled. She added flowers, a new rug, and a basket of books.

At last report, she was enjoying her mini-moments of peace and reading. It has made her feel more taken care of, and she's happier with her children.

When we're looking for alone time, we need to get creative. How can it be managed right where we are, without expending too much money or time? How can it be made doable even with small children? There's always a way to care for yourself right where you are.

When you feel cared for, you're more likely to be Present for someone else.

5—SLEEP

This is one of my favorite subjects. I've had tons of experience with this one thing!

I was a night owl. I would be up until 11:00 or 12:00 p.m. getting kids managed and into bed and putting the house back together. Afterward, I read until somewhere between 11:00 p.m. and 2:00 a.m. In the morning, I would drag myself out of bed at 6:00 or 7:00, depending on when my kids got up.

How do you think that worked out? I'll bet some of you know. It was a disaster. It's virtually impossible to parent well and be Present when you can barely see for lack of sleep.

If you had asked me, I would have told you I was busy and there wasn't enough time to get a good night's sleep. I might have said I had to stay up late to have time for myself. I believed these stories because they felt true. But they weren't true! I was choosing to be up late (Except when I had a baby and we all know what that's like!).

Periodically, over a thirty-year period, I would go in prayer and ask how I could get a better handle on my life. I would always have the same

> **"Exhaustion makes wimps out of all of us."**
>
> —James E. Loehr, performance psychologist and author

thought, *Go to bed earlier and get up earlier*. And just as regularly, I would dismiss the whole idea. I didn't want to follow that counsel. I wanted my house in order and I wanted alone time. I was convinced the only way to get either one was to stay up late. So I resisted.

After years, I got desperate. I asked a final time. The impression was the same. "Go to bed earlier and get up earlier." But this time, I didn't resist.

I made the decision I would go to bed earlier and get up earlier. Can I say it was *hard*?! It didn't get easier after the first month, or the sixth, or even the ninth. I'll be honest; I struggled for a full year to keep my commitment before it finally began to feel good. But I'd made a decision. I was choosing something different. It was about taking care of self.

I've been living this new way for quite a while now, and it's been amazing. I enjoy going to bed earlier and getting up earlier. I can't even believe it myself! My thinking is clearer. I get to do things that make my day more productive—prayer, personal study, meditation. My whole day runs better. I remain calm more often. I have more patience, and I feel less stress.

I frequently have children asleep in my living room. They're so used to hearing me up at 5:00 a.m. they don't wake up anymore. They keep on sleeping and I do my thing. Really, this is doable!

It's doable even if your kids get up at 5:30 a.m. You may not get the quiet morning routine. Your day will begin earlier. These are the hard facts. What will make this trade off worthwhile is how you'll feel during the day. You may have less alone time, but you'll find it easier to be Present. You'll find yourself feeling happy more often. You'll like yourself and your children better.

I recommend you begin going to bed at least thirty minutes earlier than you do now, an hour if you can commit to it. Don't get on the computer after 10:00 p.m. This will absolutely help you get to bed earlier! Going to bed earlier will change your days! Nevertheless, some of you will resist.

If you do resist, it will come up over and over again, until you finally get desperate for a way to feel better as a parent, to feel calmer, more in control, more patient, happier, and healthier. When that time comes, you'll remember this counsel and hopefully you'll take it. It won't be easy, but if you remember that simple things, consistently done over time, make *big* differences, you'll be able to persevere as long as it takes to make this your new habit.

6—EAT WELL

Can I say, *stop* eating over the sink! Stop calling the crusts of your children's sandwiches lunch. *Stop.* Make a better choice. Fix your food and sit down with your kids and eat. Have a mini-conversation. Laugh a bit. Savor that sandwich. It takes five minutes! Value yourself enough to sit down with a plate and eat.

I know you'll have to make a dozen trips to the kitchen, but you'll feel more nourished if, in between trips, you're sitting down.

Eat dinner as a family. Get the support of your spouse. Cook together, at least a few times a week, so mealtime feels less heavy and more fun.

When you're on the go with your kids, go prepared. Have a basket or sack of healthy snacks you can grab as you run for the car. Keep it in the pantry ready to go. It will help you avoid fast food and grumpy kids.

If you work away from home, take a lunch. This was a hard lesson for me to learn, but if I can learn it, you can learn it. I think about what I need to do for lunch before I go to bed. If I can, I prepare it before going to bed. If not, I get up a bit earlier. It's not about time. I have less time than even a few years ago. It's a decision, and I've made it, to care for myself by eating well.

Don't eat at your computer, either at home or the office. I know you're busy, but if you want to feel cared for, leave your desk. Turn on music as you eat. Sit outside if the day is warm. Even the break room and a coworker trump your desk.

Eating well should be at the top of your self-care list. It's something you can do while in the thick of parenting. Taking time to eat is one of the ways you maintain the energy to do the job you've taken on—the job of raising a family. If you give yourself this time, you'll be more motivated to be Present with your children. Besides, eating with your kids is one of the touchpoints that helps you practice being Present.

7—EXERCISE

Oh man, I don't like to exercise. I can't think of any exercise I like except swimming. But that requires a drive in the car and wet hair. Ick!

Frankly, I also believed I didn't have the time. But as I've said, when we take full responsibility for our lives, we stop using the time excuse.

Recently, my daughter and her husband decided to exercise. They have four young children. Time is an issue. So were the amount of children they have and the amount of work it takes to get them up and going in the morning. But they took responsibility for their well-being and didn't use the time excuse.

To make it happen, they both got up earlier. One went to the gym while the other got kids up and dressed. When Mom got home Dad would go to the gym and Mom would take over wherever he had left off in child care. It worked out for them for a good long time. It wasn't easy, but they had made a decision to exercise and together they made it happen.

Another way she exercised, my daughter and I left the house for a walk at 6:00 a.m. for well over a year. We walked six days a week for thirty minutes a day, consistently. Our husbands held down the fort until we got home. It wasn't easy to get up and get going early, especially in the bleak Utah winter, but we made the choice to exercise. Now that my book is done and I'm not writing at four in the morning, we've begun again.

I know half a dozen women who walk their kids to school daily. They're in a big group talking, laughing, and making it work.

I can think of another three women who get up early and head out together. They've made deals with their husbands to get kids fed so they can have this half hour before they need to send them out the door to school. They walk five days a week.

I recall one mom who did her exercising in front of the TV with a child on her back. You do whatever it takes.

I know a couple of dads who get up early to exercise; afterward, it's home to help Mom get kids off to school and then leave for work.

There are a few families that exercise after school. One family rides their bikes as long as the weather permits, each evening. Another family goes to the recreation center and swims three times a week.

None of this is easy. We all have to make time. Most of you reading this book have kids. You just need to make a decision to do it. It's a choice that, when made, feels nurturing.

Talk to your spouse. What can you do? How can you make it work? Now do it. Remember simple things, done consistently over time make *big* differences. If you can't run, walk. If you can't exercise daily, give it two or three days a week. If you can't get thirty minutes, commit to fifteen.

When you care for yourself in this way, you'll want to be Present with your children more often. You'll have more energy for it. And sometimes you can exercise with them and be Present at the same time.

IN SUMMARY

You're going to spend far more time with your children than you're going to spend without them, so it's imperative to learn how to self-care while you're in the thick of parenting. It's simple, it's doable, and it takes small amounts of time and virtually no money; but it can and will pay huge dividends. Nurturing yourself while you're doing your job of parenting is going to help you be in a place mentally where you can and will be Present more often.

Self-care can be as simple and plain as having a cup of herbal tea while you read to your children. It might be taking a few deep breaths while soothing a screaming child. You could turn on your favorite music and dance in the living room with your kids. Add laughter!

Self-care can be taking a walk with your children to take the edge off the day. Sitting in the swing and watching your children play can give you fresh air and a breather from all that you're feeling pressed to do. Go to the bathroom more often if that's what will buy you a few moments alone.

When you're on the edge of losing your temper, getting irritable, or feeling resentful, ask yourself what you need to stay in control. Pay attention to yourself.

I can vividly recall knowing when I was going to stop being the adult. It was almost always when I had pushed myself for too long, too hard, or was too tired. What I needed was to *stop* before I got to that place.

In those younger years, I didn't stop and the result was inevitable. If you find yourself moving to that place, *stop*. Stop working. Stop trying to explain, teach, reprimand, and so on. *Stop*. Sit down. Hug a child. Breathe deeply. Get a drink of water. Walk out to the yard. Be alone for three to five minutes.

Do something that will feel nurturing to you. Give yourself space to get it together. When you pay attention to how you're feeling, to what's happening in your body, that's self-care. This can be done while you're in the thick of parenting.

You're reading this book because you want to be Present with your kids. You want relationships that will stand the test of time and growth and the upheaval that come with both.

You can place yourself in a position to be Present more often when you take care of yourself—when you give yourself sleep, meals that feel nurturing, and when you move your body (and not only while you clean).

Learning to make wiser choices by avoiding the Sucker's Choice will keep you in win-win situations with your spouse and children. Laying down emotional weight and finding time to be alone right where you are go a long way to helping you have the energy to be Present.

Being kind to yourself will make life feel lighter, and your relationships will improve. You'll feel happier overall. Your self-esteem will go up. You'll be a better, more Present parent.

In short, when you care for yourself, you care for your family.

CHAPTER 13

BLESSED Are Your Eyes for They See—A Summary

I was listening to Tony Bennett on the radio. He's a singer from my mother's era and my era and, regardless of your age, from your era. He has never stopped singing. At age eighty-nine, he released a new album.

When he was ten years old, he would stand in front of his family—aunts, uncles, and cousins—who would gather at his home each Sunday for a meal, and he would sing. They told him, "We love how you sing." Tony Bennett said, "This lit a passion in me that exists to this day."

In this radio broadcast, at age eighty-nine, he commented, "I think I can get better [at singing] and I'm always searching for it" (National Public Radio Staff, "The Songs Never Die").

Imagine feeling you could still better your craft at age eighty-nine. I found his words inspiring and I believe it's true of this work we call parenting. No matter where we are in our parenting, we can get better at it.

I've always believed the family is the perfect classroom for becoming kinder, charitable, joyful, forgiving, Present, and in the end, wiser.

It doesn't matter how long you've been parenting, a few months or many years. It doesn't matter if you have all teens, many small children, or if your children have left home to build their own lives. It doesn't matter if you've never had children of your own.

We all parent and we continue to parent for our entire lives. As the great singer Tony Bennett said, "I think I can get better at it, and I'm always searching." I think we can all get better at it!

A LIFE-CHANGING MOMENT

When I was in my early forties, I had a remarkable experience that changed my life. At the time, my children ranged from ages two to twenty. Some were struggling. Our whole family was in upheaval. I felt like a failure much of the time. My husband felt the same.

One day I was driving down a quiet street going on a mundane errand. I was, miraculously, alone. My mind wasn't focused on any particular thing. I was driving and relishing the quiet.

Off to my right, as I glanced down the street, I saw a small girl, possibly four years old, skipping along towards me. She had bouncy curls and was wearing a dress and with each skip, they both puffed up. I saw her sweet little face and feet as she firmly planted each step.

Without warning, I was in a different place. I have no words to describe it. I *saw* that child as I had never seen another human being. It was as if she was clothed in a light that had previously been hidden from me.

It was overpowering, and I cannot express the feeling that filled my breast. I began weeping. It took time to get control of the emotions coursing through me.

I had been given a gift. I had seen the beauty of another human being. She was far more beautiful and precious than I had ever imagined any person could be.

I loved my children. I desired to parent them well but I was frequently lost in the doin' it, doin' it, doin' it. I couldn't clearly see or hear them. I found it challenging to be Present as often as I needed to be, but this experience changed me.

I didn't stop yelling that day or even that year. I didn't cast off my feeling of being overwhelmed, my disappointments, or my poor parenting behaviors all at once. It took time. But what sustained me was the vision of the beauty of a soul. I knew I wanted to be able to see and hear whether I was dealing with my child or any one of God's children, regardless of their age.

Since that day I've known without any question that I can and need to get better at being Present. I'm always practicing and learning. I know that no matter where you are in your parenting strengths or weakness, you can get better at it too. Keep trying, never quit. Give it all the time you need because, in reality, you have a lifetime for learning to become a great parent—a Present parent!

YOU AREN'T DOING AS BADLY AS YOU THINK

A mother emailed me after participating in a webinar on becoming a Present parent. She said, "It's a bit overwhelming because it seems like it's all about me, like I have to be in charge of it all." Well, you do have to be totally in charge—of yourself. It would be overwhelming if you thought you were responsible for your children's and spouse's choices, intentions, and responses, but you aren't. You're only responsible for your own.

You can't control another human being, not really, but you can and should control you. When you decide to take charge of *how* you are with your children, life gets better because you will be better.

However, knowing you're responsible for you isn't enough. You also need to know you aren't doing as badly as you think, no matter how it feels or looks. Knowing this is important because we can move forward better from a place of hope.

I have a friend whose mother died last year. It was a long and painful year for her and her family. They uprooted themselves and headed to a new state so she could help her dad and mom and be there at the end. It caused upheaval for their large and growing family. She was often preoccupied, sad, and discouraged. It was, in short, a hard year.

She felt bad and kept repeating that she should have been able to handle it better. Oh my, I hear that a lot from parents. We all feel that we should be handling it better, whatever *it* is.

Here's a post she wrote on her Facebook page when it was all said and done:

"A few months ago I apologized to my children for shutting down and checking out last year when we were in Utah visiting my mother as she died a little every day. My daughter piped up "Mom, you still did _____ , and we still _____ . It wasn't that bad."

Ladies, we're doing better than we think.

"It wasn't all that bad." I think my children, despite our significant heartaches, losses, trials, and occasional loneliness would say the same—It wasn't all that bad.

I know that as I think back on my family [of origin] and all the difficulty we went through and the imperfections of my parents I can soundly say—It wasn't all that bad." Liz B.

It wasn't *all that bad* because there were moments of Presence. The family made an effort to connect. She knows this is true because her children reminded her.

Despite how it may look or feel, you aren't doing as badly as you think. Children are resilient. But we can all do better. We need to pick the best 1 percent and begin.

PRESENCE IS A KEY TO MAKING LIFE BETTER

A key to making our family life better is to take the advice of Eckhart Tolle. "Most people treat the present moment as if it were an obstacle that they need to overcome. Since the present moment is Life itself, it's an insane way to live" (Tolle, "Quotes"). So get Present. See your family and your individual children now, right where you are. Hear them. See them. Take a few moments daily to be Present.

When we learn to be Present as our day unfolds, no matter what it dishes out to us, it completely changes our responses to our children and positively impacts our relationship with them. I can't resist sharing another story to help you visualize what I want you to understand and internalize.

A few years ago I was sitting at the table watching Mary. She had a small bowl of popcorn and was happily eating it. Every bite or so she would look up and give me a coy little smile. I would smile back and eat a piece of my popcorn.

After a few more bites and coy smiles, Mary got up, toddled over to me, and lifted her face for a kiss. I gave her one, and she went back to the popcorn. She took another bite, gave me that shy, coy smile, got up again, and came over for another kiss. We repeated this little drama a number of times. What made this peaceful, joyous, and gentle moment so remarkable was what had transpired twenty minutes earlier.

In our kitchen was a large bucket of thick honey. It came from my own bees and had no water added, so it was very thick and sticky. I saw that bucket earlier and thought to myself, *Hmm, that lid isn't on there tight.* Then like any busy parent, I went on my way.

Later, Mary came into the living room dripping honey from head to foot! I let out a shriek, grabbed her up, and ran for the tub. I put her under the faucet, clothes and all, as I fussed, "Mary, what did you do? Why were you in the kitchen? Just look at this mess!" and other things you would expect me to say.

As I was stripping off her clothes and washing off the honey, I made myself think about what was happening. I got *Present*! I had a real mess in the kitchen, I was sure. This was Mary's last set of clothes. She hadn't been dressed for even ten minutes. I was feeling angry, and I knew this situation was my fault.

I forced myself to calm down and look at Mary, really look at her. She was quite happy to be doused in the water, and her knowledge of the big trouble she was in had evaporated in the joy of taking a bath. She was just a baby, sixteen months old. She was interested in everything, and I mean everything! I had neglected to secure the perimeter, so to speak, and now I had a mess.

Even more, I realized that ruining this precious relationship over her childlike need to explore and my neglectful behavior would be a terrible thing to do. So I *stopped* fussing and washed her off, kissed her as I dried her, and steeled myself to face the kitchen. It was a mess!

Mattering is a universal human need and our success in sending this message to our children is dependent on being able to answer yes to these questions:

- Do you see me?

- Do you hear me?

- Do you love me?

In this scenario, I was able to answer yes to these questions, and Mary knew she mattered.

GOOD RELATIONSHIPS ARE THE KEY

Harvard University began a study on what makes us happy in the 1930s. It's the longest running study of its kind ever done. It's in its seventy-fifth year. The study has tracked the lives of 724 men from their youth until now. Most of the men are now in their nineties (Waldinger, "What makes a good life?").

These men came from two very diverse groups. One group was made up of Harvard graduates. The other consisted of boys from some of Boston's poorest neighborhoods (Waldinger, "What makes a good life?").

Robert Waldinger, the study's third director, told an audience that the clearest message of this seventy-five-year study (despite the difference in the two study groups) is, "good relationships keep us happy and healthier. Period!" ("What makes a good life?")

Waldinger pointed out the three top lessons on relationships from this study:

1. Social connections are good for us. Loneliness kills. You can be lonely in a crowd, a family, or a marriage. This leads to the second big lesson.

2. The quality of your close relationships matters. Living in warm and connected relationships is protective. The depth of our satisfaction in our relationships makes us physically healthier. This leads to the third big lesson.

3. Healthy relationships affect our brain. Feeling secure in your relationships keeps your brain functioning at a high level for longer.

These three lessons were observed when the men were in their eighties, but it isn't a stretch to know these positive outcomes of healthy relationships happened over time. If our relationships in our family are strong and healthy, it's going to benefit both parents and children long term.

Waldinger said, "This knowledge is as old as the hills. Why is it so hard to get and so easy to ignore? It's because we're human. What we want is a quick fix. Something we can get that will make our lives good and keep them that way. Relationships are messy and they're complicated. And the hard work of tending to family and friends, that's not sexy or glamorous. It's also life long, it never ends. But over the years the study has shown that the people who fared the best were those who leaned into relationships with family and friends." ("What makes a good life?")

There's no silver bullet to family success. It takes choosing relationships over mere management. It takes time and Presence.

HERE'S TO A WELL-LIVED DAY

In a recent TED talk by Candy Chang, she shared a moving experience. Chang asked the question "Before I die I want to . . . " She asked the question by turning the side of an abandoned building into a huge chalk board for people to write their responses on. In one day, the entire side of the building was filled with chalked-in answers, and it grew from there ("Before I die I want to . . . ").

Some of the responses were humorous and fun but most were poignant and many were related to the need we all have to matter and to connect with those around us.

At the end of her talk, she expressed, "Two of the most valuable things we have in life are our time and our relationships with other people. In our age of increasing distractions it's more important than ever to find ways to maintain perspective and remember life is brief and tender" (Chang, "Before I die I want to . . . ").

Being Present now with your children is a way to overcome distractions and weld firm, satisfying, and lasting relationships. Using touchpoints daily, for small amounts of time consistently, can and will make *all* the difference.

When you're older, thinking back on those earlier days when your children lived in your home will cause you very tender feelings. You're going to want to be able to call to mind moments when you held your child one more time for a little longer; when you were patient; when you allowed them to be themselves and grow; when despite the chaos or mess, you smiled and meant it.

Our homes are the perfect place to practice the art of being Present. When we're Present with our children, we send the clear and important message: I hear you. I see you. I love you. I will support you. You matter to me.

Whatever the depth of love we have for our children, if we fail to be Present, consistently over time, they will fail to feel they matter as deeply as we want them to feel it.

Regularly I pick a verse of scripture to think on and memorize. I appreciate the discipline and I like the messages. Recently I choose Matthew 13:16: "But blessed are your eyes, for they see: and your ears, for they hear."

This verse of scripture is about seeing and hearing things that cannot be seen with our temporal eyes or heard with our temporal ears. I submit that when we are Present, even if it's only a few times a week, a few minutes at a time, we will be blessed to *see* and *hear* in an extraordinary way.

Know what you want. Do the simple things. Change your story. Adjust your approach to family management. Remember that less is more. Recognize the difference between adults and kids. Watch your motives. Turn away from your technology more often. Nurture yourself right where you are. Learn to see and utilize touchpoints. Get *Present*.

May we all be blessed in our relationships as we practice the art of being Present.

Here's to a well-lived day,

Mary Ann

BIBLIOGRAPHY

American Beauty. Directed by Sam Mendes, written by Alan Ball. Performed by Kevin Spacey and Annette Bening. France: Dreamworks, 1999.

Arnold, Jeanne E., Anthony P. Graesch, Enzo Ragazzini, and Elinor Ochs. *Life at Home in the Twenty-First Century: 32 Families Open Their Doors.* Los Angeles: The Cotsen Institute of Archaeology Press, 2012.

Associated Press and MTV. "Youth Happiness Study." *Associated Press*, August 2007, http://surveys.ap.org/data/ KnowledgeNetworks/2007-08-20%20AP-MTV%20Youth%20 Happiness.pdf.

Bauerlein, Mark. "Why Gen-Y Johnny Can't Read Nonverbal Cues." *The Wall Street Journal,* September 4, 2009, http://www.wsj.com/articles/ SB10001424052970203863204574348493483201758.

Bhandarkar, Sumitha. "101 Fun Things to Do with Kids to Enjoy Everyday Family Life." *A Fine Parent*, November 17, 2014, https://afineparent. com/lighten-up/fun-things-to-do-with-kids.html.

Campbell, Desirée. "10 Things Children Will Always Remember." *The 36th Avenue*, October 14, 2012, http://www.the36thavenue. com/10-things-children-will-always-remember.

Carter, Christine. *Raising Happiness: 10 Simple Steps for More Joyful Kids and Happier Parents.* New York: Ballantine Books, 2010.

Chang, Candy. "Before I die I want to . . ." *TED Talks*, September 4, 2012.

Clear, James. "Being Consistent Is Not the Same as Being Perfect." *Entrepreneur*, June 5, 2014, https://www.entrepreneur.com/ article/234325.

Clear, James. "The Science of Positive Thinking: How Positive Thoughts Build Your Skills, Boost Your Health, and Improve Your Work." *The Huffington Post*, September 8, 2013, http://www.huffingtonpost.com/ james-clear/positive-thinking_b_3512202.html.

Clement, Debbie. "Children's Art: Process VERSUS Product." Pre-K and K Sharing, February 1, 2012, http://prekandksharing.blogspot. com/2012/02/childrens-art-process-versus-product.html.

Coolidge, Calvin. "Quotations." Calvin Coolidge Presidential Foundation, accessed February 6, 2017, https://coolidgefoundation.org/quote/ quotations-o.

Covey, Stephen R. *First Things First*. New York City: Covey Leadership Center, 1994.

Delistraty, Cody C. "The Importance of Eating Together: Family dinners build relationships, and help kids do better in school." *The Atlantic*, July 18, 2014. http://www.theatlantic.com/health/archive/2014/07/the-importance-of-eating-together/374256.

"Don't Text While Parenting—It Will Make You Cranky." Truly Viral News, May 12, 2016. http://trueviralnews.com/dont-text-while-parenting-it-will-make-you-cranky-2.

Dyer, Wayne. "Why the Inside Matters." *Wayne's Blog*, May 15, 2013, http://www.drwaynedyer.com/blog/why-the-inside-matters.

Edwards, Jaroldeen. *Daffodil Principle: One Woman, Two Hands, One Bulb at a Time*. China: Shadow Mountain, 2004.

Feiler, Bruce. "Want to Give Your Family Value and Purpose? Write a Mission Statement." *The Atlantic*, February 25, 2013, http://www.theatlantic.com/sexes/archive/2013/02/want-to-give-your-family-value-and-purpose-write-a-mission-statement/273491.

Fishel, Anne. "FAQ." The Family Dinner Project. Accessed November 23, 2016. http://thefamilydinnerproject.org/resources/faq.

Frankl, Viktor E. *Man's Search for Meaning*. Boston: Beacon Press, 1959.

Fredrickson, Barbara L., Michael A. Cohn, Kimberly A. Coffey, Jolynn Pek, and Sandra M. Finkel, "Open Hearts Build Lives: Positive Emotions, Induced Through Loving-Kindness Meditation, Build Consequential Personal Resources." *Journal of Personality and Social Psychology* 95, no. 5 (2008): 1045-1062, https://www.ncbi.nlm.nih.gov/pmc/articles/PMC3156028.

Freeman, Hana. Quoted in "Listening and responding to children." *The Home School Coach*, February 3, 2011, http://home-school-coach.com/listening-and-responding-to-children.

Gerber, Michael E. *The E-Myth: Why Most Small Businesses Don't Work and What to Do about It*. Ballinger Publishing, 1985.

Gray, Marjory R. and Laurence Steinberg. "Unpacking Authoritative Parenting: Reassessing a Multidimensional Construct." *Journal of Marriage and Family*, 61(3):574-87, 1999.

Goodwyn, Hannah. "Make Memories with Your Kids." Christian Broadcasting Network, accessed February 2, 2017, http://www1.cbn.com/family/make-memories-with-your-kids.

Hardy, Kathy, M.Ed. "Children's Art: It's the Process, Not the Product, that Counts." The Alliance for Early Childhood, accessed February 1, 2017, http://www.theallianceforec.org/library.php?c=7&news=114.

Harriman, Vince. "What Can Kids Learn from a Failed Science Project? Everything!" *CWIST,* October 21, 2013, http://blog.cwist.com/science-kids-learning-to-fail.

Harrison, Clancy. "Cooking With Kids Is About The Process Not The Meal." Fields of Flavor, July 15, 2015, http://www.fieldsofflavor.com/simple-tips-make-cooking-kids-easier.

Henn, Steve. "When Parents Are The Ones Too Distracted By Devices." National Public Radio, April 14, 2014, http://www.npr.org/sections/alltechconsidered/2014/04/16/303749247/when-parents-are-the-ones-too-distracted-by-devices.

Highlights for Children. "The State of the Kid 2014." *Highlights,* 2014, https://www.highlights.com/sites/default/files/public/sotk2014.pdf.

Humphries, Alysia McCausland. "The Power of focus ie. Being Present." *The Home School Coach,* March 5, 2012, http://home-school-coach.com/wednesday-the-power-of-focus-ie-being-present.

Johnson, Amy. "Why You Should Read Aloud to Older Kids." *What Do We Do All Day?,* April 29, 2015, http://www.whatdowedoallday.com/why-you-should-read-aloud-to-older-kids.

Johnson, Emma. "The Real Cost of Your Shopping Habits." *Forbes,* January 15, 2015, http://www.forbes.com/sites/emmajohnson/2015/01/15/the-real-cost-of-your-shopping-habits/#2206f9fd21ae.

Johnson, Kenneth. "We All Have a Father in Whom We Can Trust." *Ensign,* May 1994, 30.

Johnson, Mary Ann. "What matters most in life." *The Home School Coach,* July 29, 2011, http://home-school-coach.com/what-matters-most-in-life.

Kristen. Quoted in "What Do You Wish You Had Known about Kids Art Projects?" Tinker Lab, February 1, 2012, http://tinkerlab.com/what-do-you-wish-you-had-known-about-making-art-with-children.

Lamb, Marguerite. "7 Secrets to Raising a Happy Child," *American Baby,* May 2008, http://www.parents.com/toddlers-preschoolers/development/fear/raising-happy-children.

McGlynn, David. "Please Forgive My Spotless Home." *New York Times,* November 28, 2014, http://www.nytimes.com/2014/11/30/fashion/modern-love-please-forgive-my-spotless-home.html?_r=1.

McKay, Brett and Kate. "Fathering with Intentionality: The Importance of Creating a Family Culture. The Art of Manliness, July 22, 2013, http://www.artofmanliness.com/2013/07/22/family-culture.

McLeod, S.A. "Skinner—Operant Conditioning." Simply Psychology, last modified 2015, http://www.simplypsychology.org/operant-conditioning.html.

McMillan, Ron. "Master Your Stories and You Master Your Life." *Meridian Magazine*, November 25, 2013, http://ldsmag.com/article-1-13595.

Moore, Kimberly. "What I learn while driving . . . " *Learning along the way* . . . . April 20, 2012, https://kimberlymoore.wordpress.com/2012/04/20/what-i-learn-while-driving.

National Center on Addiction and Substance Abuse at Columbia University. "The Importance of Family Dinners." National Court Appointed Special Advocate Association, September 2011, http://www.centeronaddiction.org/addiction-research/reports/importance-of-family-dinners-2011.

National Public Radio Staff. " 'The Songs Never Die': Tony Bennett And Bill Charlap On Staying Power." National Public Radio, October 10, 2015, http://www.npr.org/2015/10/10/446973670/the-songs-never-die-tony-bennett-and-bill-charlap-on-staying-power.

"National Survey Reveals 62% of Kids Think Parents Are Too Distracted to Listen." Highlights Newsroom, October 8, 2014. https://www.highlights.com/newsroom/national-survey-reveals-62-kids-think-parents-are-too-distracted-listen.

Neighmond, Patti. "For the Children's Sake, Put Down That Smartphone." National Public Radio, April 21, 2014, http://www.npr.org/sections/health-shots/2014/04/21/304196338/for-the-childrens-sake-put-down-that-smartphone.

Oaks, Dallin H. "Good, Better Best." *Ensign*, November 2007, 104–8.

Palmer, Jodie. "Concentrate on one RIGHT thing for consistent improvement." The Home School Coach, January 4, 2011, http://home-school-coach.com/concentrate-one-right-thing-consistent-improvement.

Palmer, Jodie. "Family Mission Statement: Part I." The Home School Coach, June 13, 2010, http://home-school-coach.com/a-family-mission-statement-part-1.

Palmer, Jodie. "Family Mission Statement: Part II." The Home School Coach, June 14, 2010, http://home-school-coach.com/family-mission-statement.

Palmer, Jodie. "Family Mission Statement: Part III." The Home School Coach, June 17, 2010, http://home-school-coach.com/family-mission-statement-part-iii.

Palmer, Jodie. "Family Mission Statement: Part IV." The Home School Coach, June 21, 2010, http://home-school-coach.com/family-mission-statement-part-iv.

Patterson, Kerry, Joseph Grenny, Ron McMillan, and Al Switzler. *Crucial Conversations,* McGraw-Hill, 2002.

Pinborough, Jan. "Keeping Safe and Balanced in a Google-YouTube-Twitter-Facebook-iEverything World." *Ensign,* February 2012, 18. https://www.lds.org/ensign/2012/02/keeping-safe-and-balanced-in-a-google-youtube-twitter-facebook-ieverything-world?lang=eng

Pinegar, Rex D. "The Small and Simple Things." *Ensign,* November 1994.

Radesky, Jenny S., Caroline J. Kistin, Barry Zuckerman, Katie Nitzberg, Jamie Gross, Margot Kaplan-Sanoff, Marilyn Augustyn, and Michael Silverstein. "Patterns of Mobile Device Use by Caregivers and Children During Meals in Fast Food Restaurants." *Pediatrics,* vol. 133, no. 4 (2014): e843-e849, http://pediatrics.aappublications.org/content/early/2014/03/05/peds.2013-3703.full.pdf+html.

Resnick, MD, PS Bearman, RW Blum, KE Bauman, KM Harris, J Jones, J Tabor, T Beuhring, RE Sieving, M Shew, M Ireland, LH Bearinger, and JR Udry. "Protecting Adolescents from Harm: Findings from the National Longitudinal Study on Adolescent Health." *Journal of the American Medical Association* 278(10):823-32, 1997.

Robison, Kimberli Pelo. "A Dangerous Woman." *Meridian Magazine,* June 18, 2010. http://ldsmag.com/article-1-5736.

Rosen, Larry. "Why Would Kids Who Spend More Time on Facebook Display More Empathy Online and in Real Life?" *Science and Religion Today,* August 25, 2011, http://www.scienceandreligiontoday.com/2011/08/25/why-would-kids-who-spend-more-time-on-facebook-display-more-empathy-online-and-in-real-life.

Rudkin, Angharad. "The Top Five Parenting Regrets." *The Guardian,* March 22, 2013, https://www.theguardian.com/lifeandstyle/2013/mar/22/top-five-parenting-regrets.

Rustand, Warren. Quoted in "What Is Your Family's Culture?" Successful Culture, accessed February 6, 2017, http://successfulculture.com/what-is-your-familys-culture.

Schetzel, Dionne. "Being Present: My Cure for a Busy Life." The Home School Coach, May 13, 2011, http://home-school-coach.com/being-present-cure-for-busy-life.

Scholastic Inc. and YouGov. 2014. "Kids and Family Reading Report: U.S. Edition." *Scholastic.* http://www.scholastic.com/readingreport/key-findings.htm.

Sheila Seifert and Jeanne Gowen Dennis. "Writing a Family Mission Statement." Focus on the Family, http://www.focusonthefamily.com/parenting/spiritual-growth-for-kids/writing-a-family-mission-statement, 2013.

Shute, Nancy. "Parents, Not Kids, Are the Biggest Abusers of Technology." *US News and World Report,* February 9, 2011. http://health.usnews.com/health-news/blogs/on-parenting/2011/02/09/parents-not-kids-are-the-biggest-abusers-of-technology.

Silver, Sharon. "How to Stop Dumping Your Stress onto Your Kids." POPSUGAR, June 28, 2015, http://www.popsugar.com/moms/How-Less-Stressed-Around-Your-Kids-27330725.

Silver, Sharon. "4 Minute Way to De-Stress." Proactive Parenting, November 20, 2015, http://proactiveparenting.net/4-minute-way-to-de-stress.

Spencer, Leah. Quoted in "Example of learning style in children--The Spencer Sparks." The Home School Coach, November 11, 2010, http://home-school-coach.com/learning-style-in-children.

Spencer, Leah. Quoted in "How to assist your child's love for learning by responding to their sparks." The Home School Coach, October 12, 2010, http://home-school-coach.com/howto-identify-childs-love-learning-responding-sparks.

Taylor, Jim. "The Best Messages to Send Your Kids." *Psychology Today,* July 21, 2011. https://www.psychologytoday.com/blog/the-power-prime/201107/parenting-the-best-messages-send-your-children.

Tolle, Eckhart. "Quotes." Eckhart Tolle Now, accessed February 8, 2017, https://www.eckharttollenow.com/eckhart-tolle-quotes/p18.

Waldinger, Robert. "What makes a good life? Lessons from the longest study on happiness." *TED Talks,* January 25, 2016.

Waterlow, Lucy. "From not taking enough photos to working too hard, what parents 'truly' regret from their child's early years." *The Daily Mail,* August 20, 2012, http://www.dailymail.co.uk/femail/article-2191049/From-taking-photos-working-hard-parents-truly-regret-childs-early-years.html#ixzz4QrHrr3IJ.

INDEX OF TERMS

ABOUT THE
AUTHOR

Mary Ann Cazier Johnson was born into a large and bois-terous family of nine children and survived to become the mother of seven equally boisterous and busy children. She has been happily married to her husband, Don, for forty-six years and has thirteen grandchildren ages two to twenty-nine. She started college at nineteen and finally finished with a masters degree in her forties.

Mary Ann has helped thousands of individuals and families to build better relationships. She is the founder of Relationship Transformations for Busy Parents, an online community reaching thousands of people each week. She is the creator and president of Family Connection Mentoring—a service of one-on-one mentoring for parents and their families. She is also well known in the home-school community as The Home School Coach.

Becoming a Present Parent is her first book on what she knows and does best – helping children and parents connect. She has been blogging and presenting her Presence concepts across the country in workshops and webinars for over seven years.

Mary Ann is a Montana transplant to Salt Lake City, Utah, where she lives with her husband, Don. Her favorite pastime is reading and learning.

Scan to visit

www.becomingapresentparent.com